THE SILVER PYRAMID
DOC SAVAGE

DENNIS O'NEIL
WRITER

ADAM KUBERT
& ANDY KUBERT
ARTISTS

PETRA SCOTESE
COLORIST

JOHN COSTANZA
ANDY KUBERT
LETTERERS

BASED ON CHARACTERS CREATED BY
LESTER DENT

DAN DiDIO
SVP-Executive Editor

MIKE CARLIN
Editor-original series

GEORG BREWER
VP-Design & DC Direct Creative

BOB HARRAS
Group Editor-Collected Editions / Editor

ROBBIN BROSTERMAN
Design Director-Books

CURTIS KING JR.
Senior Art Director

DC COMICS

PAUL LEVITZ
President & Publisher

RICHARD BRUNING
SVP-Creative Director

PATRICK CALDON
EVP-Finance & Operations

AMY GENKINS
SVP-Business & Legal Affairs

JIM LEE
Editorial Director-WildStorm

GREGORY NOVECK
SVP-Creative Affairs

STEVE ROTTERDAM
SVP-Sales & Marketing

CHERYL RUBIN
SVP-Brand Management

Cover by Andy Kubert

DOC SAVAGE: THE SILVER PYRAMID

DC Comics, 1700 Broadway, New York, NY 10019
A Warner Bros. Entertainment Company

Printed by World Color Press, Inc.,
St-Romuald, QC, Canada 12/16/09. First Printing.
ISBN: 978-1-4012-2621-3

SUSTAINABLE   Certified Fiber
FORESTRY   Sourcing
INITIATIVE
www.sfiprogram.org
Fiber used in this product line meets the sourcing requirements
of the SFI program. www.sfiprogram.org PWC-SFICOC-260

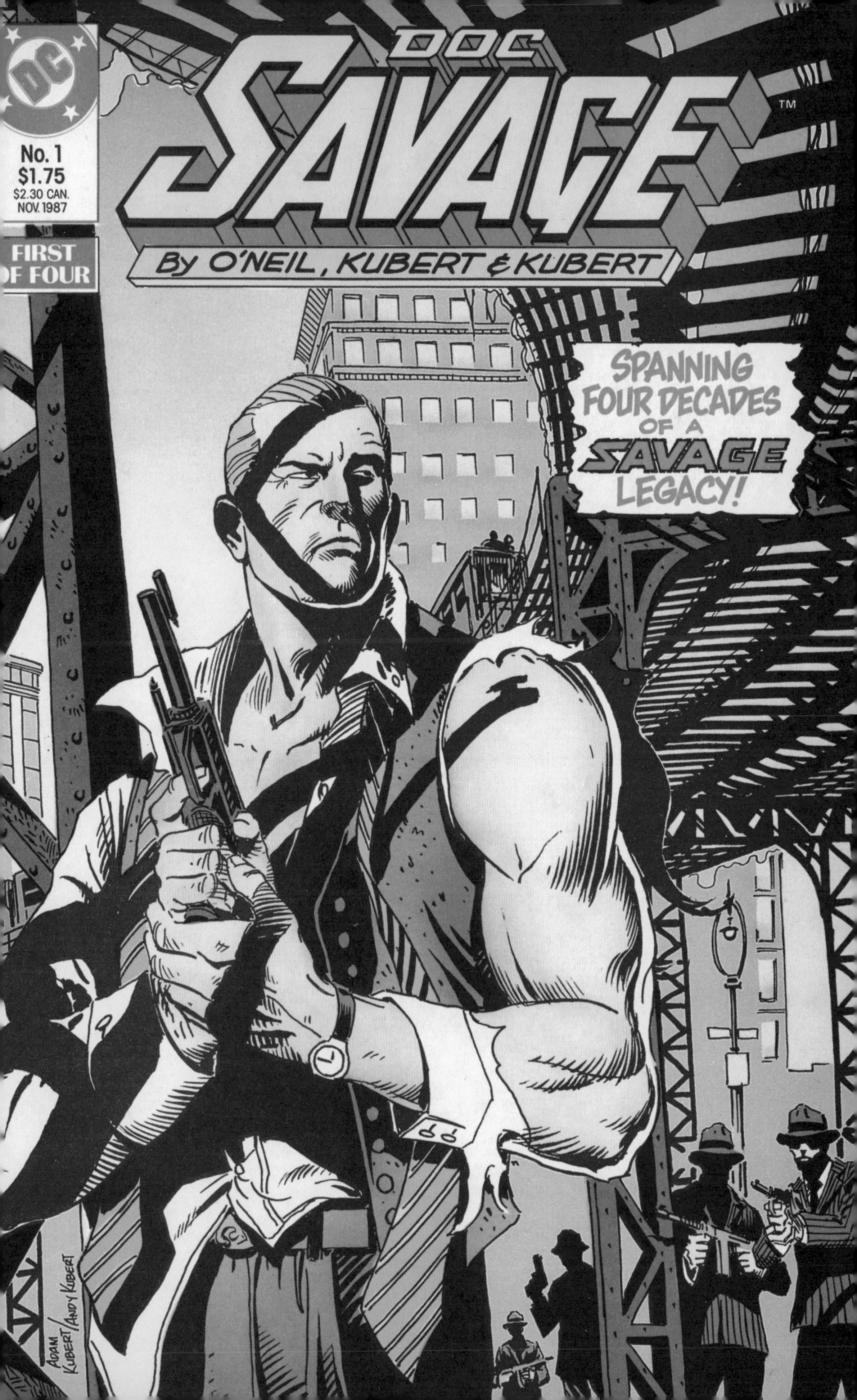
DC
DOC
SAVAGE™
No. 1
$1.75
$2.30 CAN.
NOV. 1987
FIRST OF FOUR
By O'NEIL, KUBERT & KUBERT
SPANNING FOUR DECADES OF A SAVAGE LEGACY!
ADAM KUBERT / ANDY KUBERT

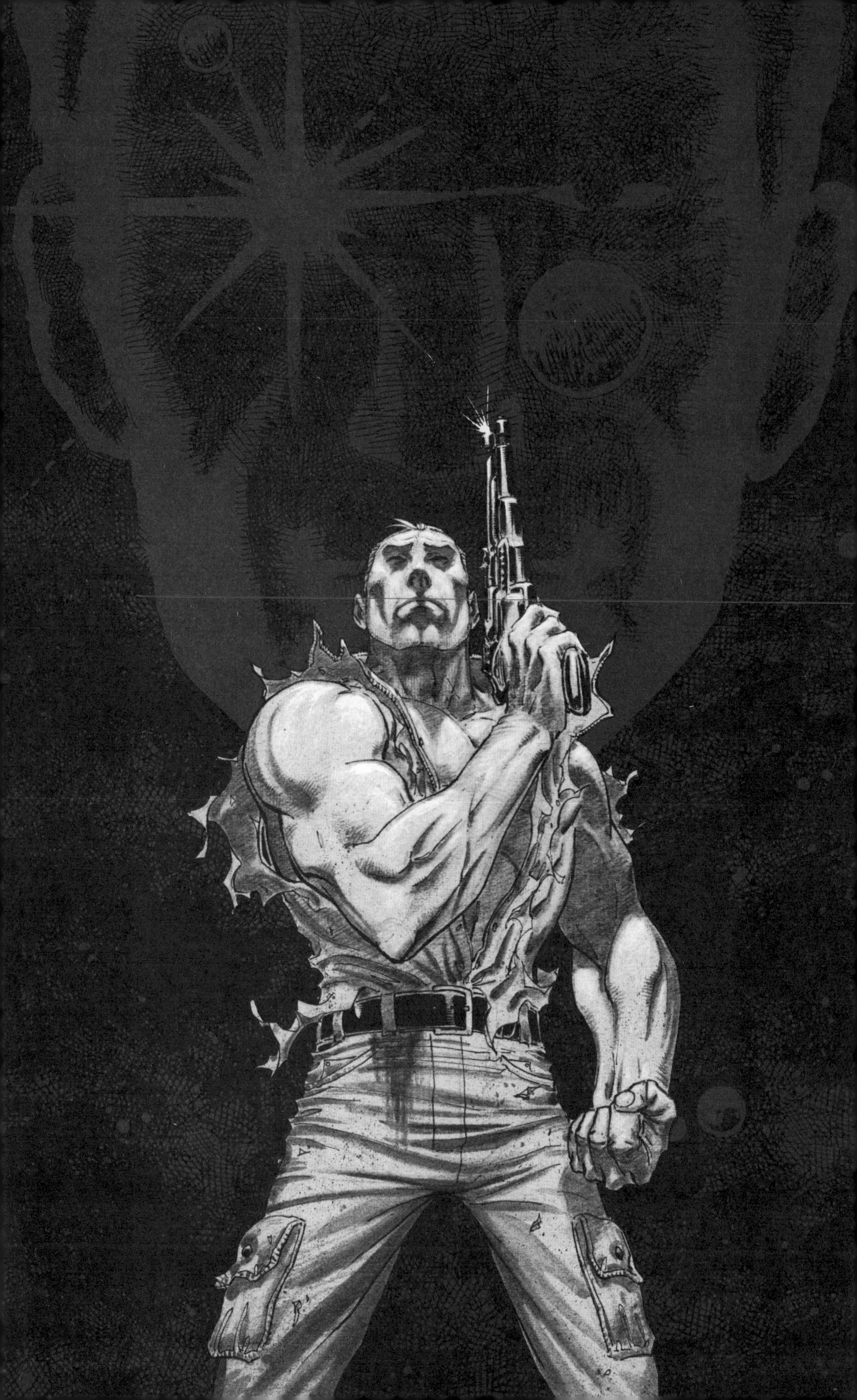

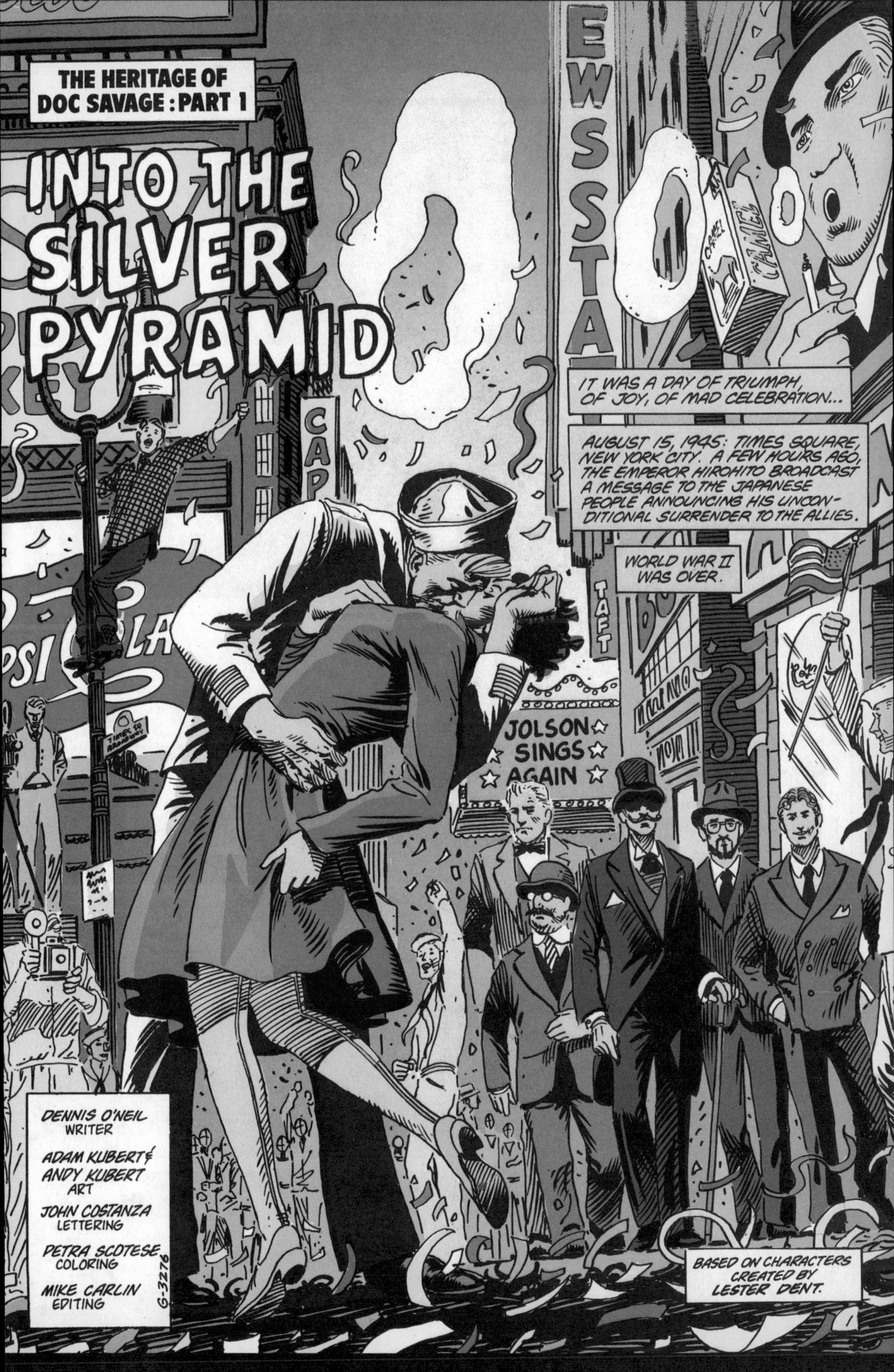

THE HERITAGE OF DOC SAVAGE : PART 1
INTO THE SILVER PYRAMID
IT WAS A DAY OF TRIUMPH, OF JOY, OF MAD CELEBRATION...
AUGUST 15, 1945: TIMES SQUARE, NEW YORK CITY. A FEW HOURS AGO, THE EMPEROR HIROHITO BROADCAST A MESSAGE TO THE JAPANESE PEOPLE ANNOUNCING HIS UNCONDITIONAL SURRENDER TO THE ALLIES.
WORLD WAR II WAS OVER.
CAMEL
TAFT
JOLSON SINGS AGAIN
DENNIS O'NEIL WRITER
ADAM KUBERT & ANDY KUBERT ART
JOHN COSTANZA LETTERING
PETRA SCOTESE COLORING
MIKE CARLIN EDITING
G-3276
BASED ON CHARACTERS CREATED BY LESTER DENT.

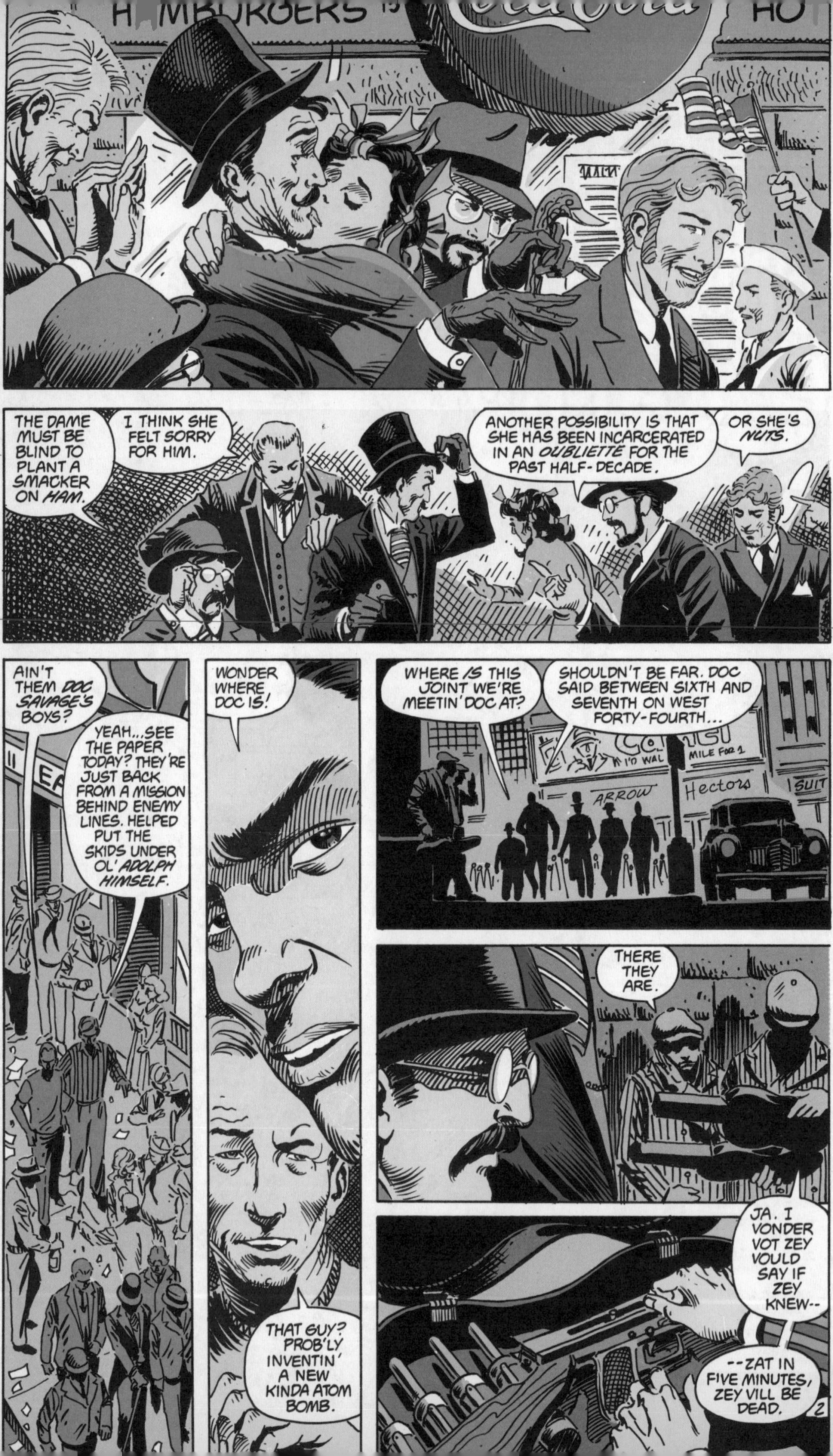

THE DAME MUST BE BLIND TO PLANT A SMACKER ON *HAM*.
I THINK SHE FELT SORRY FOR HIM.
ANOTHER POSSIBILITY IS THAT SHE HAS BEEN INCARCERATED IN AN *OUBLIETTE* FOR THE PAST HALF-DECADE.
OR SHE'S *NUTS*.
AIN'T THEM *DOC SAVAGE'S* BOYS?
YEAH...SEE THE PAPER TODAY? THEY'RE JUST BACK FROM A MISSION BEHIND ENEMY LINES. HELPED PUT THE SKIDS UNDER OL' *ADOLPH HIMSELF*.
WONDER WHERE DOC IS!
THAT GUY? PROB'LY INVENTIN' A NEW KINDA ATOM BOMB.
WHERE *IS* THIS JOINT WE'RE MEETIN' DOC AT?
SHOULDN'T BE FAR. DOC SAID BETWEEN SIXTH AND SEVENTH ON WEST FORTY-FOURTH...
THERE THEY ARE.
JA. I VONDER VOT ZEY VOULD SAY IF ZEY KNEW--
--ZAT IN FIVE MINUTES, ZEY VILL BE DEAD.

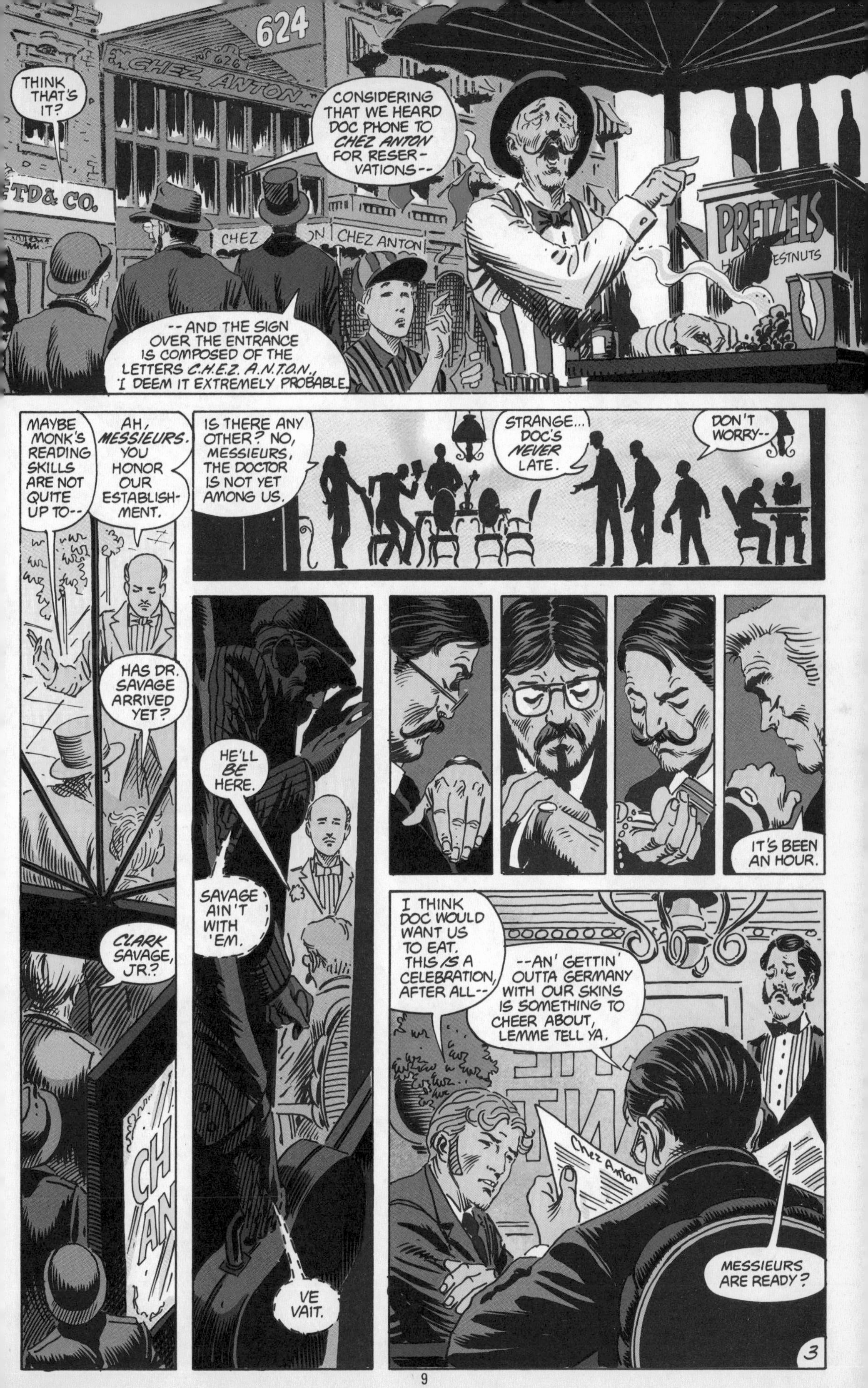
624
CHEZ ANTON
626
TD& CO.
THINK THAT'S IT?
CONSIDERING THAT WE HEARD DOC PHONE TO CHEZ ANTON FOR RESER-VATIONS--
PRETZELS
--AND THE SIGN OVER THE ENTRANCE IS COMPOSED OF THE LETTERS C.H.E.Z. A.N.T.O.N., I DEEM IT EXTREMELY PROBABLE.
MAYBE MONK'S READING SKILLS ARE NOT QUITE UP TO--
AH, MESSIEURS. YOU HONOR OUR ESTABLISH-MENT.
HAS DR. SAVAGE ARRIVED YET?
CLARK SAVAGE, JR.?
IS THERE ANY OTHER? NO, MESSIEURS, THE DOCTOR IS NOT YET AMONG US.
STRANGE... DOC'S NEVER LATE.
DON'T WORRY--
HE'LL BE HERE.
SAVAGE AIN'T WITH 'EM.
VE VAIT.
IT'S BEEN AN HOUR.
I THINK DOC WOULD WANT US TO EAT. THIS IS A CELEBRATION, AFTER ALL--
--AN' GETTIN' OUTTA GERMANY WITH OUR SKINS IS SOMETHING TO CHEER ABOUT, LEMME TELL YA.
Chez Anton
MESSIEURS ARE READY?
3

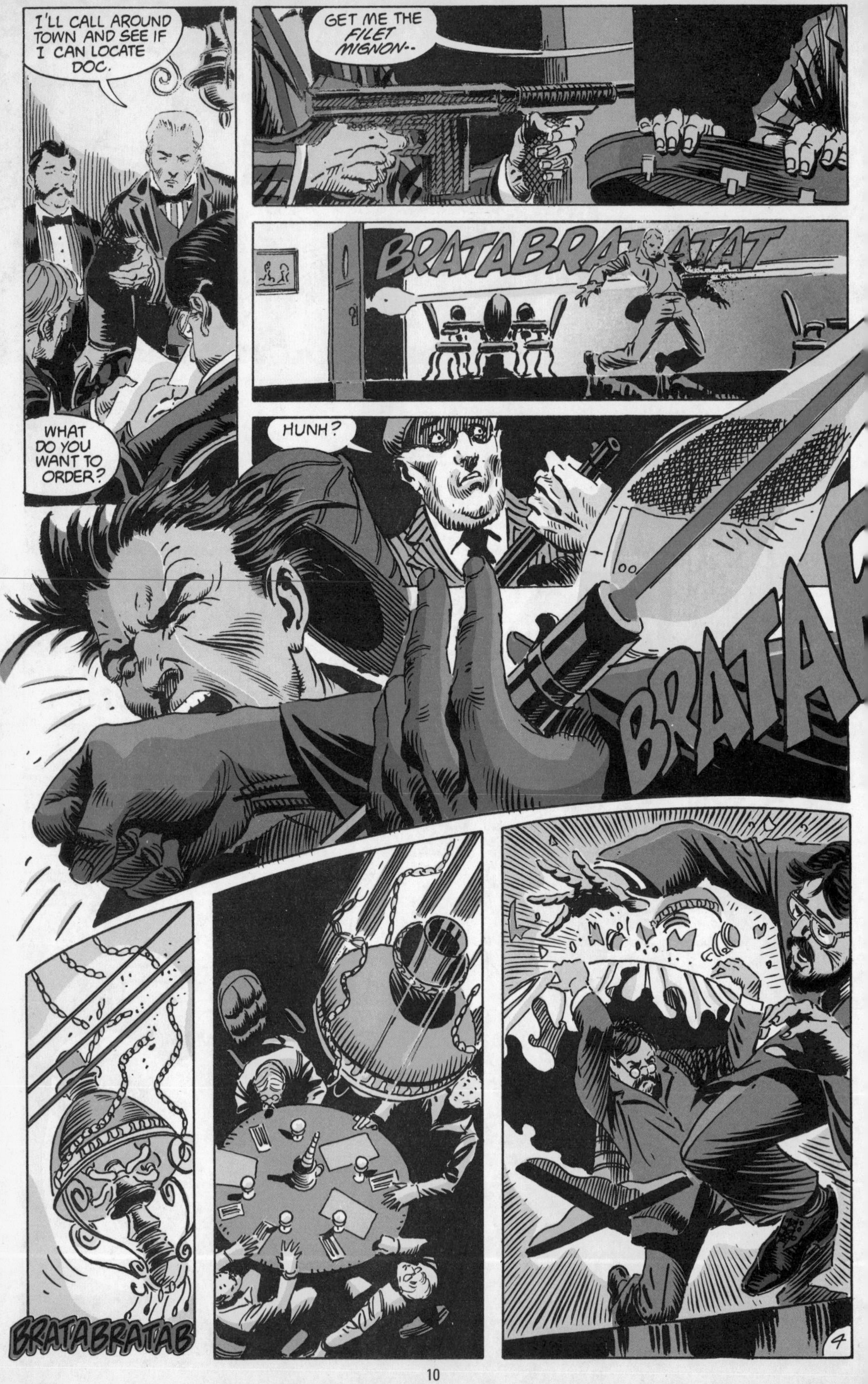
I'LL CALL AROUND TOWN AND SEE IF I CAN LOCATE DOC.
GET ME THE FILET MIGNON--
BRATABRATATAT
WHAT DO YOU WANT TO ORDER?
HUNH?
BRATA
BRATABRATAB
4

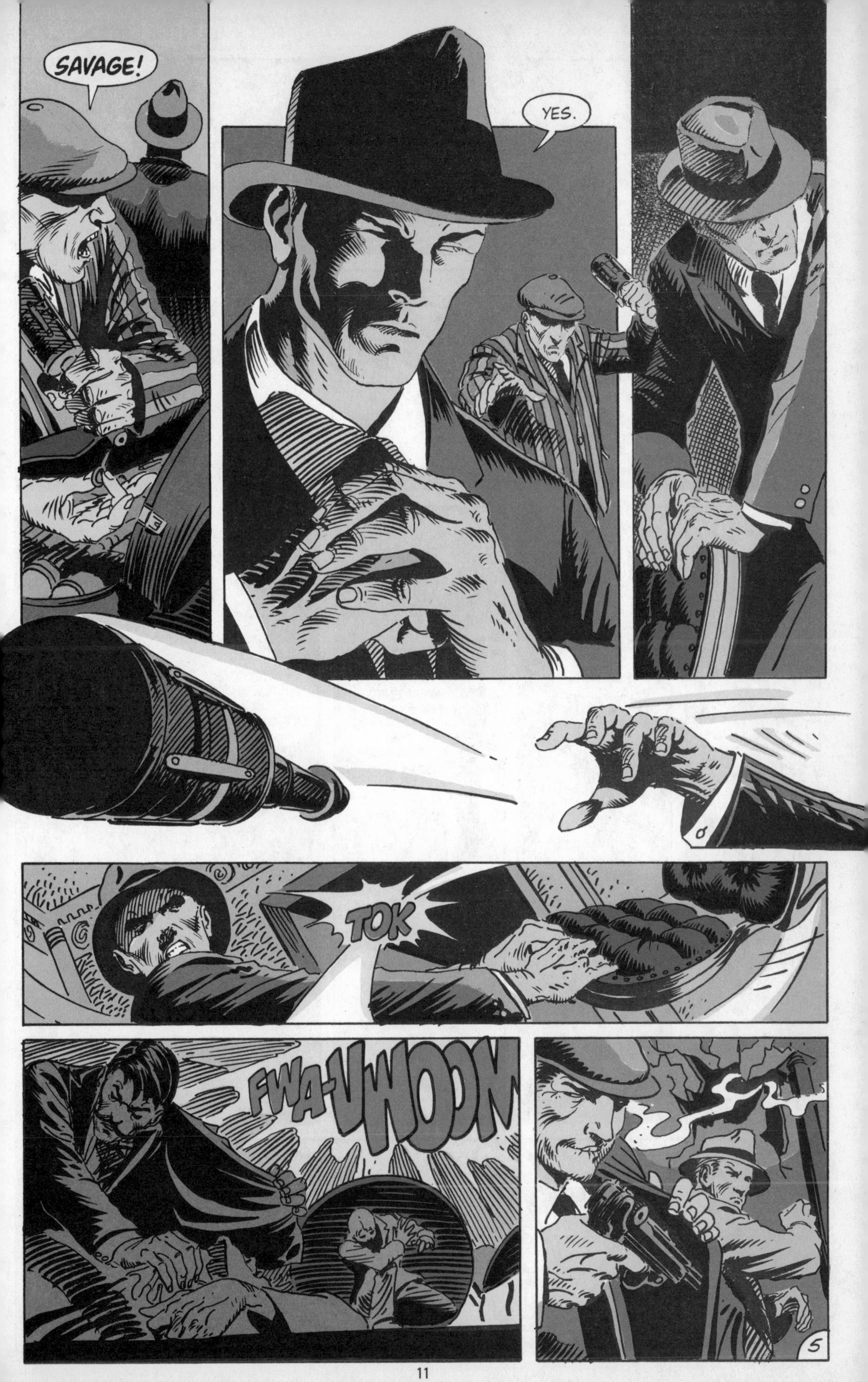
SAVAGE!
YES.
TOK
FWA-VWOON
5

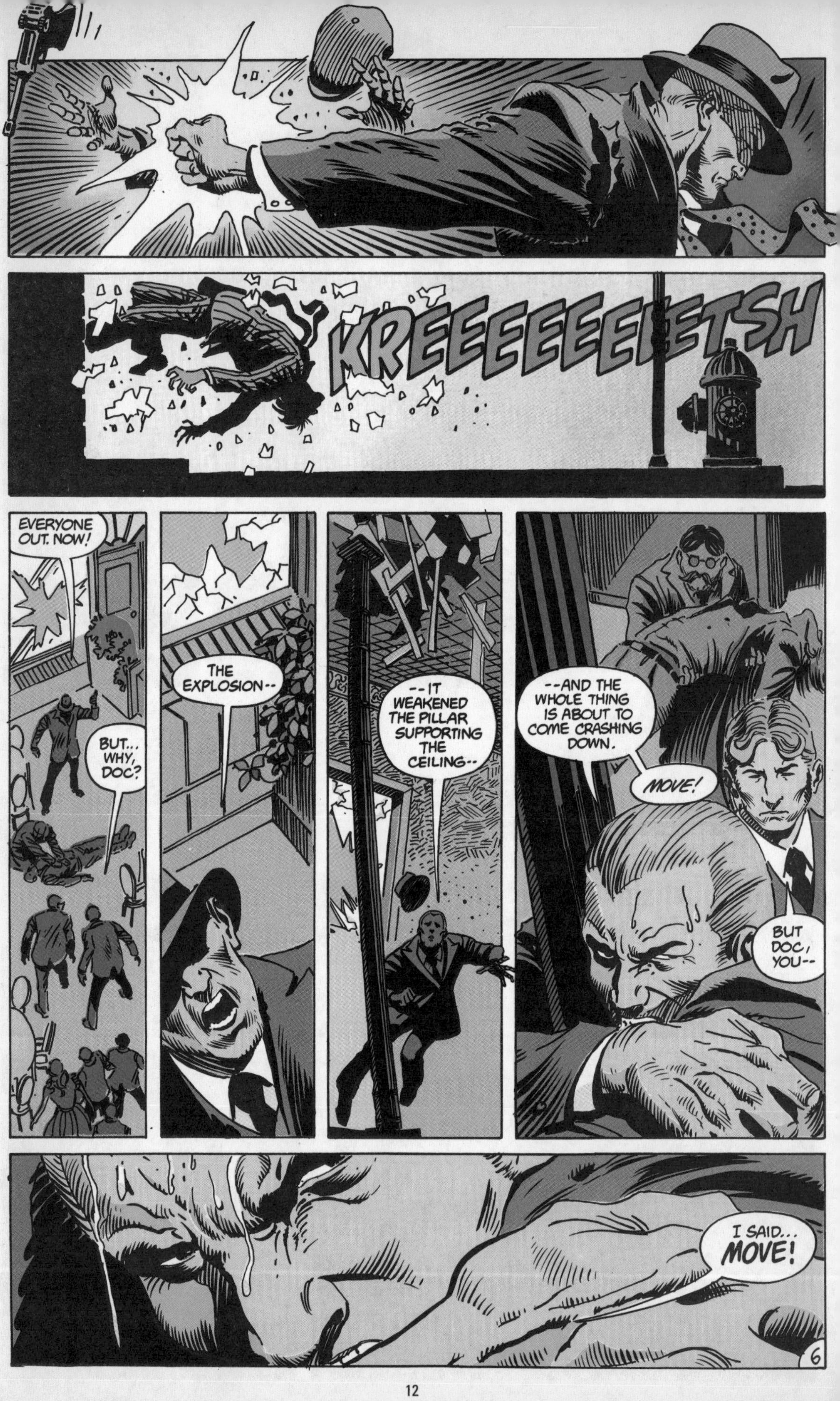
KREEEEEEEETSH
EVERYONE OUT. NOW!
BUT... WHY, DOC?
THE EXPLOSION--
--IT WEAKENED THE PILLAR SUPPORTING THE CEILING--
--AND THE WHOLE THING IS ABOUT TO COME CRASHING DOWN.
MOVE!
BUT DOC, YOU--
I SAID... MOVE!
6

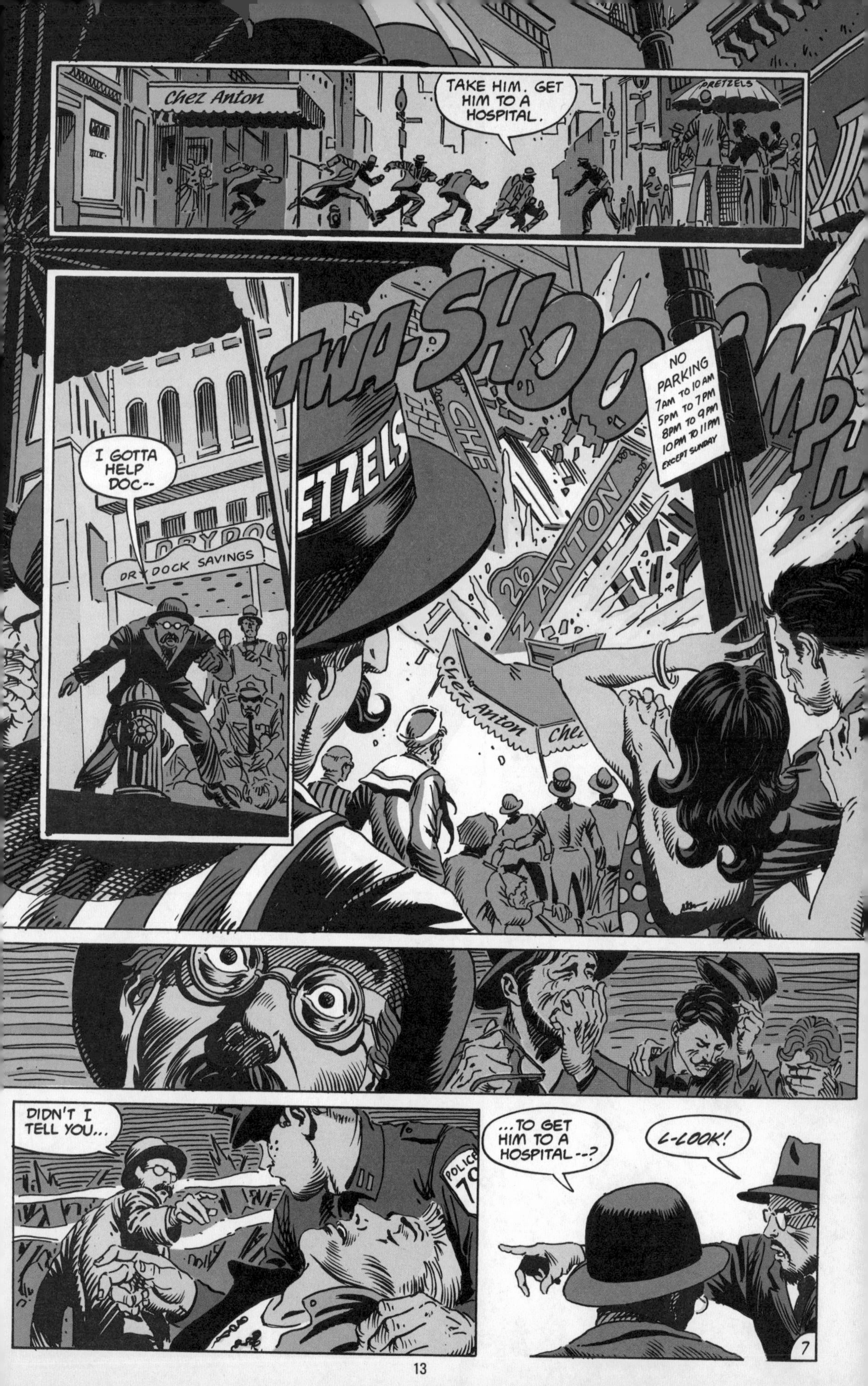
Chez Anton
PRETZELS
TAKE HIM. GET HIM TO A HOSPITAL.
I GOTTA HELP DOC--
DRY DOCK SAVINGS
TWA-SHOOOOMMH
NO PARKING
7AM TO 10AM
5PM TO 7PM
8PM TO 9PM
10PM TO 11PM
EXCEPT SUNDAY
ETZELS
ANTON
26
Chez Anton
DIDN'T I TELL YOU...
POLICE 70
...TO GET HIM TO A HOSPITAL--?
L-LOOK!
7

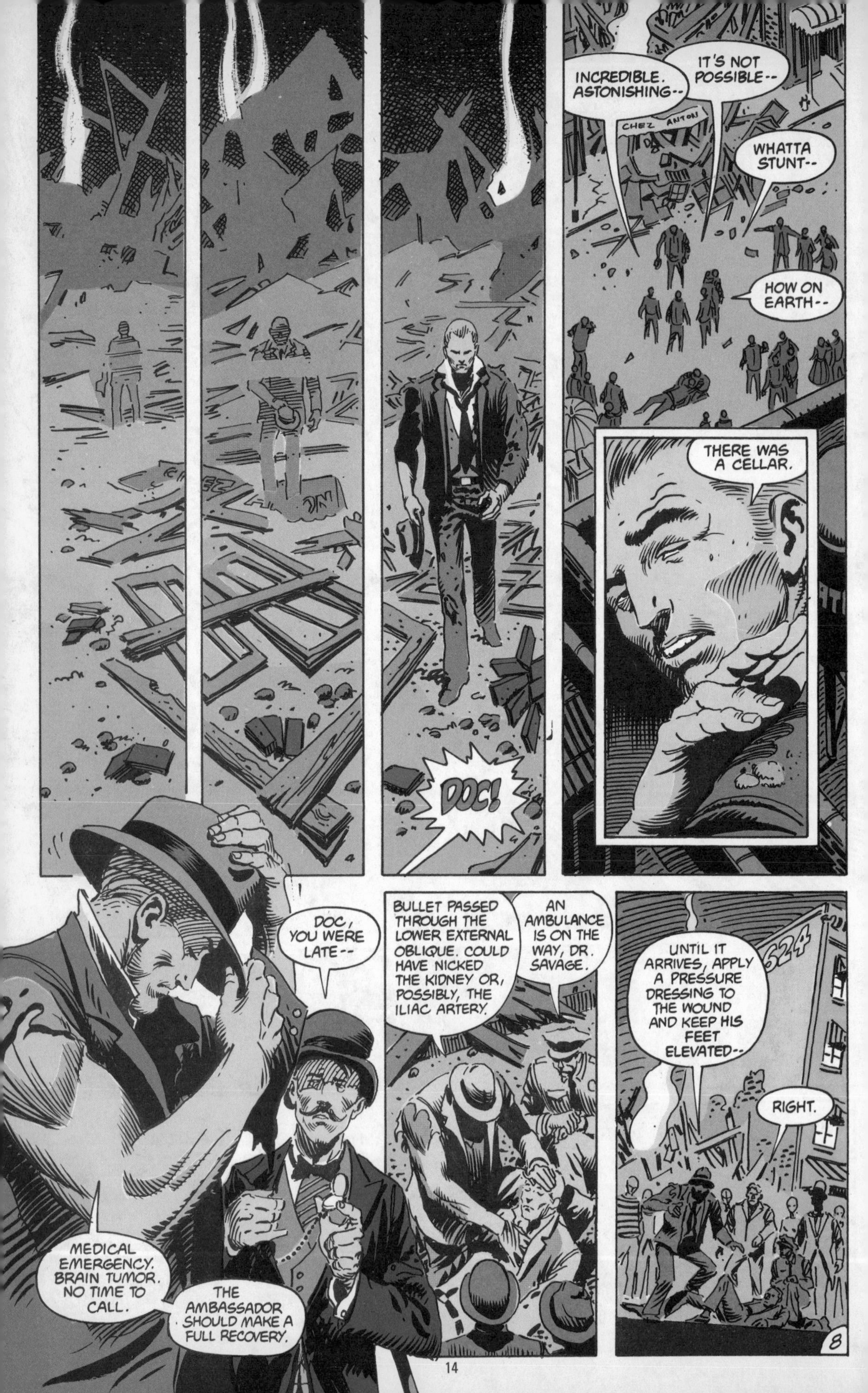
INCREDIBLE. ASTONISHING--
IT'S NOT POSSIBLE--
CHEZ ANTONI
WHATTA STUNT--
HOW ON EARTH--
THERE WAS A CELLAR.
DOC!
DOC, YOU WERE LATE--
MEDICAL EMERGENCY. BRAIN TUMOR. NO TIME TO CALL.
THE AMBASSADOR SHOULD MAKE A FULL RECOVERY.
BULLET PASSED THROUGH THE LOWER EXTERNAL OBLIQUE. COULD HAVE NICKED THE KIDNEY OR, POSSIBLY, THE ILIAC ARTERY.
AN AMBULANCE IS ON THE WAY, DR. SAVAGE.
UNTIL IT ARRIVES, APPLY A PRESSURE DRESSING TO THE WOUND AND KEEP HIS FEET ELEVATED--
RIGHT.
624
8

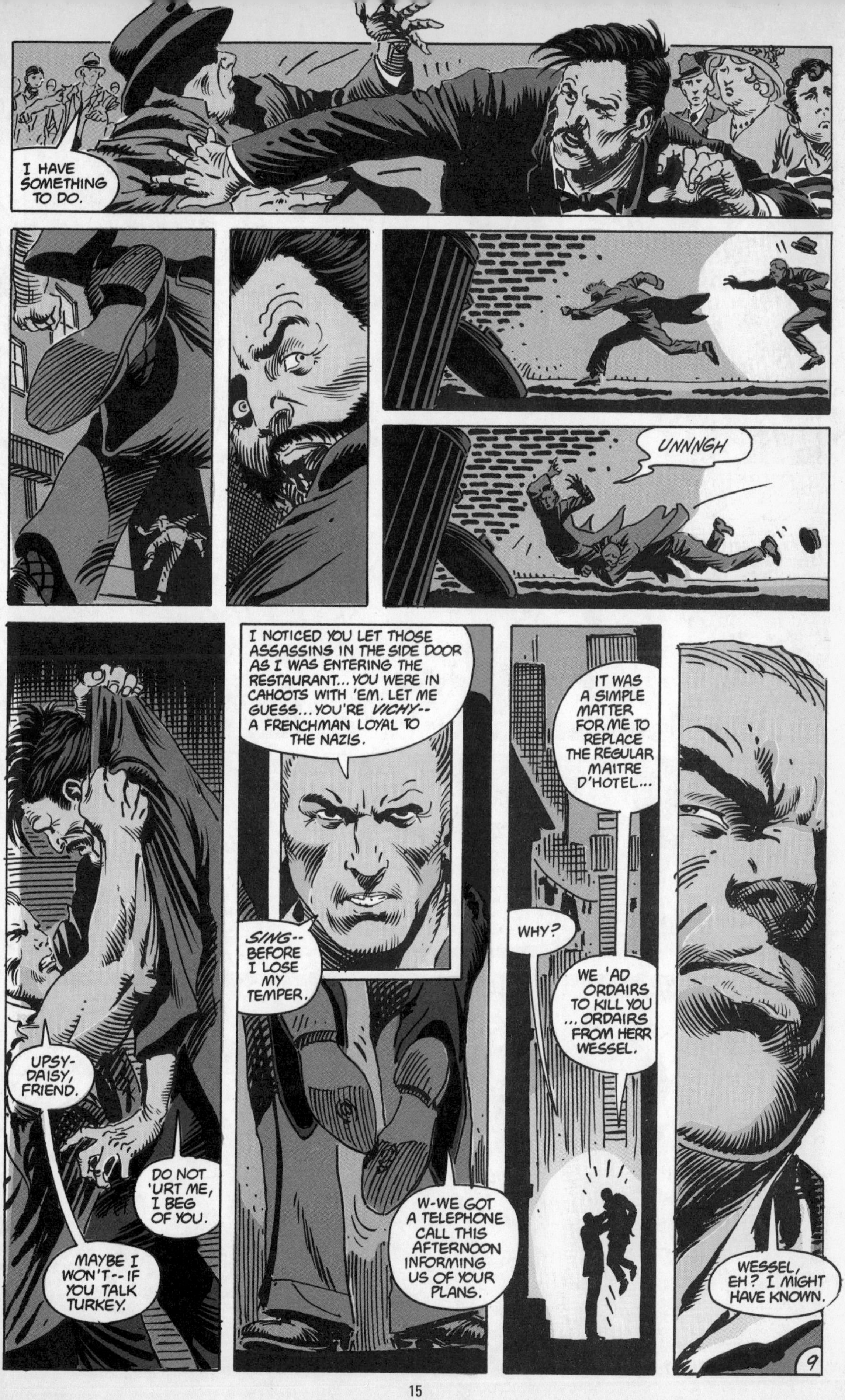

I HAVE SOMETHING TO DO.
UNNNGH
UPSY-DAISY, FRIEND.
DO NOT 'URT ME, I BEG OF YOU.
MAYBE I WON'T--IF YOU TALK TURKEY.
I NOTICED YOU LET THOSE ASSASSINS IN THE SIDE DOOR AS I WAS ENTERING THE RESTAURANT... YOU WERE IN CAHOOTS WITH 'EM. LET ME GUESS... YOU'RE *VICHY*-- A FRENCHMAN LOYAL TO THE NAZIS.
SING-- BEFORE I LOSE MY TEMPER.
W-WE GOT A TELEPHONE CALL THIS AFTERNOON INFORMING US OF YOUR PLANS.
IT WAS A SIMPLE MATTER FOR ME TO REPLACE THE REGULAR MAITRE D'HOTEL...
WHY?
WE 'AD ORDAIRS TO KILL YOU ...ORDAIRS FROM HERR WESSEL.
WESSEL, EH? I MIGHT HAVE KNOWN.
9

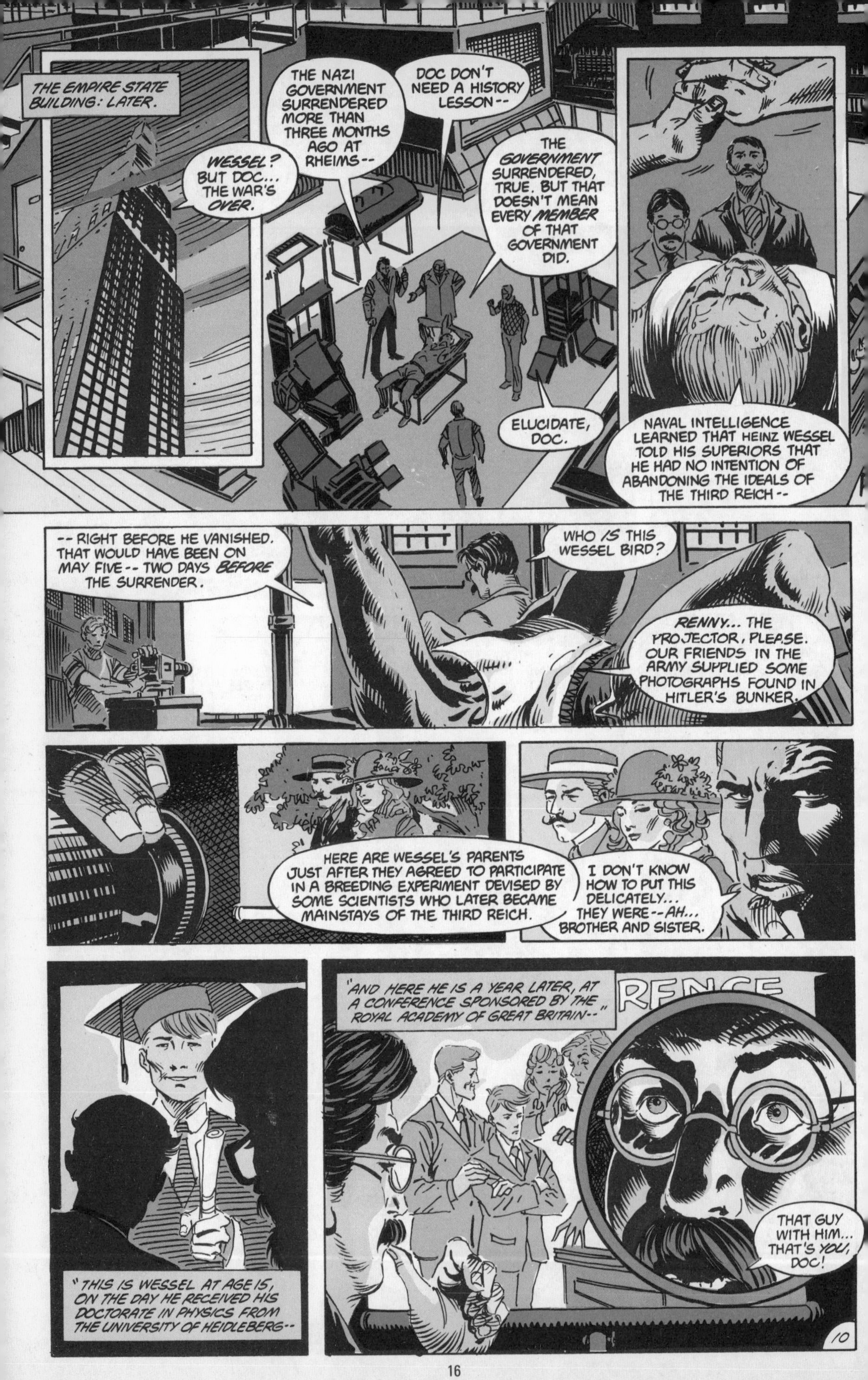
THE EMPIRE STATE BUILDING: LATER.
WESSEL? BUT DOC... THE WAR'S OVER.
THE NAZI GOVERNMENT SURRENDERED MORE THAN THREE MONTHS AGO AT RHEIMS--
DOC DON'T NEED A HISTORY LESSON--
THE GOVERNMENT SURRENDERED, TRUE. BUT THAT DOESN'T MEAN EVERY MEMBER OF THAT GOVERNMENT DID.
ELUCIDATE, DOC.
NAVAL INTELLIGENCE LEARNED THAT HEINZ WESSEL TOLD HIS SUPERIORS THAT HE HAD NO INTENTION OF ABANDONING THE IDEALS OF THE THIRD REICH--
--RIGHT BEFORE HE VANISHED. THAT WOULD HAVE BEEN ON MAY FIVE--TWO DAYS BEFORE THE SURRENDER.
WHO IS THIS WESSEL BIRD?
RENNY... THE PROJECTOR, PLEASE. OUR FRIENDS IN THE ARMY SUPPLIED SOME PHOTOGRAPHS FOUND IN HITLER'S BUNKER.
HERE ARE WESSEL'S PARENTS JUST AFTER THEY AGREED TO PARTICIPATE IN A BREEDING EXPERIMENT DEVISED BY SOME SCIENTISTS WHO LATER BECAME MAINSTAYS OF THE THIRD REICH.
I DON'T KNOW HOW TO PUT THIS DELICATELY... THEY WERE--AH... BROTHER AND SISTER.
"THIS IS WESSEL AT AGE 15, ON THE DAY HE RECEIVED HIS DOCTORATE IN PHYSICS FROM THE UNIVERSITY OF HEIDLEBERG--
"AND HERE HE IS A YEAR LATER, AT A CONFERENCE SPONSORED BY THE ROYAL ACADEMY OF GREAT BRITAIN--"
RENCE
THAT GUY WITH HIM... THAT'S YOU, DOC!
10

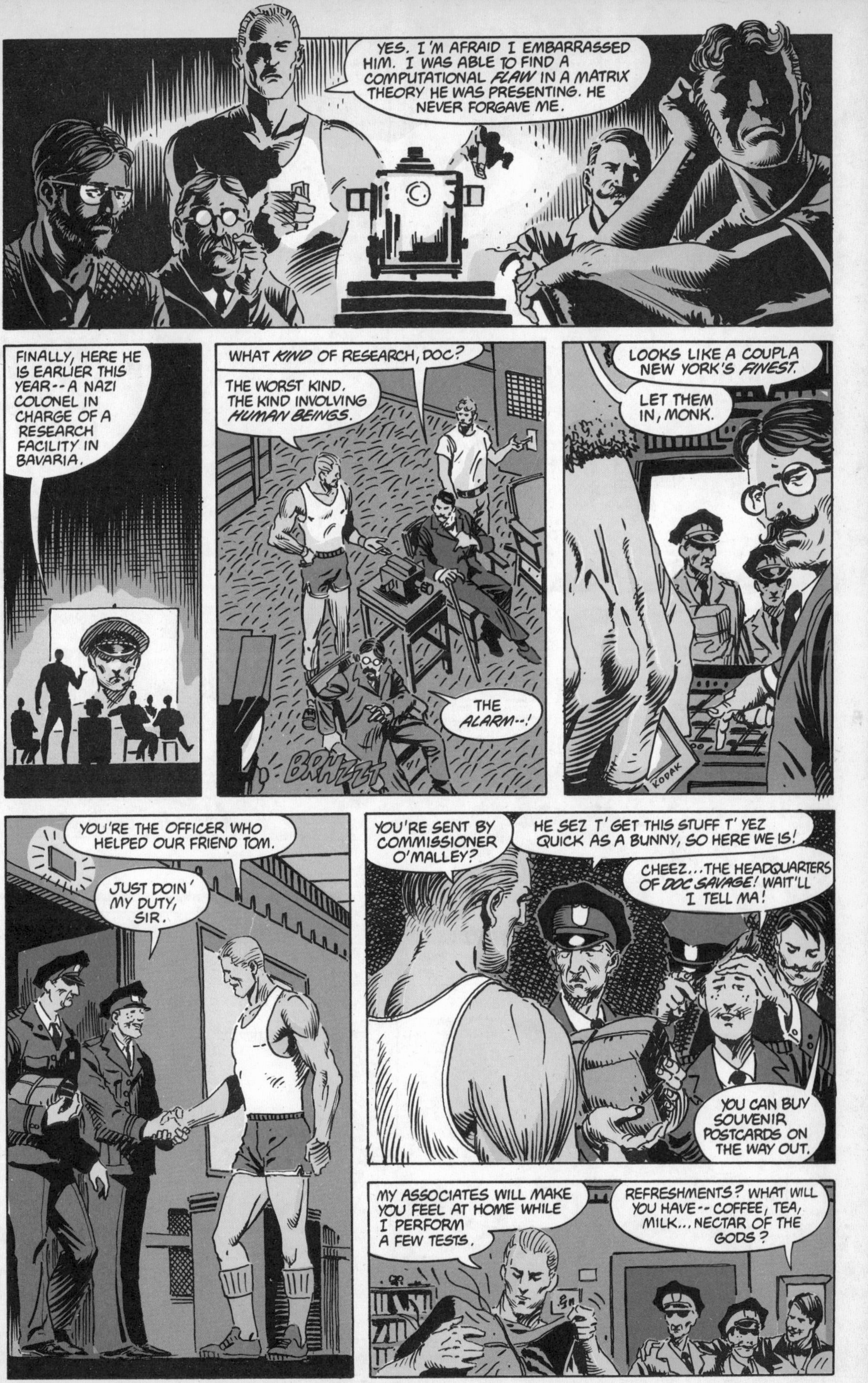
YES. I'M AFRAID I EMBARRASSED HIM. I WAS ABLE TO FIND A COMPUTATIONAL FLAW IN A MATRIX THEORY HE WAS PRESENTING. HE NEVER FORGAVE ME.
FINALLY, HERE HE IS EARLIER THIS YEAR--A NAZI COLONEL IN CHARGE OF A RESEARCH FACILITY IN BAVARIA.
WHAT KIND OF RESEARCH, DOC?
THE WORST KIND. THE KIND INVOLVING HUMAN BEINGS.
THE ALARM--!
BRHZZZT
LOOKS LIKE A COUPLA NEW YORK'S FINEST.
LET THEM IN, MONK.
KODAK
YOU'RE THE OFFICER WHO HELPED OUR FRIEND TOM.
JUST DOIN' MY DUTY, SIR.
YOU'RE SENT BY COMMISSIONER O'MALLEY?
HE SEZ T' GET THIS STUFF T' YEZ QUICK AS A BUNNY, SO HERE WE IS!
CHEEZ... THE HEADQUARTERS OF DOC SAVAGE! WAIT'LL I TELL MA!
YOU CAN BUY SOUVENIR POSTCARDS ON THE WAY OUT.
MY ASSOCIATES WILL MAKE YOU FEEL AT HOME WHILE I PERFORM A FEW TESTS.
REFRESHMENTS? WHAT WILL YOU HAVE--COFFEE, TEA, MILK... NECTAR OF THE GODS?

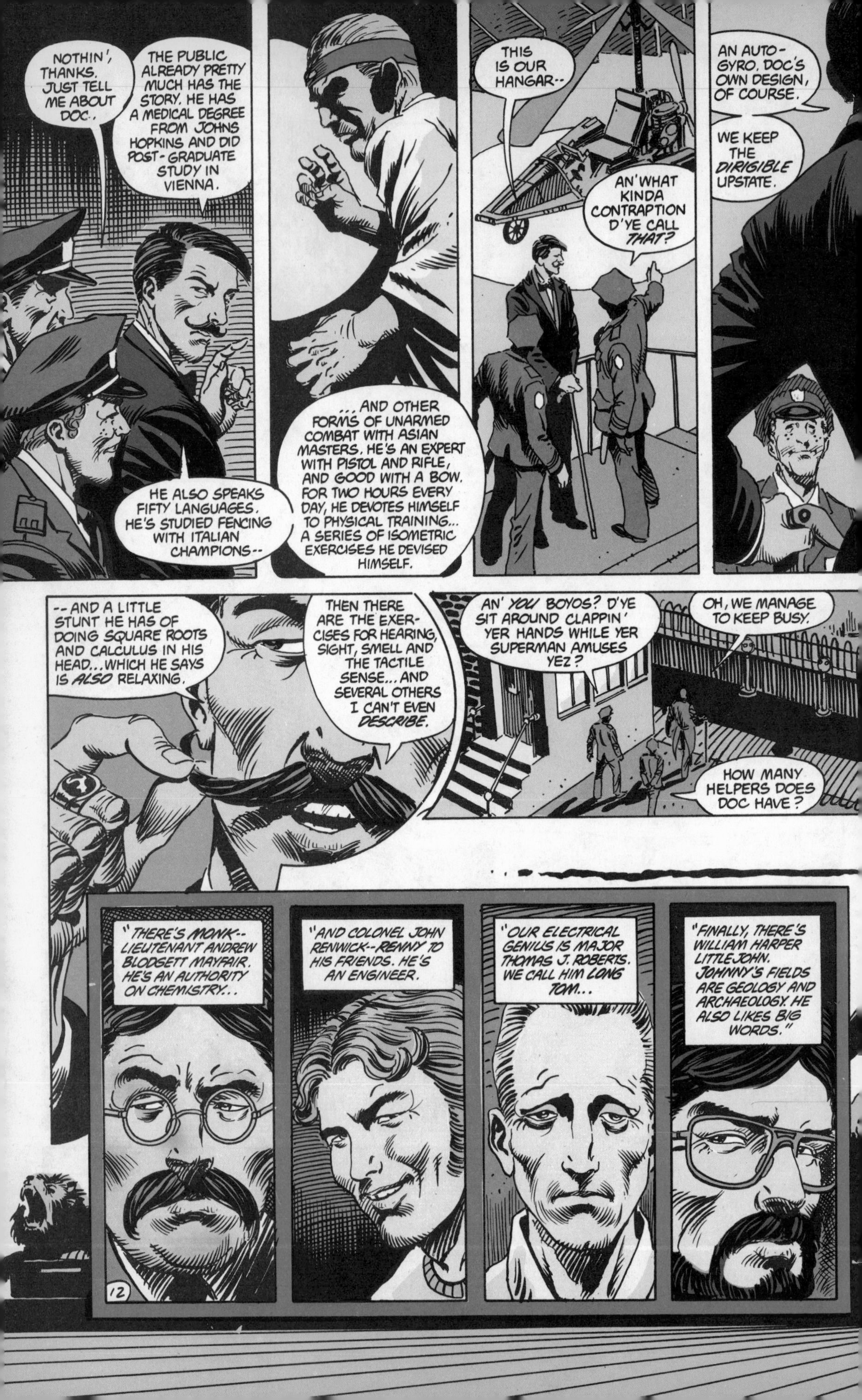
NOTHIN', THANKS. JUST TELL ME ABOUT DOC.
THE PUBLIC ALREADY PRETTY MUCH HAS THE STORY. HE HAS A MEDICAL DEGREE FROM JOHNS HOPKINS AND DID POST-GRADUATE STUDY IN VIENNA.
HE ALSO SPEAKS FIFTY LANGUAGES. HE'S STUDIED FENCING WITH ITALIAN CHAMPIONS--
...AND OTHER FORMS OF UNARMED COMBAT WITH ASIAN MASTERS. HE'S AN EXPERT WITH PISTOL AND RIFLE, AND GOOD WITH A BOW. FOR TWO HOURS EVERY DAY, HE DEVOTES HIMSELF TO PHYSICAL TRAINING... A SERIES OF ISOMETRIC EXERCISES HE DEVISED HIMSELF.
THIS IS OUR HANGAR--
AN' WHAT KINDA CONTRAPTION D'YE CALL *THAT*?
AN AUTO-GYRO, DOC'S OWN DESIGN, OF COURSE.
WE KEEP THE *DIRIGIBLE* UPSTATE.
--AND A LITTLE STUNT HE HAS OF DOING SQUARE ROOTS AND CALCULUS IN HIS HEAD... WHICH HE SAYS IS *ALSO* RELAXING.
THEN THERE ARE THE EXER-CISES FOR HEARING, SIGHT, SMELL AND THE TACTILE SENSE... AND SEVERAL OTHERS I CAN'T EVEN *DESCRIBE*.
AN' *YOU* BOYOS? D'YE SIT AROUND CLAPPIN' YER HANDS WHILE YER SUPERMAN AMUSES YEZ?
OH, WE MANAGE TO KEEP BUSY.
HOW MANY HELPERS DOES DOC HAVE?
"THERE'S *MONK*-- LIEUTENANT ANDREW BLODGETT MAYFAIR. HE'S AN AUTHORITY ON CHEMISTRY...
"AND COLONEL JOHN RENWICK--*RENNY* TO HIS FRIENDS. HE'S AN ENGINEER.
"OUR ELECTRICAL GENIUS IS MAJOR THOMAS J. ROBERTS. WE CALL HIM *LONG TOM*...
"FINALLY, THERE'S WILLIAM HARPER LITTLEJOHN. JOHNNY'S FIELDS ARE GEOLOGY AND ARCHAEOLOGY. HE ALSO LIKES BIG WORDS."
12

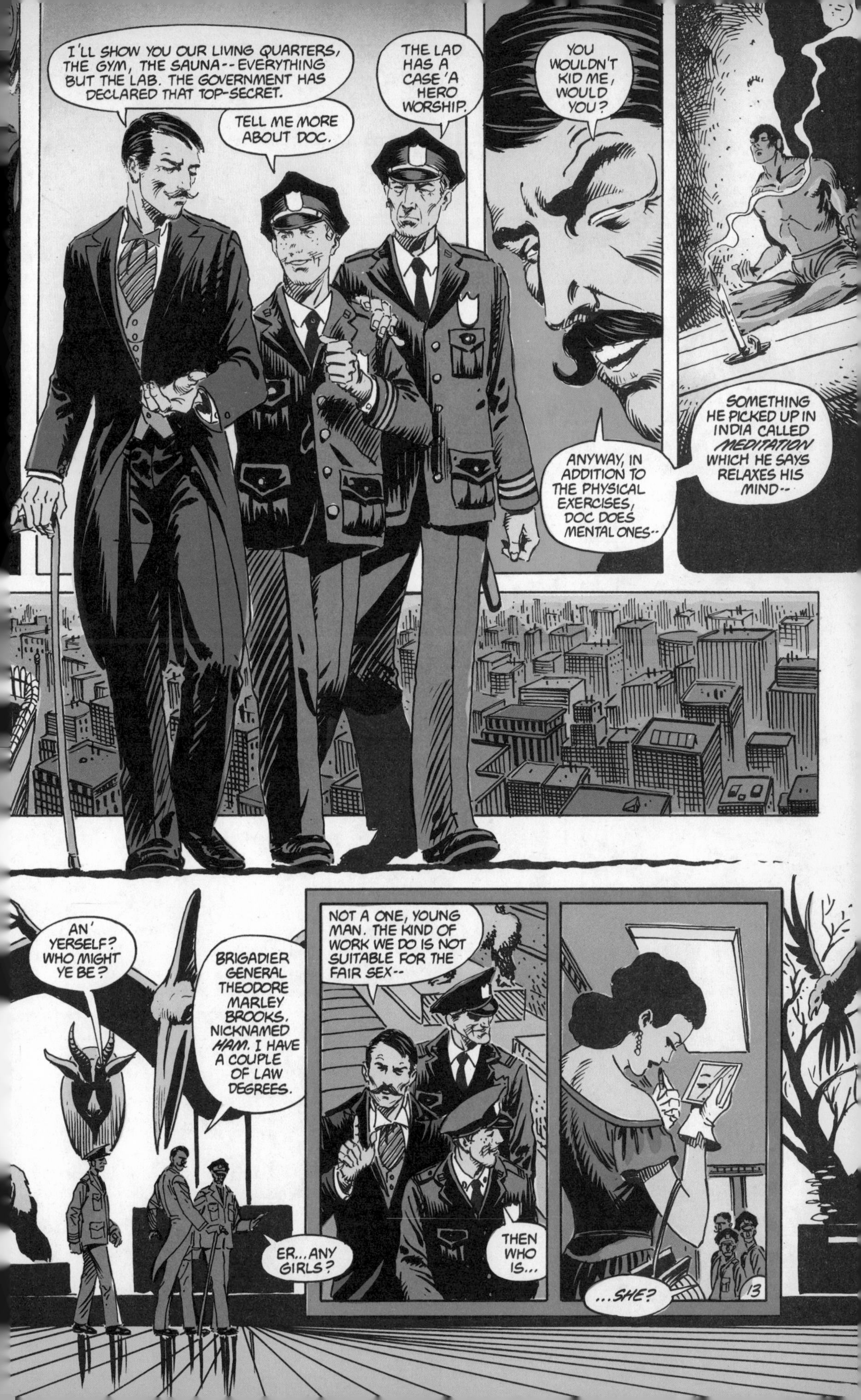
I'LL SHOW YOU OUR LIVING QUARTERS, THE GYM, THE SAUNA-- EVERYTHING BUT THE LAB. THE GOVERNMENT HAS DECLARED THAT TOP-SECRET.
TELL ME MORE ABOUT DOC.
THE LAD HAS A CASE 'A HERO WORSHIP.
YOU WOULDN'T KID ME, WOULD YOU?
ANYWAY, IN ADDITION TO THE PHYSICAL EXERCISES, DOC DOES MENTAL ONES--
SOMETHING HE PICKED UP IN INDIA CALLED MEDITATION WHICH HE SAYS RELAXES HIS MIND--
AN' YERSELF? WHO MIGHT YE BE?
BRIGADIER GENERAL THEODORE MARLEY BROOKS. NICKNAMED HAM. I HAVE A COUPLE OF LAW DEGREES.
ER... ANY GIRLS?
NOT A ONE, YOUNG MAN. THE KIND OF WORK WE DO IS NOT SUITABLE FOR THE FAIR SEX--
THEN WHO IS...
...SHE?
13

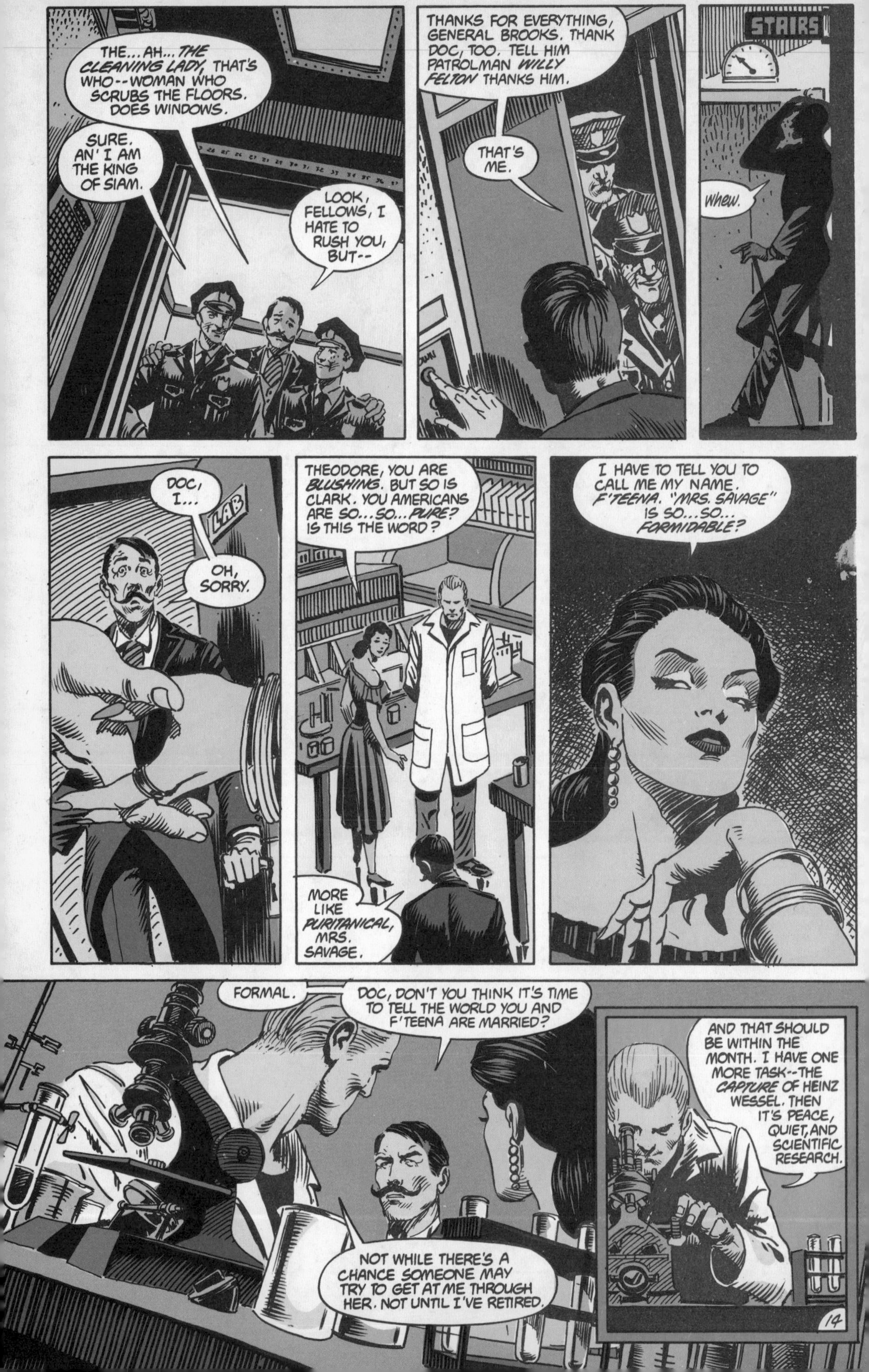
THE... AH... THE CLEANING LADY, THAT'S WHO--WOMAN WHO SCRUBS THE FLOORS. DOES WINDOWS.
SURE. AN' I AM THE KING OF SIAM.
LOOK, FELLOWS, I HATE TO RUSH YOU, BUT--
THANKS FOR EVERYTHING, GENERAL BROOKS. THANK DOC, TOO. TELL HIM PATROLMAN WILLY FELTON THANKS HIM.
THAT'S ME.
STAIRS
Whew.
DOC, I...
LAB
OH, SORRY.
THEODORE, YOU ARE BLUSHING. BUT SO IS CLARK. YOU AMERICANS ARE SO... SO... PURE? IS THIS THE WORD?
MORE LIKE PURITANICAL, MRS. SAVAGE.
I HAVE TO TELL YOU TO CALL ME MY NAME. F'TEENA. "MRS. SAVAGE" IS SO... SO... FORMIDABLE?
FORMAL.
DOC, DON'T YOU THINK IT'S TIME TO TELL THE WORLD YOU AND F'TEENA ARE MARRIED?
NOT WHILE THERE'S A CHANCE SOMEONE MAY TRY TO GET AT ME THROUGH HER. NOT UNTIL I'VE RETIRED.
AND THAT SHOULD BE WITHIN THE MONTH. I HAVE ONE MORE TASK--THE CAPTURE OF HEINZ WESSEL. THEN IT'S PEACE, QUIET, AND SCIENTIFIC RESEARCH.
14

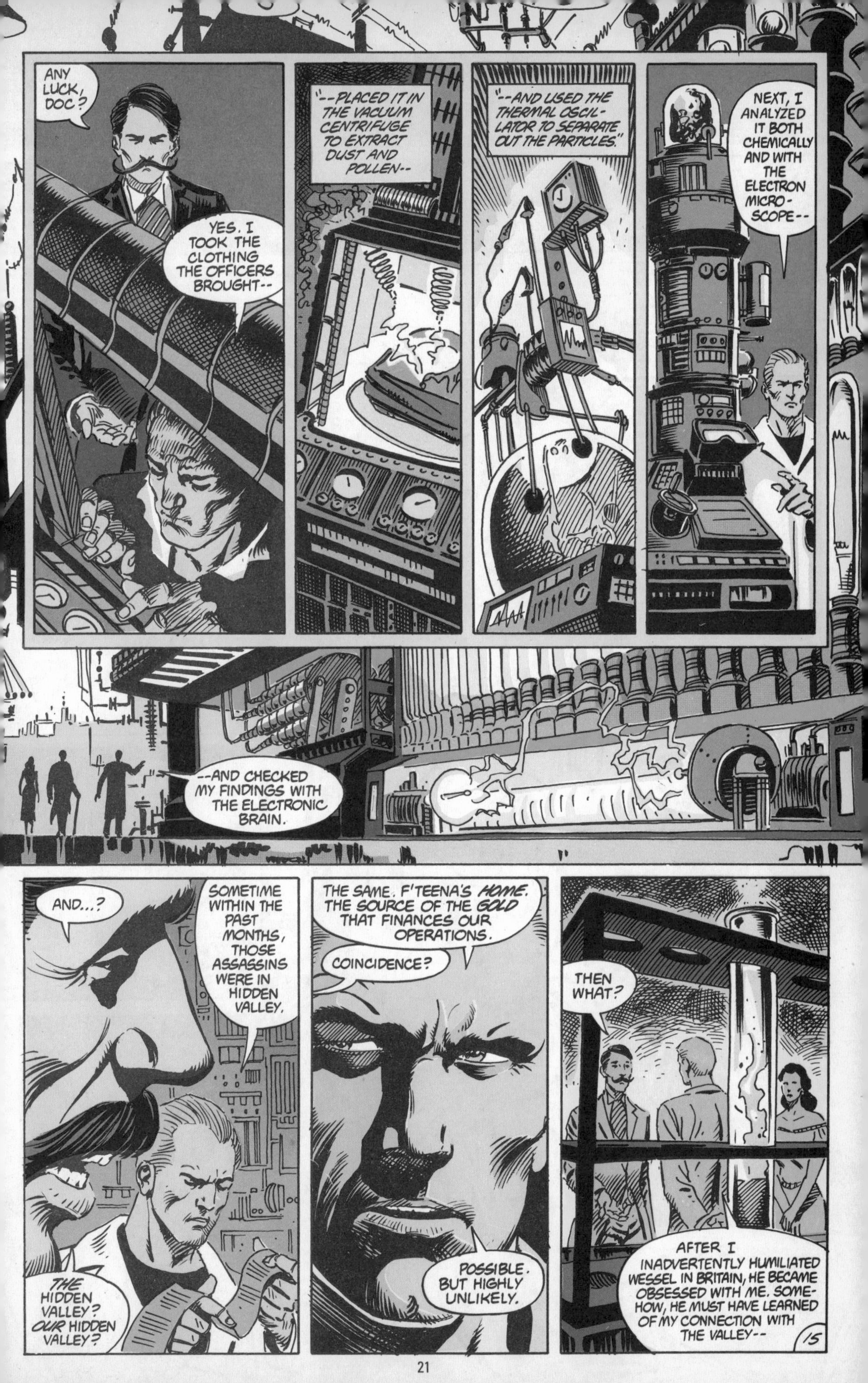

ANY LUCK, DOC?
YES. I TOOK THE CLOTHING THE OFFICERS BROUGHT--
"--PLACED IT IN THE VACUUM CENTRIFUGE TO EXTRACT DUST AND POLLEN--
"--AND USED THE THERMAL OSCILLATOR TO SEPARATE OUT THE PARTICLES."
NEXT, I ANALYZED IT BOTH CHEMICALLY AND WITH THE ELECTRON MICRO-SCOPE--
--AND CHECKED MY FINDINGS WITH THE ELECTRONIC BRAIN.
AND...?
SOMETIME WITHIN THE PAST MONTHS, THOSE ASSASSINS WERE IN HIDDEN VALLEY.
THE HIDDEN VALLEY? OUR HIDDEN VALLEY?
THE SAME. F'TEENA'S HOME. THE SOURCE OF THE GOLD THAT FINANCES OUR OPERATIONS.
COINCIDENCE?
POSSIBLE. BUT HIGHLY UNLIKELY.
THEN WHAT?
AFTER I INADVERTENTLY HUMILIATED WESSEL IN BRITAIN, HE BECAME OBSESSED WITH ME. SOME-HOW, HE MUST HAVE LEARNED OF MY CONNECTION WITH THE VALLEY--
15

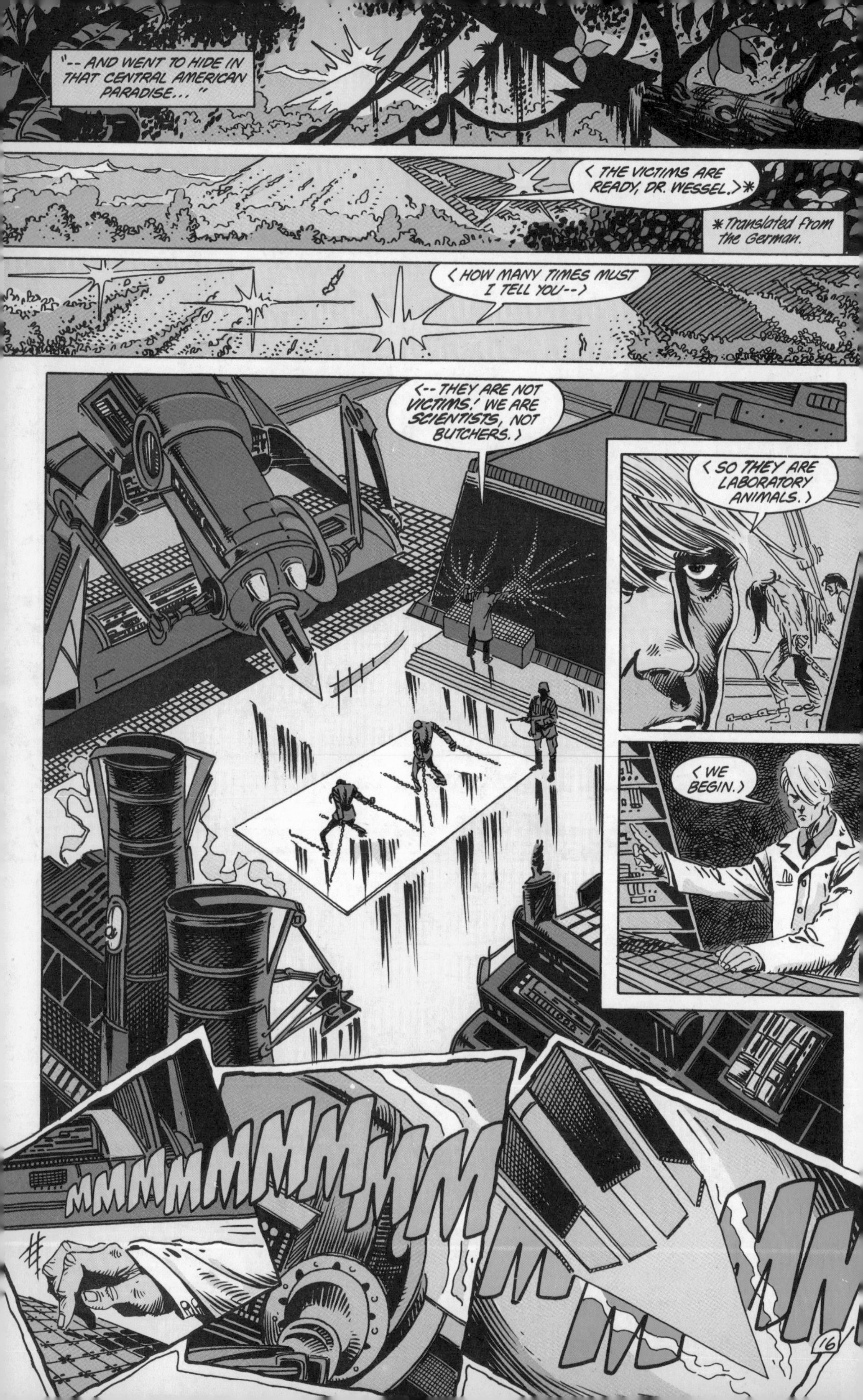
"-- AND WENT TO HIDE IN THAT CENTRAL AMERICAN PARADISE..."
< THE VICTIMS ARE READY, DR. WESSEL. >*
*Translated from the German.
< HOW MANY TIMES MUST I TELL YOU-- >
<-- THEY ARE NOT VICTIMS! WE ARE SCIENTISTS, NOT BUTCHERS. >
< SO THEY ARE LABORATORY ANIMALS. >
< WE BEGIN. >
MMMMMMMMMMMMMMMMMM
16

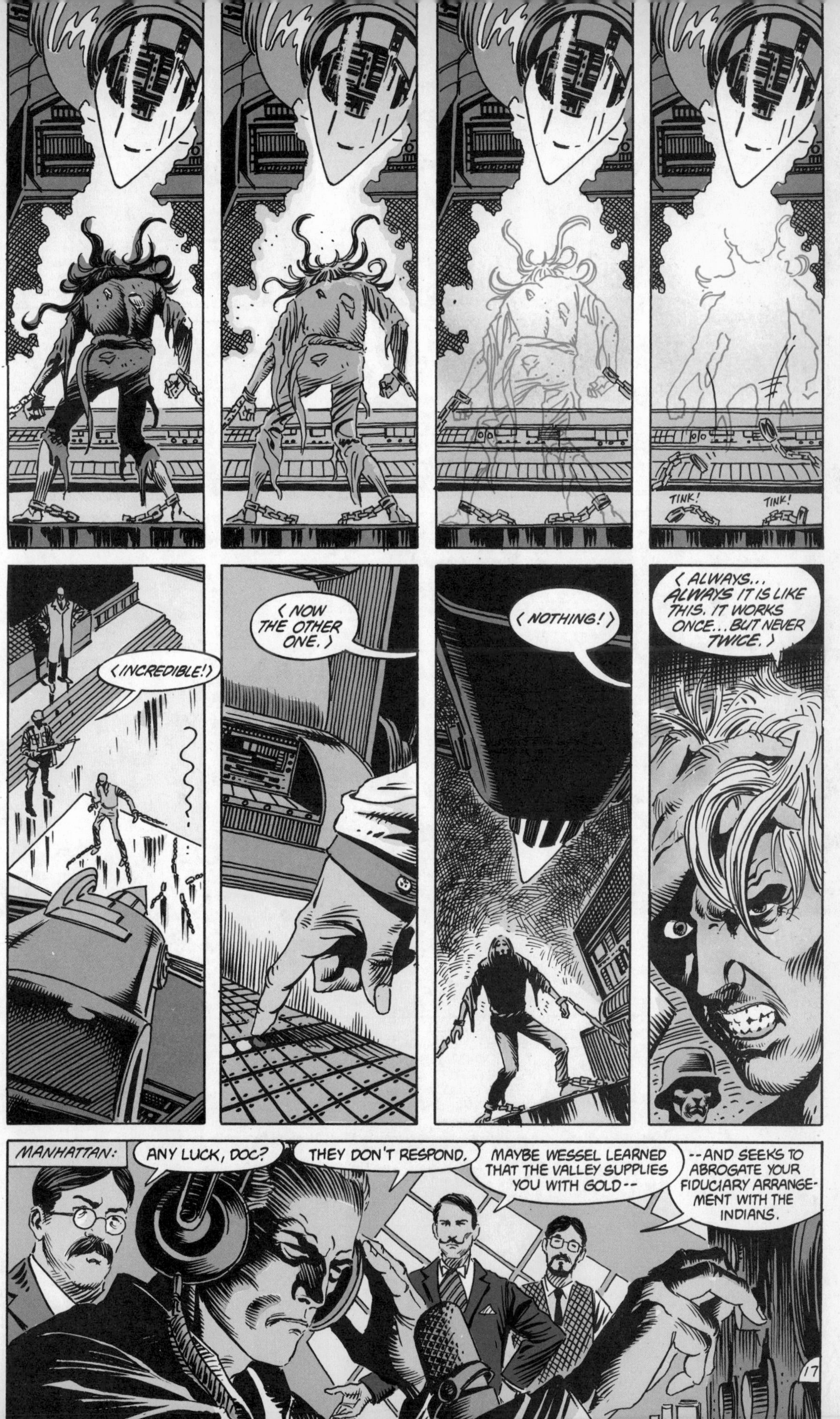
TINK!
TINK!
⟨INCREDIBLE!⟩
⟨NOW THE OTHER ONE.⟩
⟨NOTHING!⟩
⟨ALWAYS... ALWAYS IT IS LIKE THIS. IT WORKS ONCE... BUT NEVER TWICE.⟩
MANHATTAN:
ANY LUCK, DOC?
THEY DON'T RESPOND.
MAYBE WESSEL LEARNED THAT THE VALLEY SUPPLIES YOU WITH GOLD--
--AND SEEKS TO ABROGATE YOUR FIDUCIARY ARRANGEMENT WITH THE INDIANS.

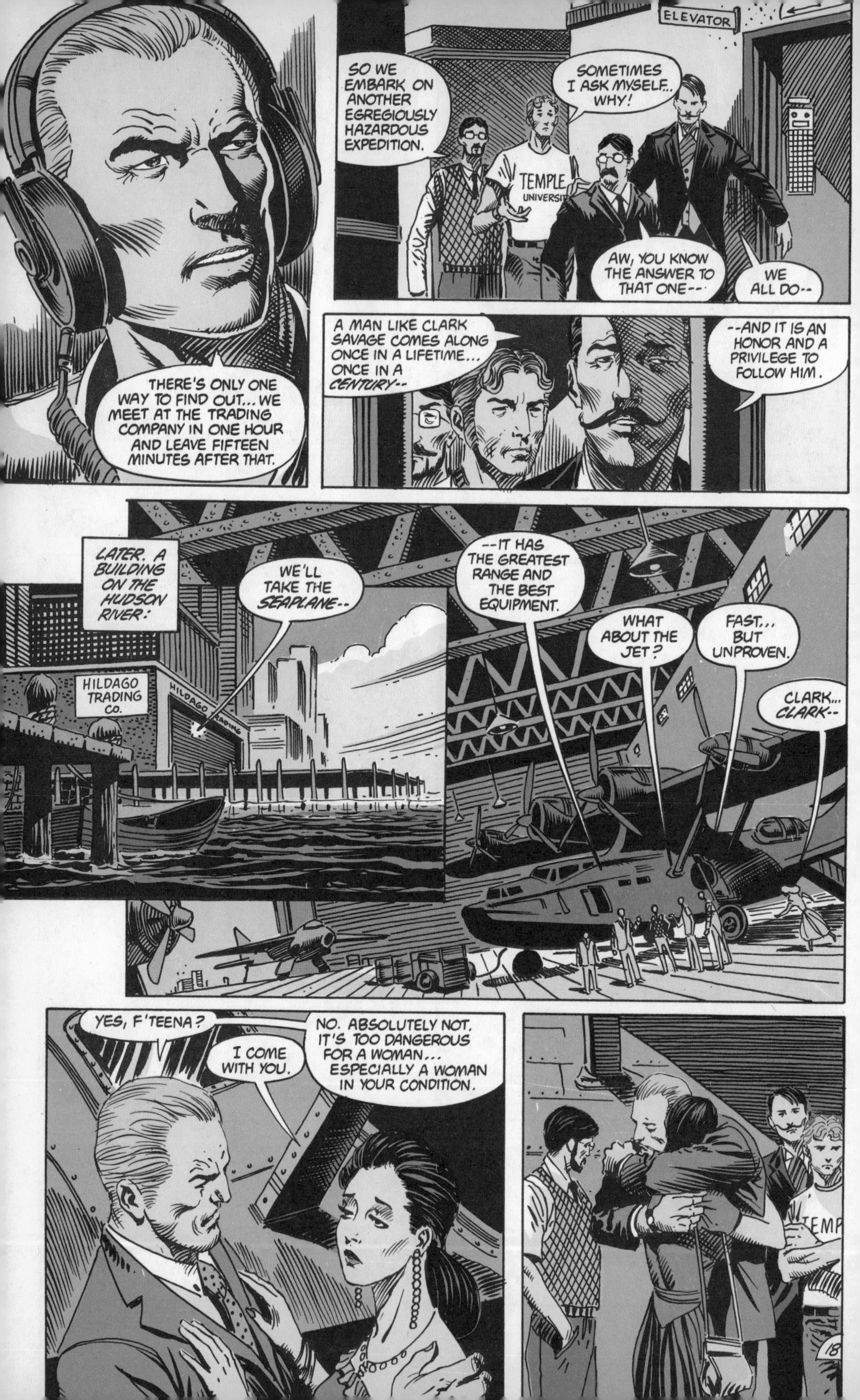
THERE'S ONLY ONE WAY TO FIND OUT... WE MEET AT THE TRADING COMPANY IN ONE HOUR AND LEAVE FIFTEEN MINUTES AFTER THAT.
ELEVATOR
SO WE EMBARK ON ANOTHER EGREGIOUSLY HAZARDOUS EXPEDITION.
SOMETIMES I ASK MYSELF... WHY!
TEMPLE UNIVERSITY
AW, YOU KNOW THE ANSWER TO THAT ONE--
WE ALL DO--
A MAN LIKE CLARK SAVAGE COMES ALONG ONCE IN A LIFETIME... ONCE IN A CENTURY--
--AND IT IS AN HONOR AND A PRIVILEGE TO FOLLOW HIM.
LATER. A BUILDING ON THE HUDSON RIVER:
HILDAGO TRADING CO.
WE'LL TAKE THE SEAPLANE--
--IT HAS THE GREATEST RANGE AND THE BEST EQUIPMENT.
WHAT ABOUT THE JET?
FAST... BUT UNPROVEN.
CLARK... CLARK--
YES, F'TEENA?
I COME WITH YOU.
NO. ABSOLUTELY NOT. IT'S TOO DANGEROUS FOR A WOMAN... ESPECIALLY A WOMAN IN YOUR CONDITION.
18

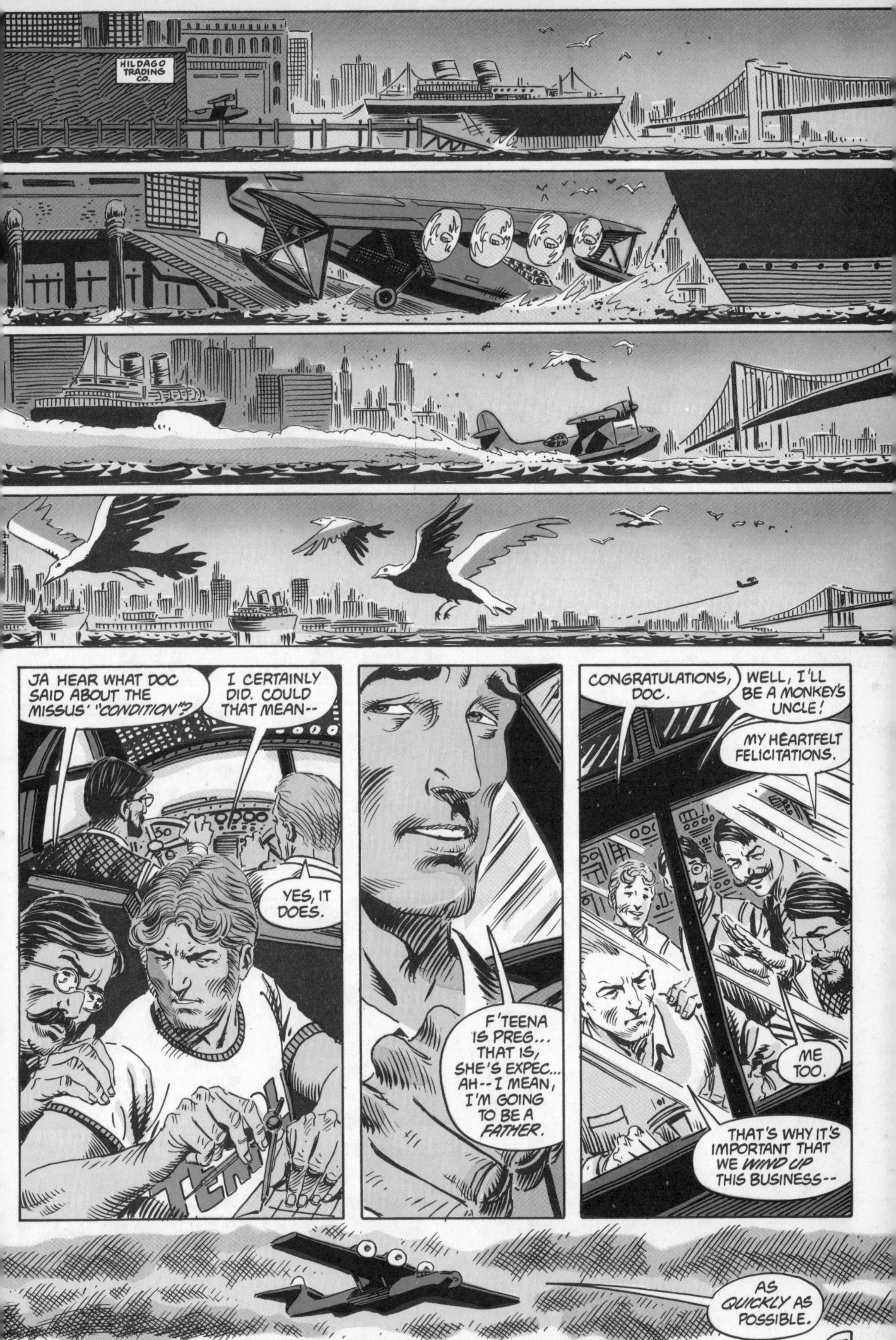
HILDAGO TRADING CO.
JA HEAR WHAT DOC SAID ABOUT THE MISSUS' "CONDITION"?
I CERTAINLY DID. COULD THAT MEAN--
YES, IT DOES.
F'TEENA IS PREG... THAT IS, SHE'S EXPEC... AH--I MEAN, I'M GOING TO BE A FATHER.
CONGRATULATIONS, DOC.
WELL, I'LL BE A MONKEY'S UNCLE!
MY HEARTFELT FELICITATIONS.
ME TOO.
THAT'S WHY IT'S IMPORTANT THAT WE WIND UP THIS BUSINESS--
AS QUICKLY AS POSSIBLE.
19

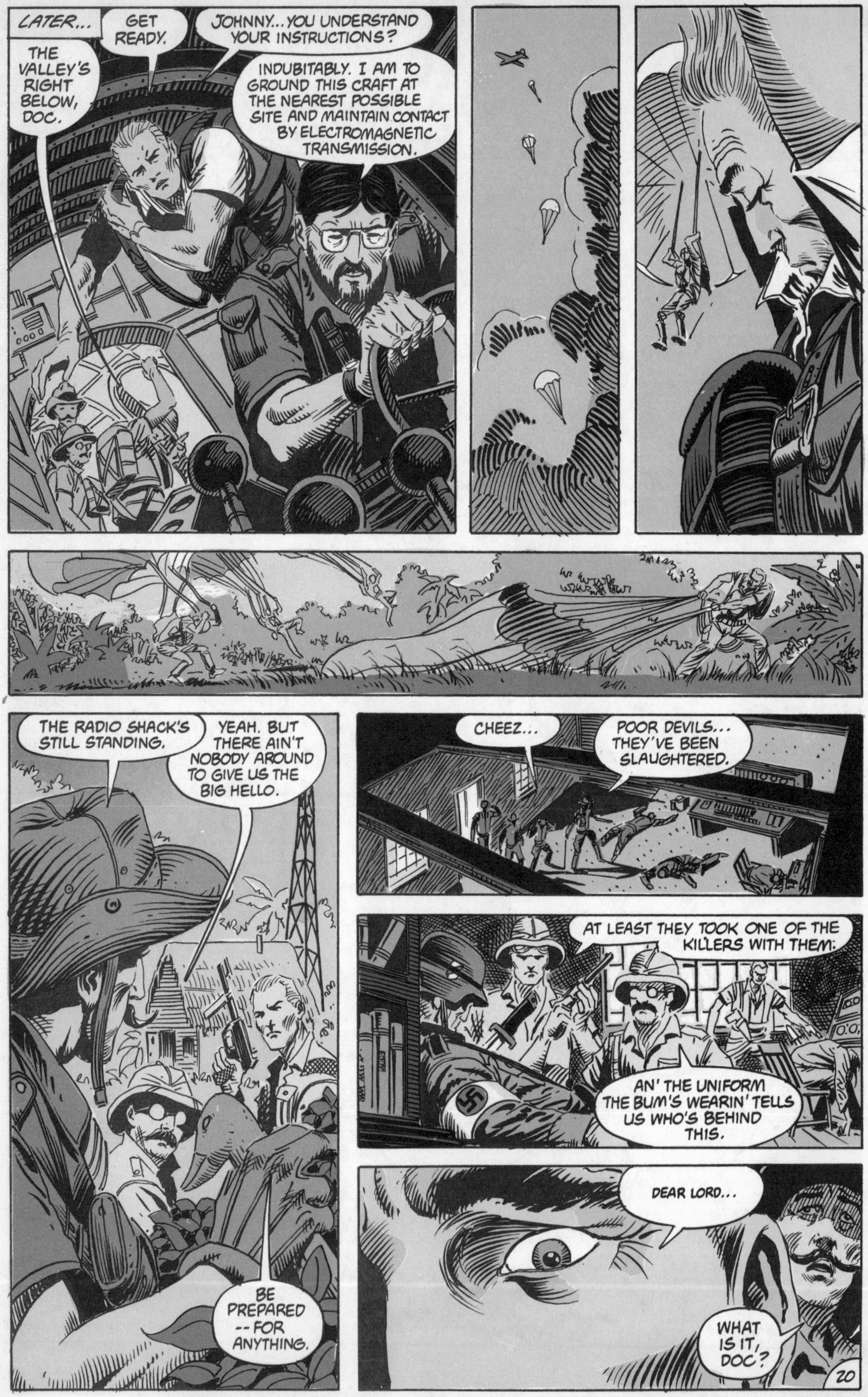

LATER...
THE VALLEY'S RIGHT BELOW, DOC.
GET READY.
JOHNNY... YOU UNDERSTAND YOUR INSTRUCTIONS?
INDUBITABLY. I AM TO GROUND THIS CRAFT AT THE NEAREST POSSIBLE SITE AND MAINTAIN CONTACT BY ELECTROMAGNETIC TRANSMISSION.
THE RADIO SHACK'S STILL STANDING.
YEAH. BUT THERE AIN'T NOBODY AROUND TO GIVE US THE BIG HELLO.
BE PREPARED -- FOR ANYTHING.
CHEEZ...
POOR DEVILS... THEY'VE BEEN SLAUGHTERED.
AT LEAST THEY TOOK ONE OF THE KILLERS WITH THEM.
AN' THE UNIFORM THE BUM'S WEARIN' TELLS US WHO'S BEHIND THIS.
DEAR LORD...
WHAT IS IT, DOC?
20

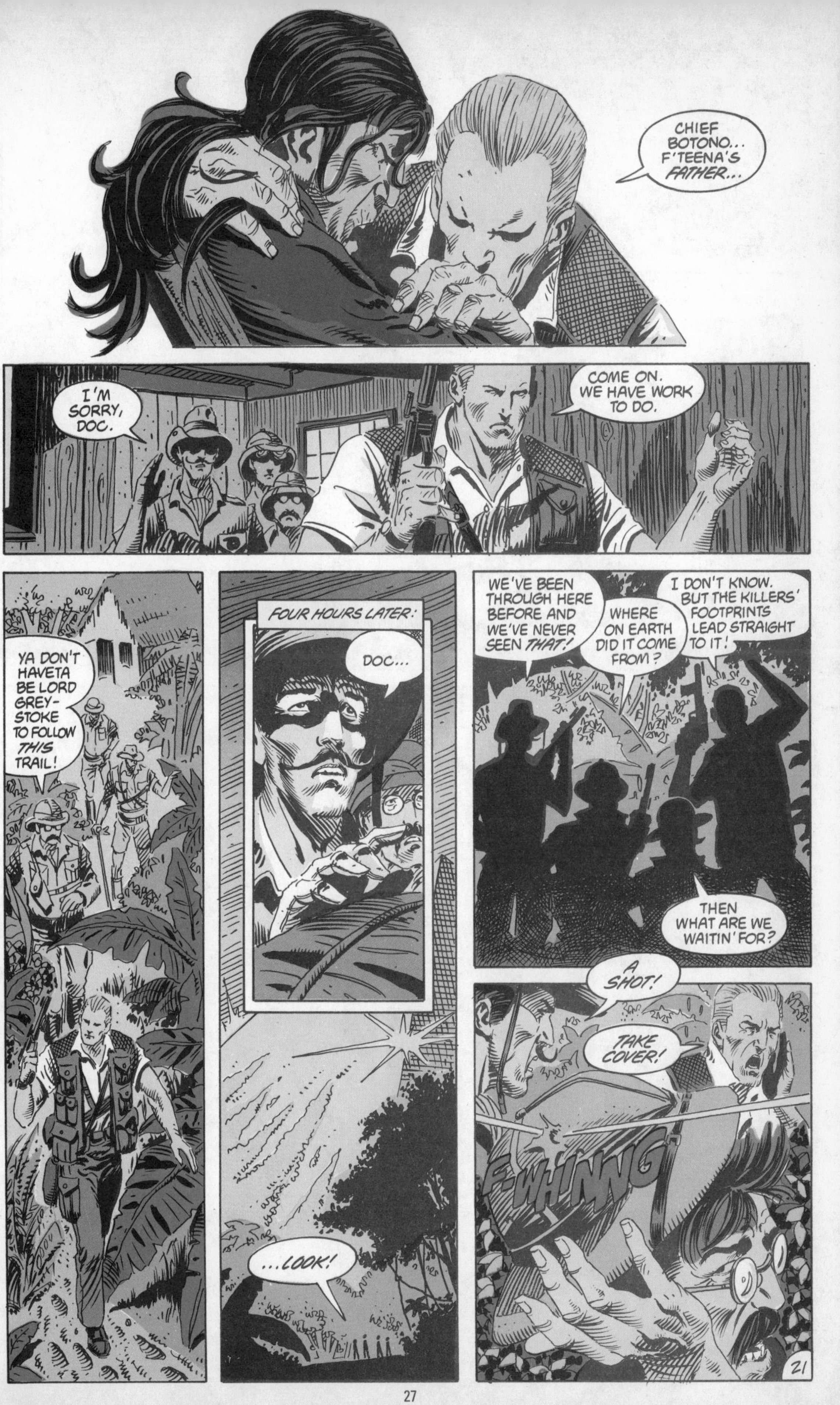
CHIEF BOTONO... F'TEENA'S *FATHER*...
I'M SORRY, DOC.
COME ON. WE HAVE WORK TO DO.
YA DON'T HAVETA BE LORD GREY-STOKE TO FOLLOW *THIS* TRAIL!
FOUR HOURS LATER:
DOC...
...LOOK!
WE'VE BEEN THROUGH HERE BEFORE AND WE'VE NEVER SEEN *THAT*!
WHERE ON EARTH DID IT COME FROM?
I DON'T KNOW. BUT THE KILLERS' FOOTPRINTS LEAD STRAIGHT TO IT!
THEN WHAT ARE WE WAITIN' FOR?
A SHOT!
TAKE COVER!
F-WHINNG
21

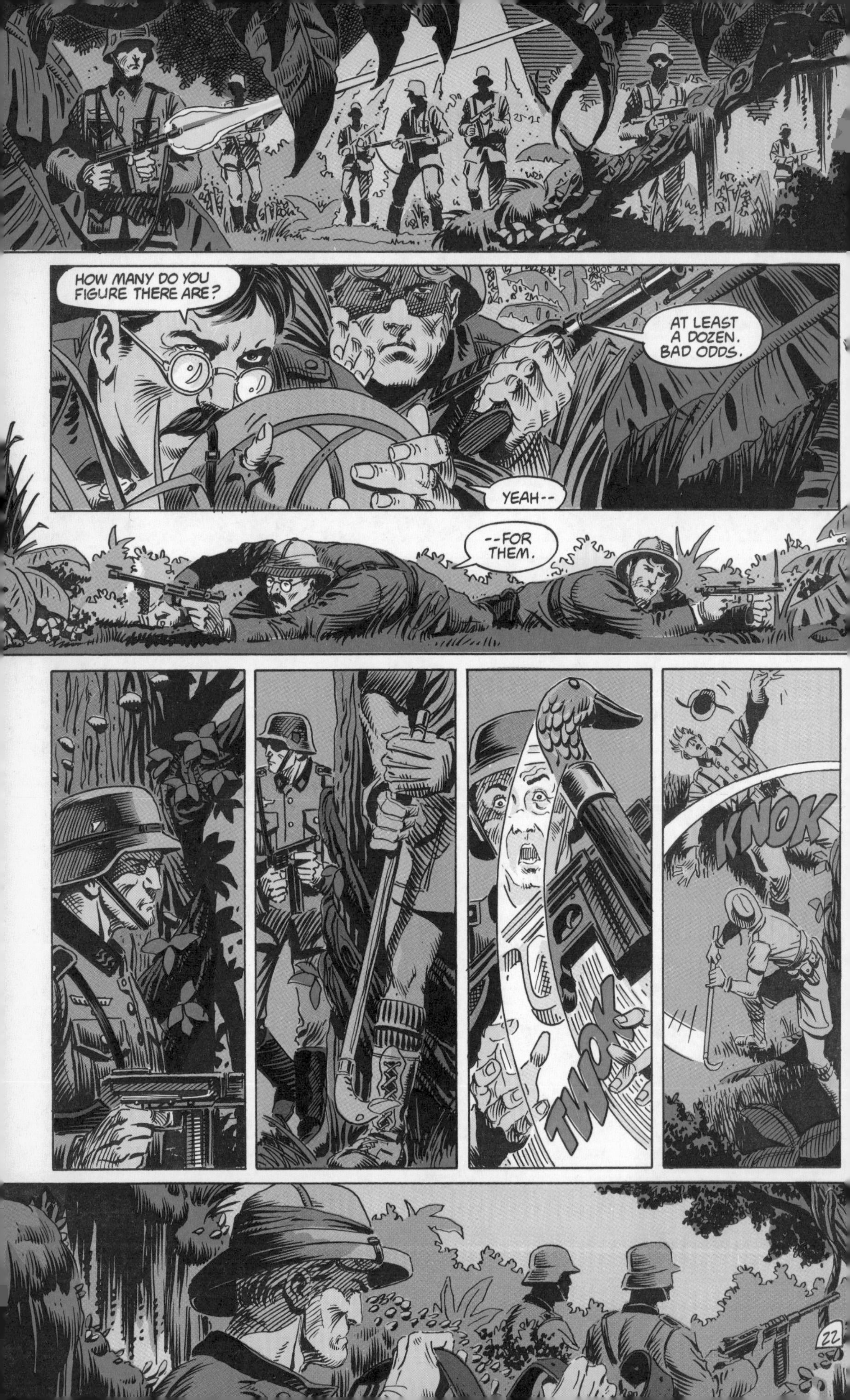

HOW MANY DO YOU FIGURE THERE ARE?
AT LEAST A DOZEN. BAD ODDS.
YEAH--
--FOR THEM.
KNOK
TWOK

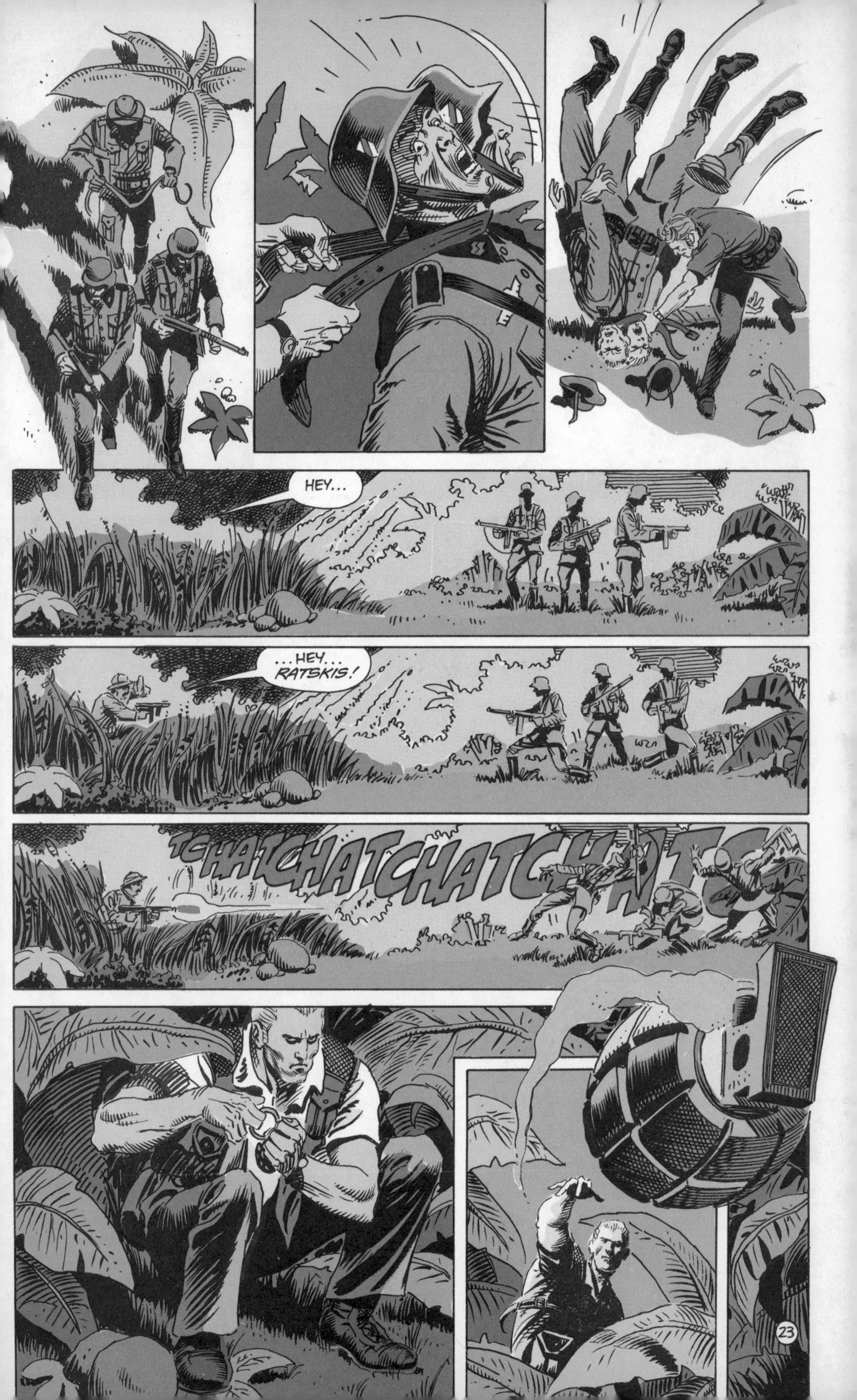
HEY...
...HEY... RATSKIS!
TCHATCHATCHATCHATS
23

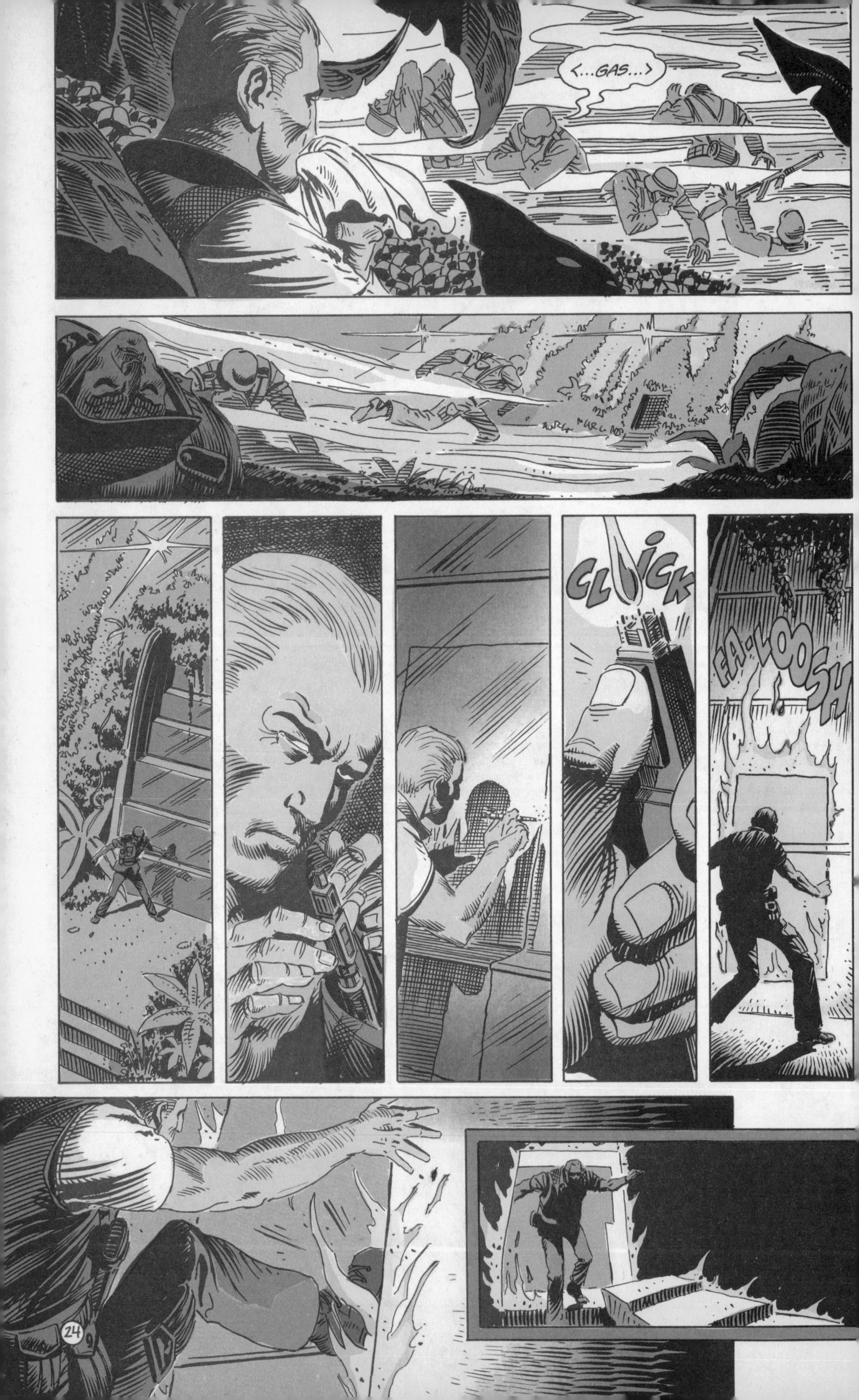

<...GAS...>
CLICK
FA-LOOSH

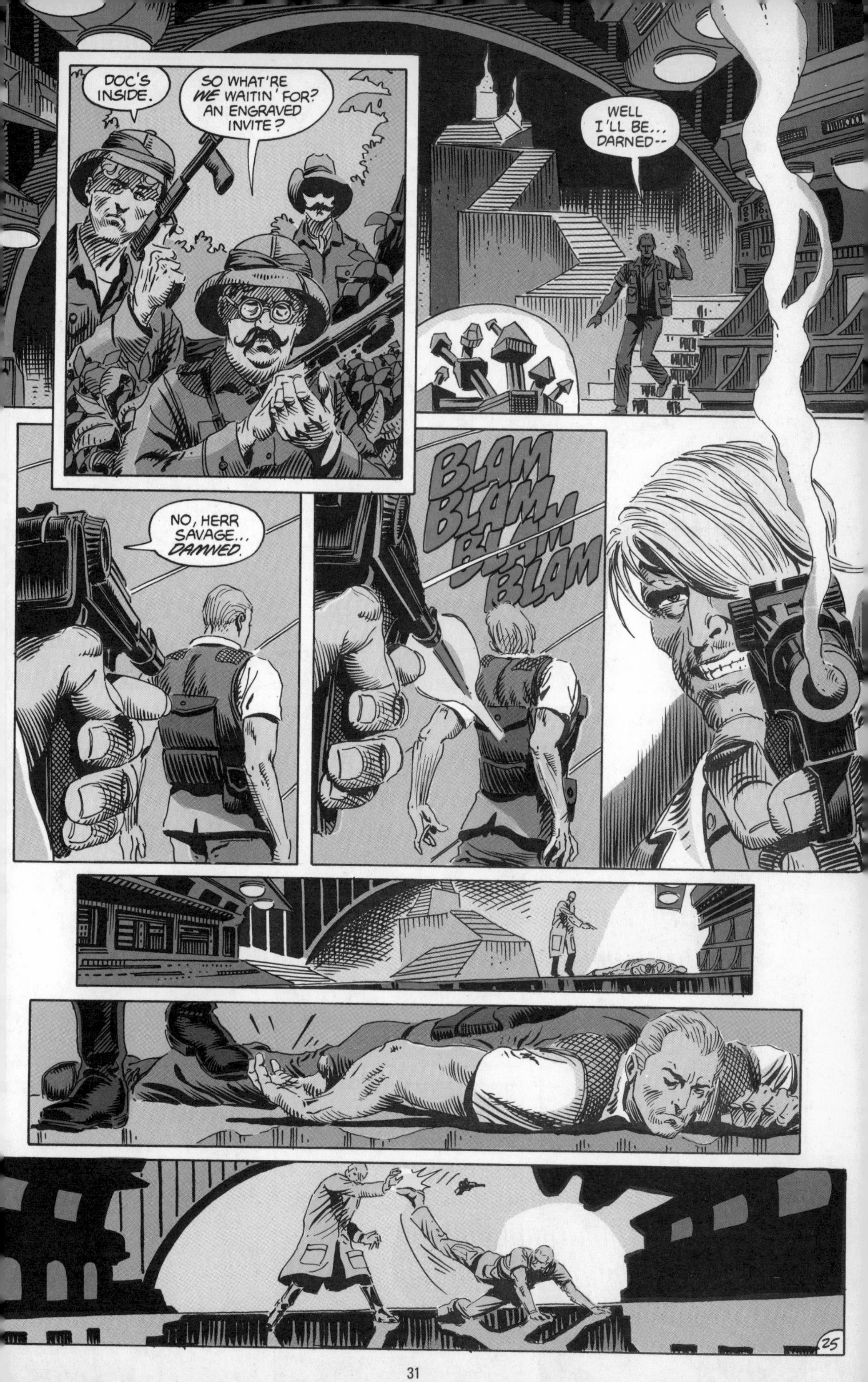
DOC'S INSIDE.
SO WHAT'RE WE WAITIN' FOR? AN ENGRAVED INVITE?
WELL I'LL BE... DARNED--
NO, HERR SAVAGE... DAMNED.
BLAM BLAM BLAM BLAM
25

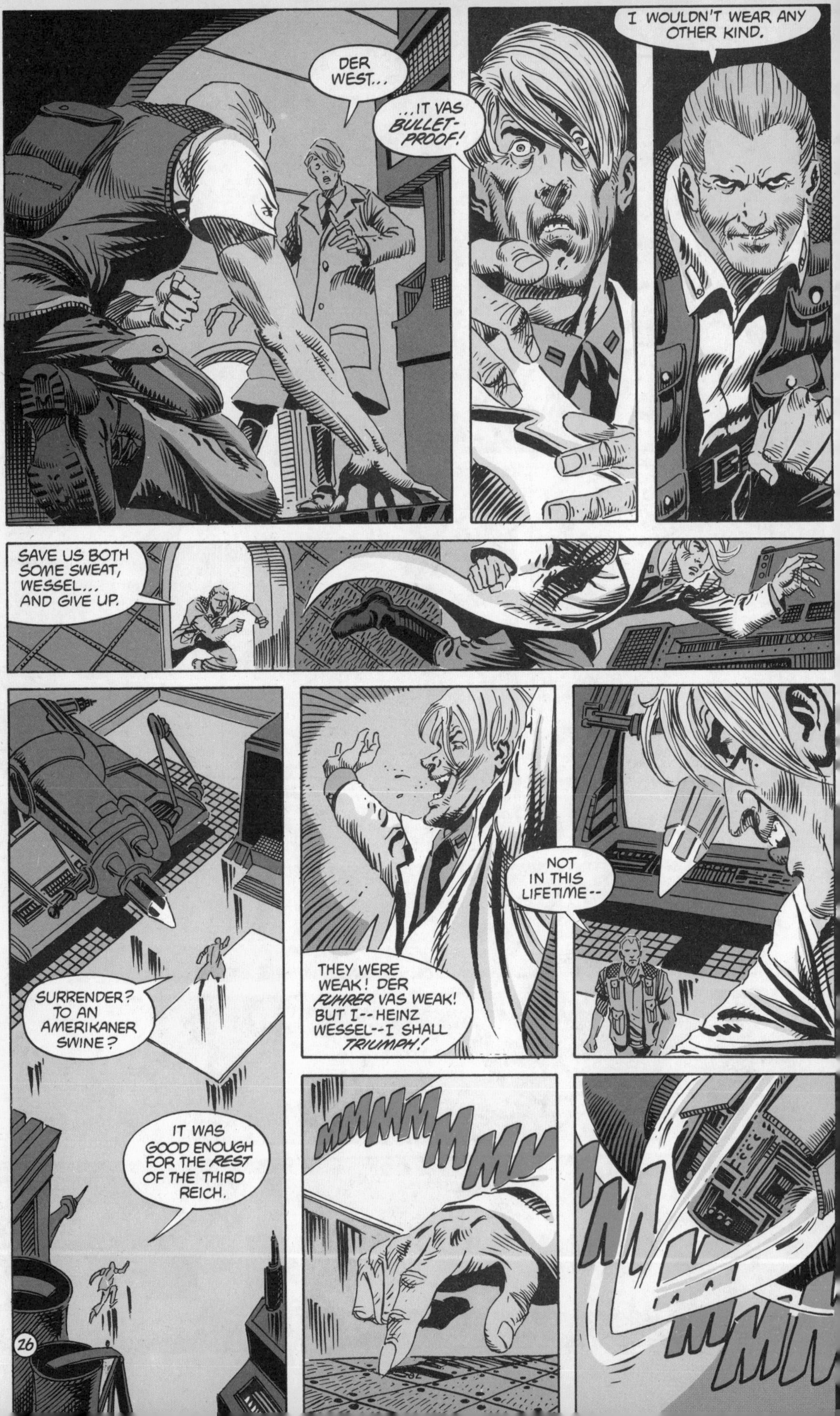

DER WEST...
...IT VAS BULLET-PROOF!
I WOULDN'T WEAR ANY OTHER KIND.
SAVE US BOTH SOME SWEAT, WESSEL... AND GIVE UP.
SURRENDER? TO AN AMERIKANER SWINE?
THEY WERE WEAK! DER FUHRER VAS WEAK! BUT I--HEINZ WESSEL--I SHALL TRIUMPH!
NOT IN THIS LIFETIME--
IT WAS GOOD ENOUGH FOR THE REST OF THE THIRD REICH.
MMMMMMMMM
MMMMMMM

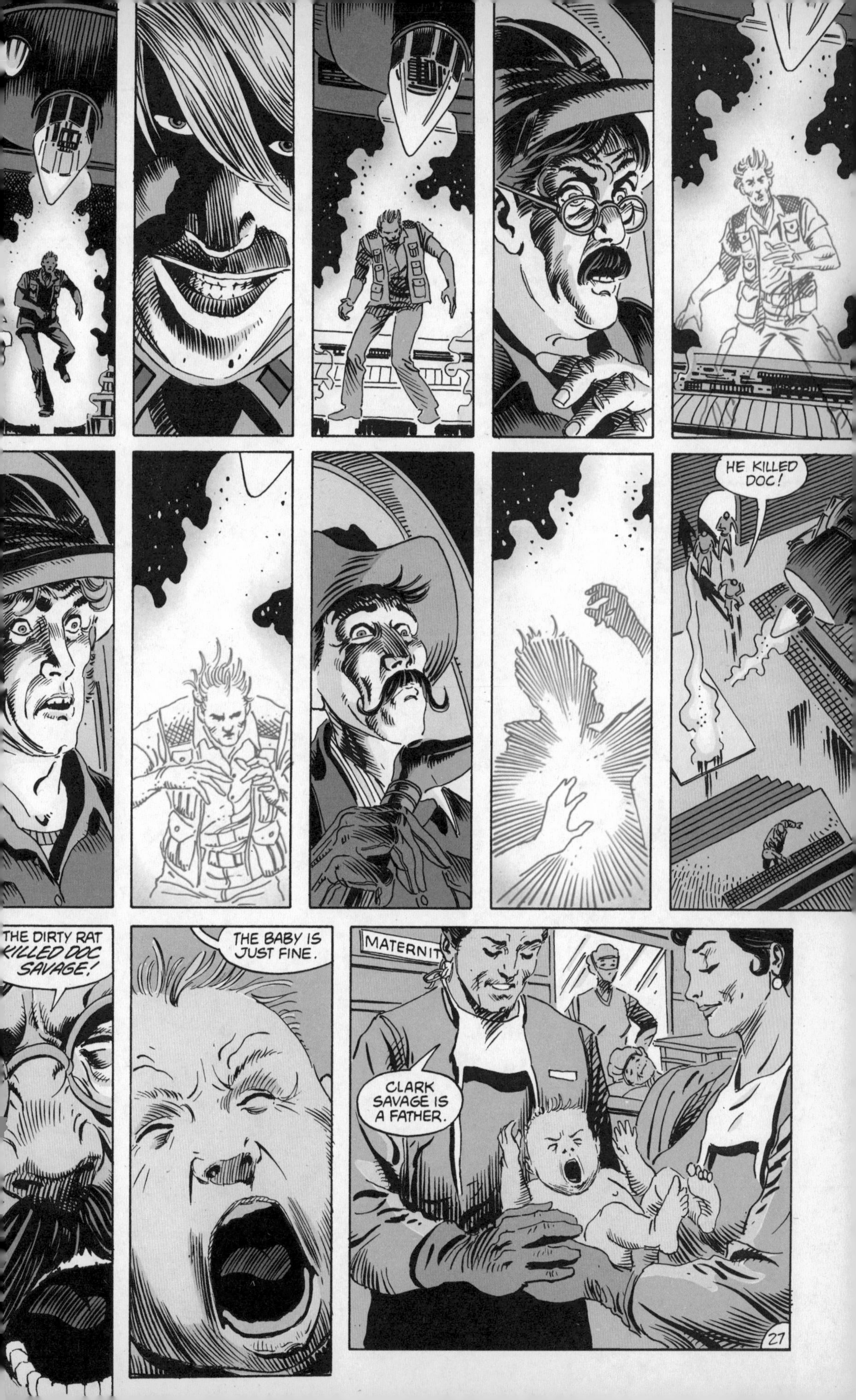
HE KILLED DOC!
THE DIRTY RAT KILLED DOC SAVAGE!
THE BABY IS JUST FINE.
MATERNIT
CLARK SAVAGE IS A FATHER.
27

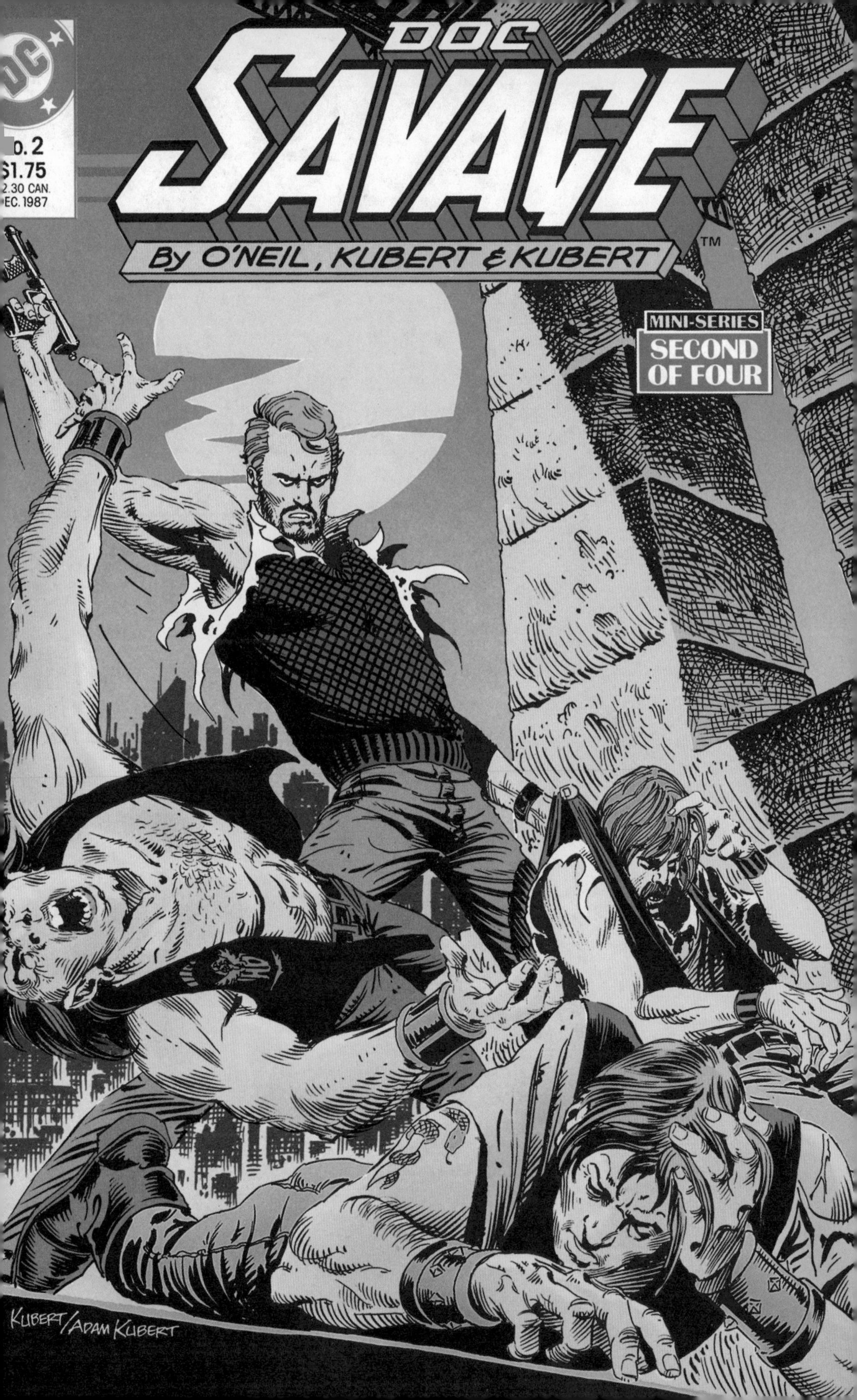

DOC
SAVAGE
o. 2
$1.75
2.30 CAN.
EC. 1987
TM
By O'NEIL, KUBERT & KUBERT
MINI-SERIES
SECOND OF FOUR
KUBERT/ADAM KUBERT

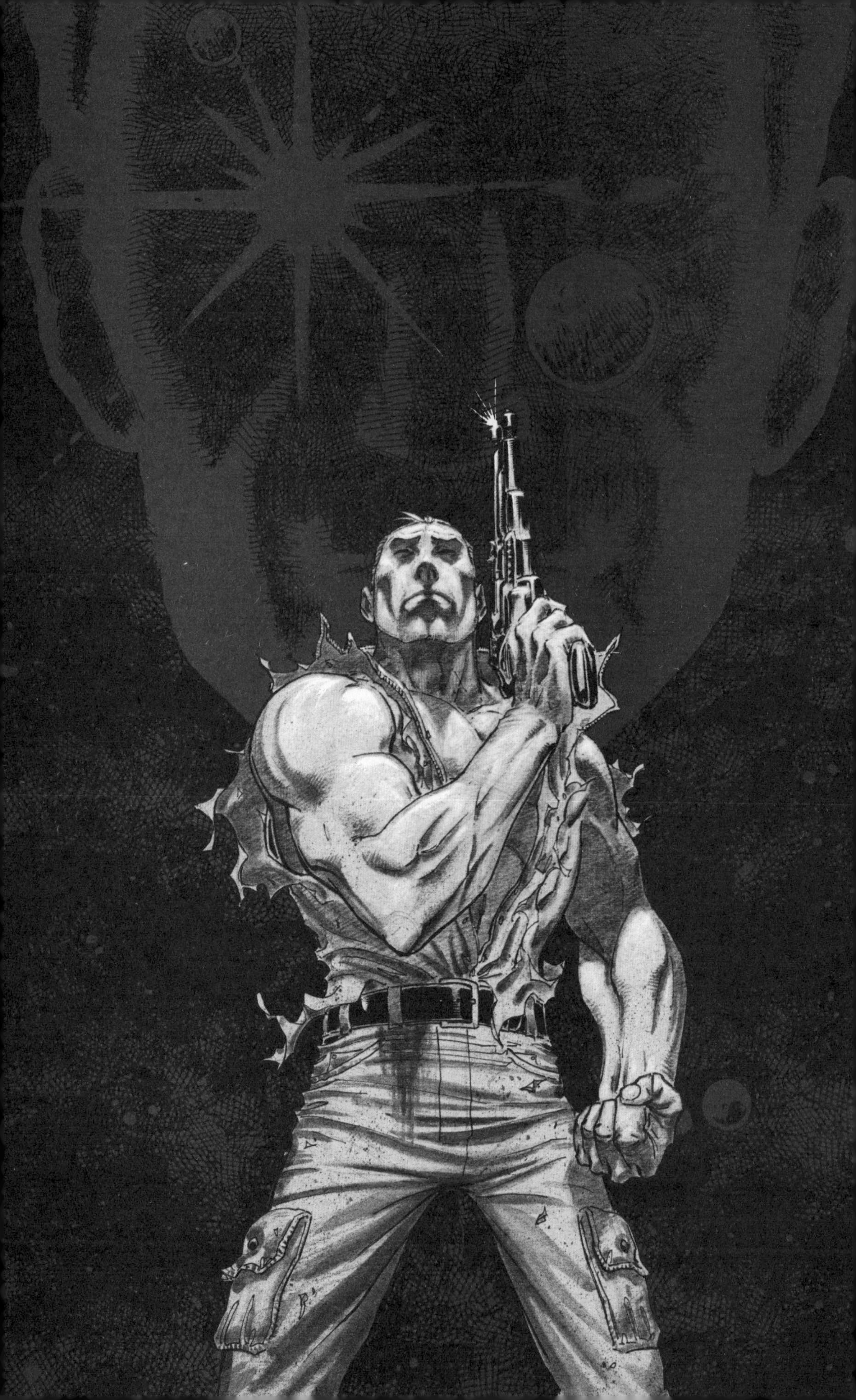

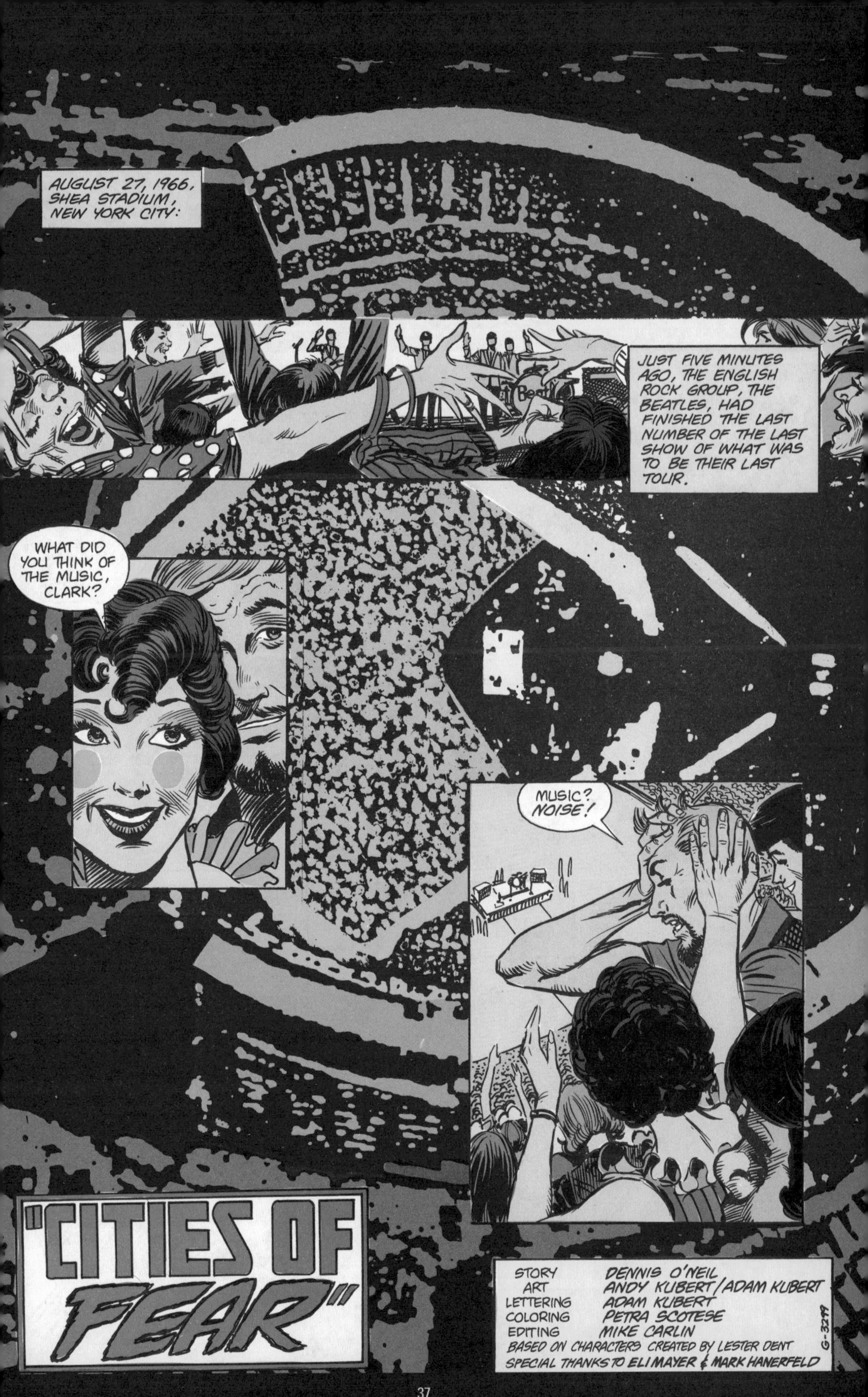

AUGUST 27, 1966, SHEA STADIUM, NEW YORK CITY:
JUST FIVE MINUTES AGO, THE ENGLISH ROCK GROUP, THE BEATLES, HAD FINISHED THE LAST NUMBER OF THE LAST SHOW OF WHAT WAS TO BE THEIR LAST TOUR.
WHAT DID YOU THINK OF THE MUSIC, CLARK?
MUSIC? NOISE!
"CITIES OF FEAR"
STORY DENNIS O'NEIL
ART ANDY KUBERT/ADAM KUBERT
LETTERING ADAM KUBERT
COLORING PETRA SCOTESE
EDITING MIKE CARLIN
BASED ON CHARACTERS CREATED BY LESTER DENT
SPECIAL THANKS TO ELI MAYER & MARK HANERFELD
G-3299

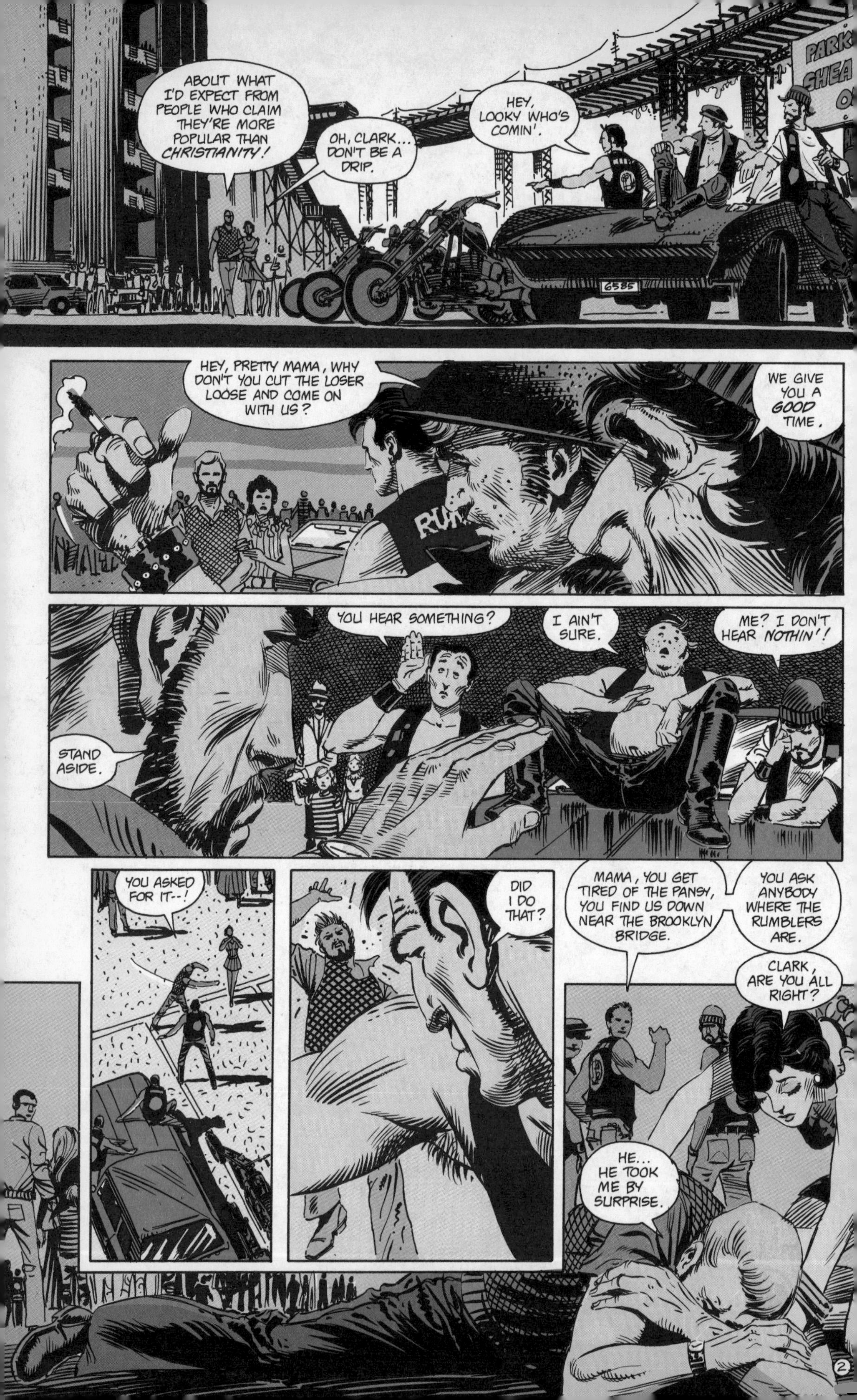
PARK
SHEA
ABOUT WHAT I'D EXPECT FROM PEOPLE WHO CLAIM THEY'RE MORE POPULAR THAN CHRISTIANITY!
OH, CLARK... DON'T BE A DRIP.
HEY, LOOKY WHO'S COMIN'.
6585
HEY, PRETTY MAMA, WHY DON'T YOU CUT THE LOSER LOOSE AND COME ON WITH US?
WE GIVE YOU A GOOD TIME.
YOU HEAR SOMETHING?
I AIN'T SURE.
ME? I DON'T HEAR NOTHIN'!
STAND ASIDE.
YOU ASKED FOR IT--!
DID I DO THAT?
MAMA, YOU GET TIRED OF THE PANSY, YOU FIND US DOWN NEAR THE BROOKLYN BRIDGE.
YOU ASK ANYBODY WHERE THE RUMBLERS ARE.
CLARK, ARE YOU ALL RIGHT?
HE... HE TOOK ME BY SURPRISE.
2

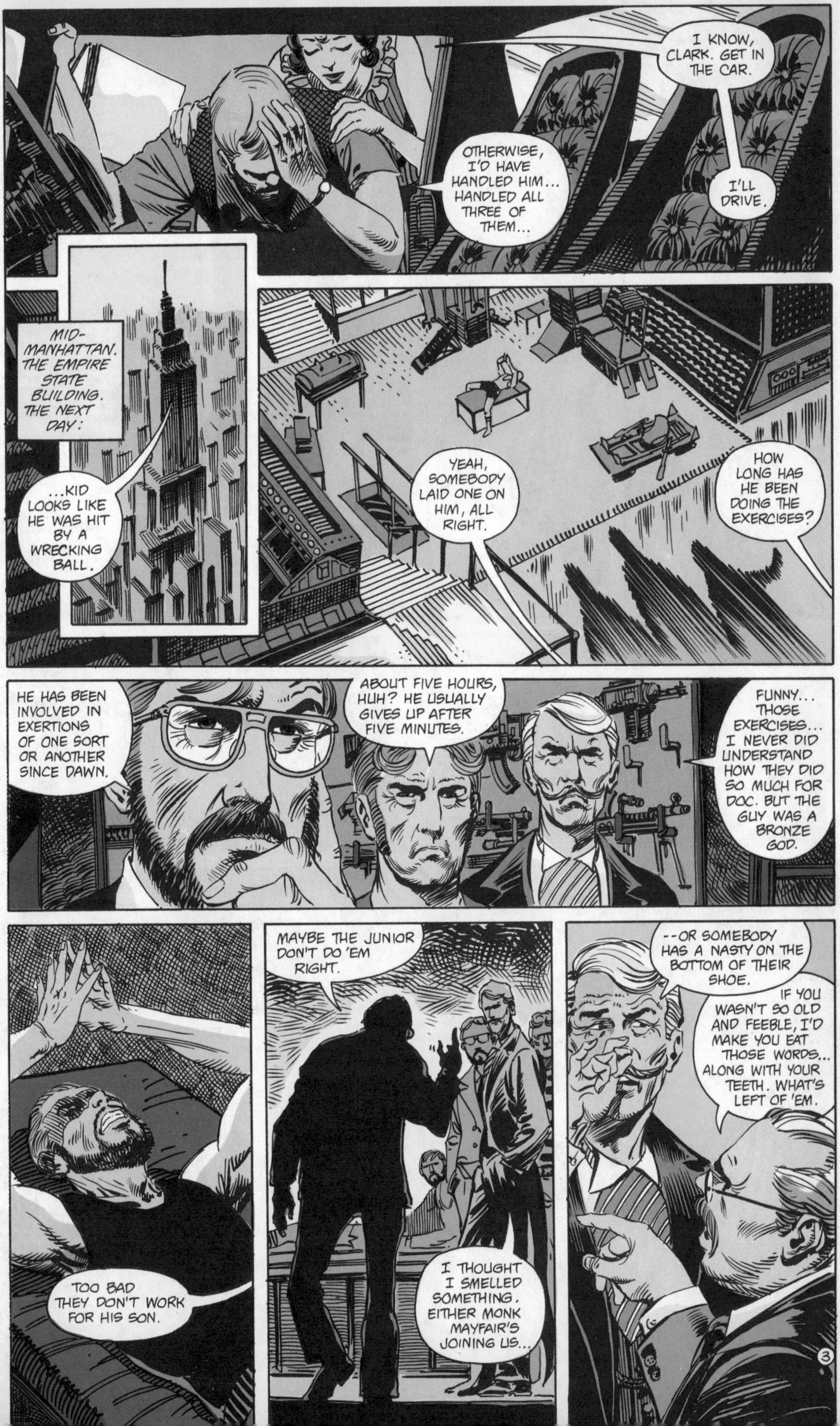
OTHERWISE, I'D HAVE HANDLED HIM... HANDLED ALL THREE OF THEM...
I KNOW, CLARK. GET IN THE CAR.
I'LL DRIVE.
MID-MANHATTAN. THE EMPIRE STATE BUILDING. THE NEXT DAY:
...KID LOOKS LIKE HE WAS HIT BY A WRECKING BALL.
YEAH, SOMEBODY LAID ONE ON HIM, ALL RIGHT.
HOW LONG HAS HE BEEN DOING THE EXERCISES?
HE HAS BEEN INVOLVED IN EXERTIONS OF ONE SORT OR ANOTHER SINCE DAWN.
ABOUT FIVE HOURS, HUH? HE USUALLY GIVES UP AFTER FIVE MINUTES.
FUNNY... THOSE EXERCISES... I NEVER DID UNDERSTAND HOW THEY DID SO MUCH FOR DOC. BUT THE GUY WAS A BRONZE GOD.
TOO BAD THEY DON'T WORK FOR HIS SON.
MAYBE THE JUNIOR DON'T DO 'EM RIGHT.
I THOUGHT I SMELLED SOMETHING. EITHER MONK MAYFAIR'S JOINING US...
--OR SOMEBODY HAS A NASTY ON THE BOTTOM OF THEIR SHOE.
IF YOU WASN'T SO OLD AND FEEBLE, I'D MAKE YOU EAT THOSE WORDS... ALONG WITH YOUR TEETH. WHAT'S LEFT OF 'EM.
3

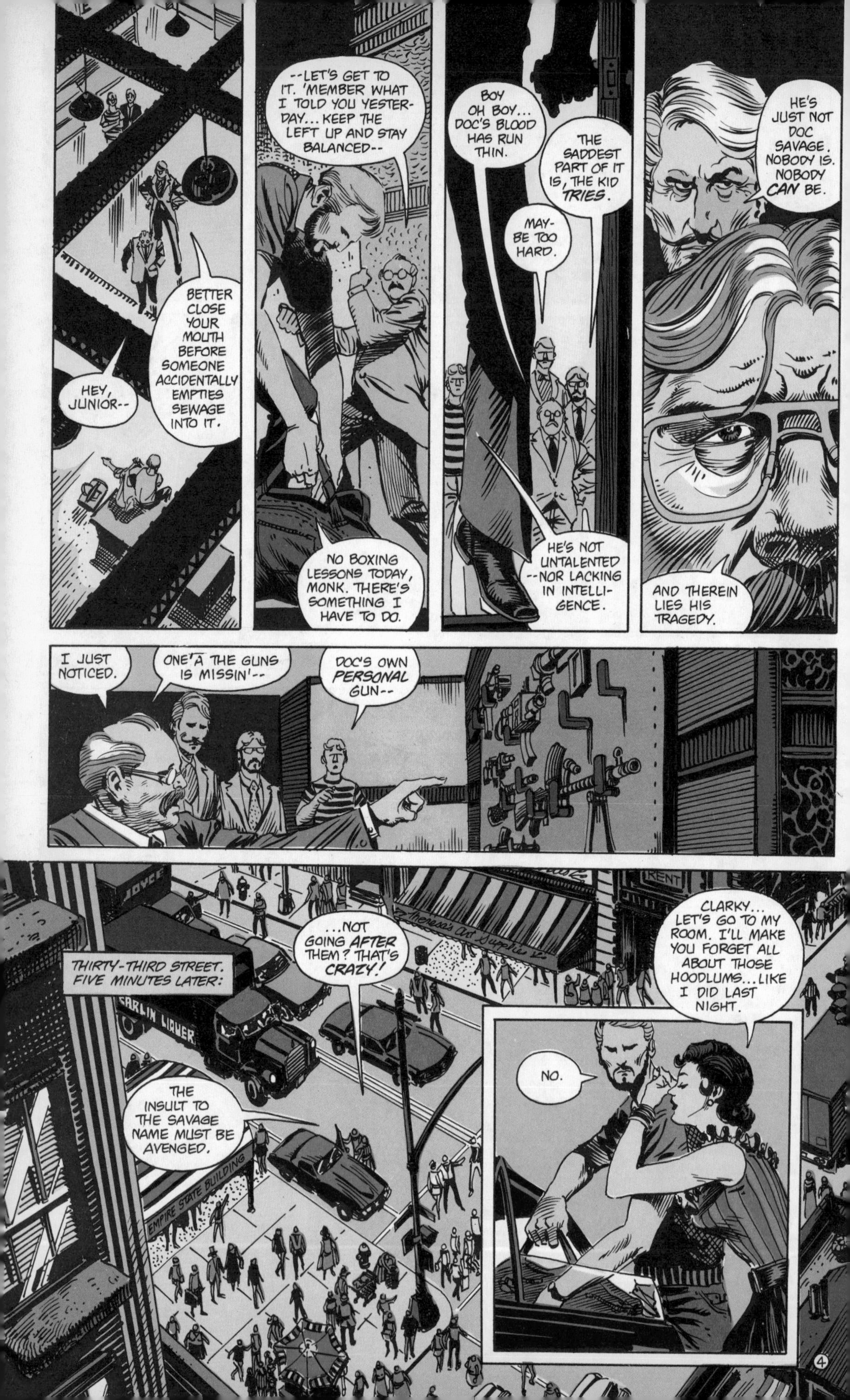
HEY, JUNIOR--
BETTER CLOSE YOUR MOUTH BEFORE SOMEONE ACCIDENTALLY EMPTIES SEWAGE INTO IT.
--LET'S GET TO IT. 'MEMBER WHAT I TOLD YOU YESTER-DAY... KEEP THE LEFT UP AND STAY BALANCED--
NO BOXING LESSONS TODAY, MONK. THERE'S SOMETHING I HAVE TO DO.
BOY OH BOY... DOC'S BLOOD HAS RUN THIN.
THE SADDEST PART OF IT IS, THE KID TRIES.
MAY-BE TOO HARD.
HE'S NOT UNTALENTED --NOR LACKING IN INTELLI-GENCE.
HE'S JUST NOT DOC SAVAGE. NOBODY IS. NOBODY CAN BE.
AND THEREIN LIES HIS TRAGEDY.
I JUST NOTICED.
ONE'A THE GUNS IS MISSIN'--
DOC'S OWN PERSONAL GUN--
THIRTY-THIRD STREET. FIVE MINUTES LATER:
JOYCE
RENT
THE INSULT TO THE SAVAGE NAME MUST BE AVENGED.
...NOT GOING AFTER THEM? THAT'S CRAZY!
EMPIRE STATE BUILDING
CLARKY... LET'S GO TO MY ROOM. I'LL MAKE YOU FORGET ALL ABOUT THOSE HOODLUMS... LIKE I DID LAST NIGHT.
NO.

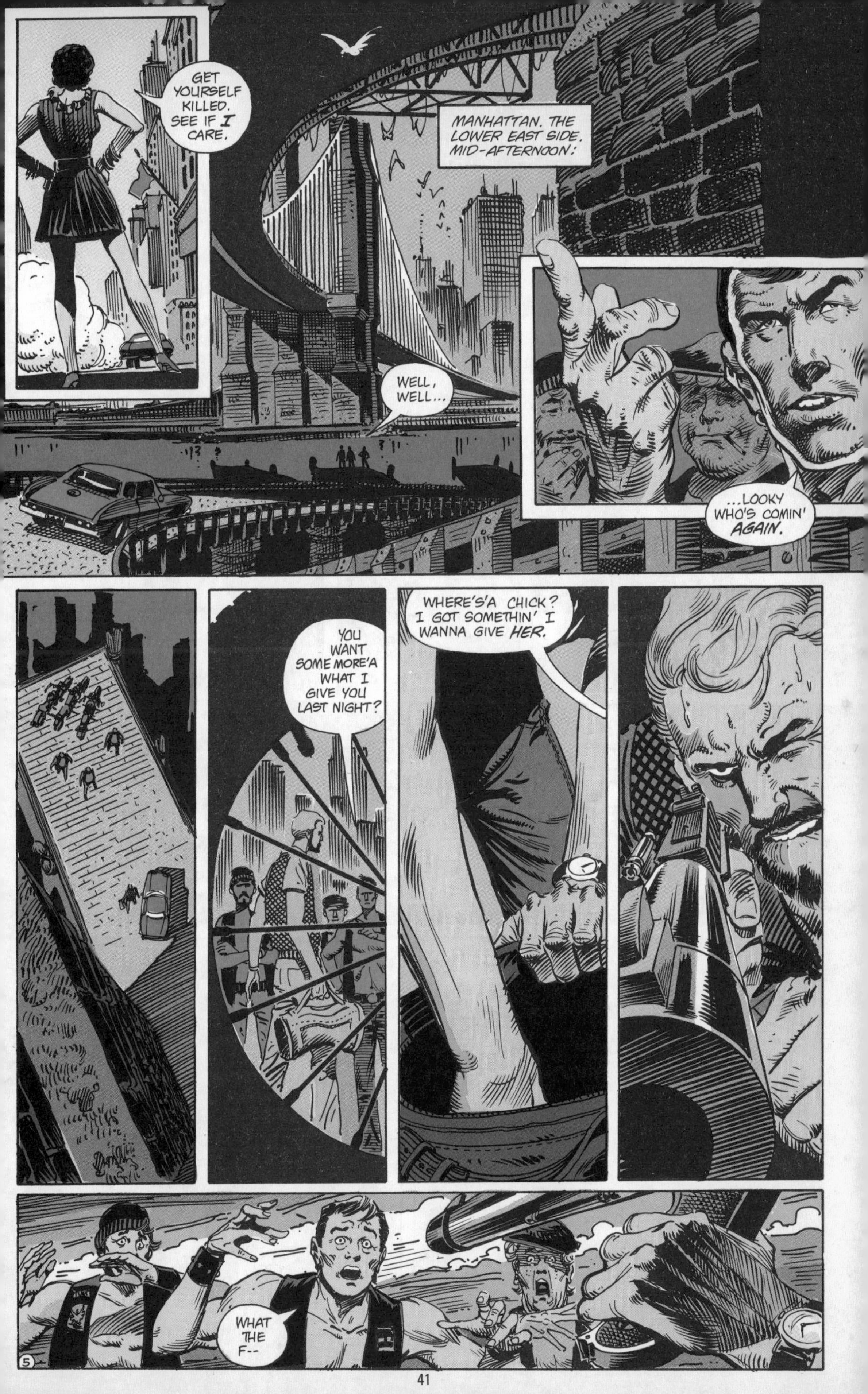
GET YOURSELF KILLED. SEE IF I CARE.
MANHATTAN. THE LOWER EAST SIDE. MID-AFTERNOON:
WELL, WELL...
...LOOKY WHO'S COMIN' AGAIN.
YOU WANT SOME MORE'A WHAT I GIVE YOU LAST NIGHT?
WHERE'S'A CHICK? I GOT SOMETHIN' I WANNA GIVE HER.
WHAT THE F--

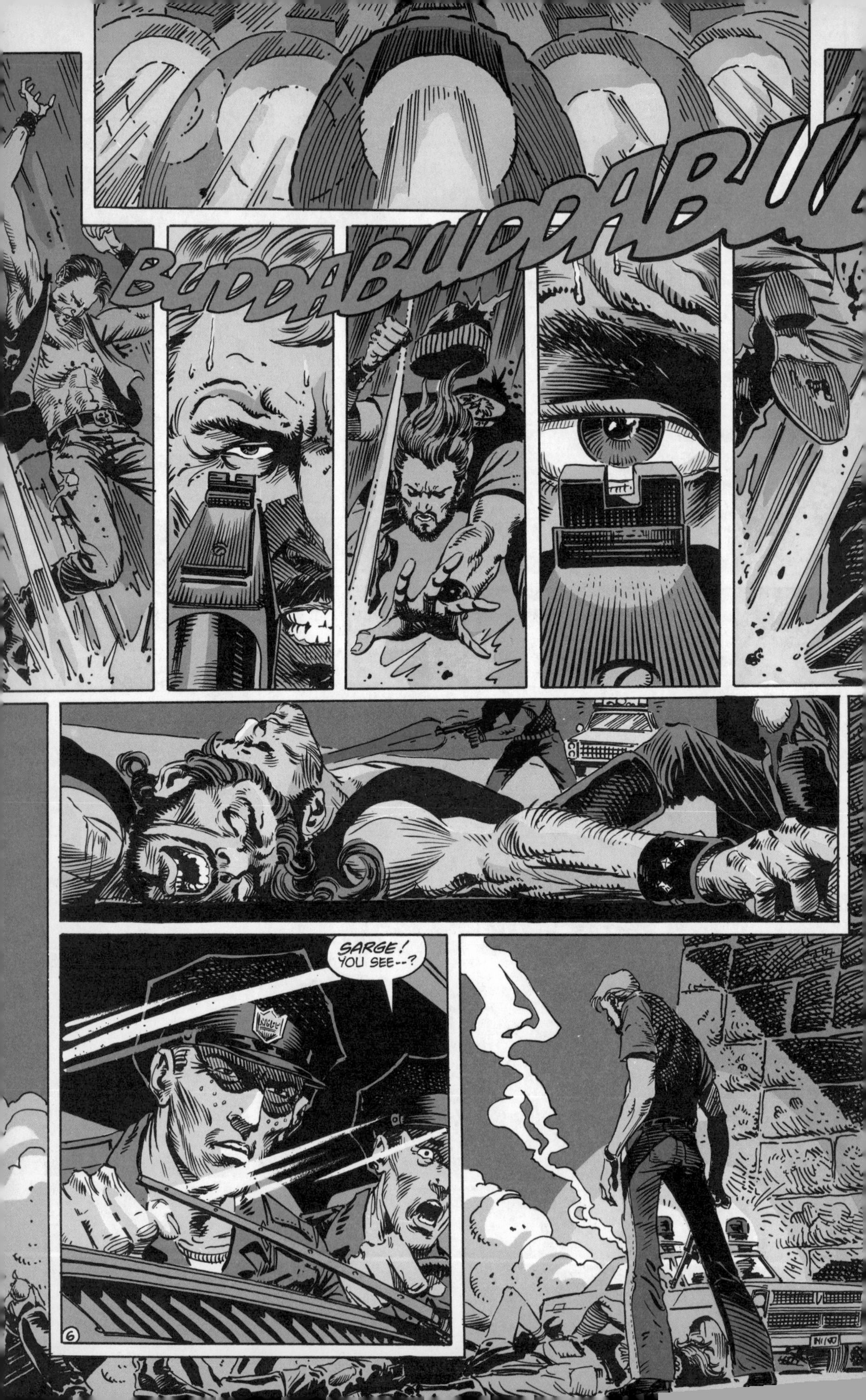
BUDDABUDDABUDDA
SARGE! YOU SEE--?
6

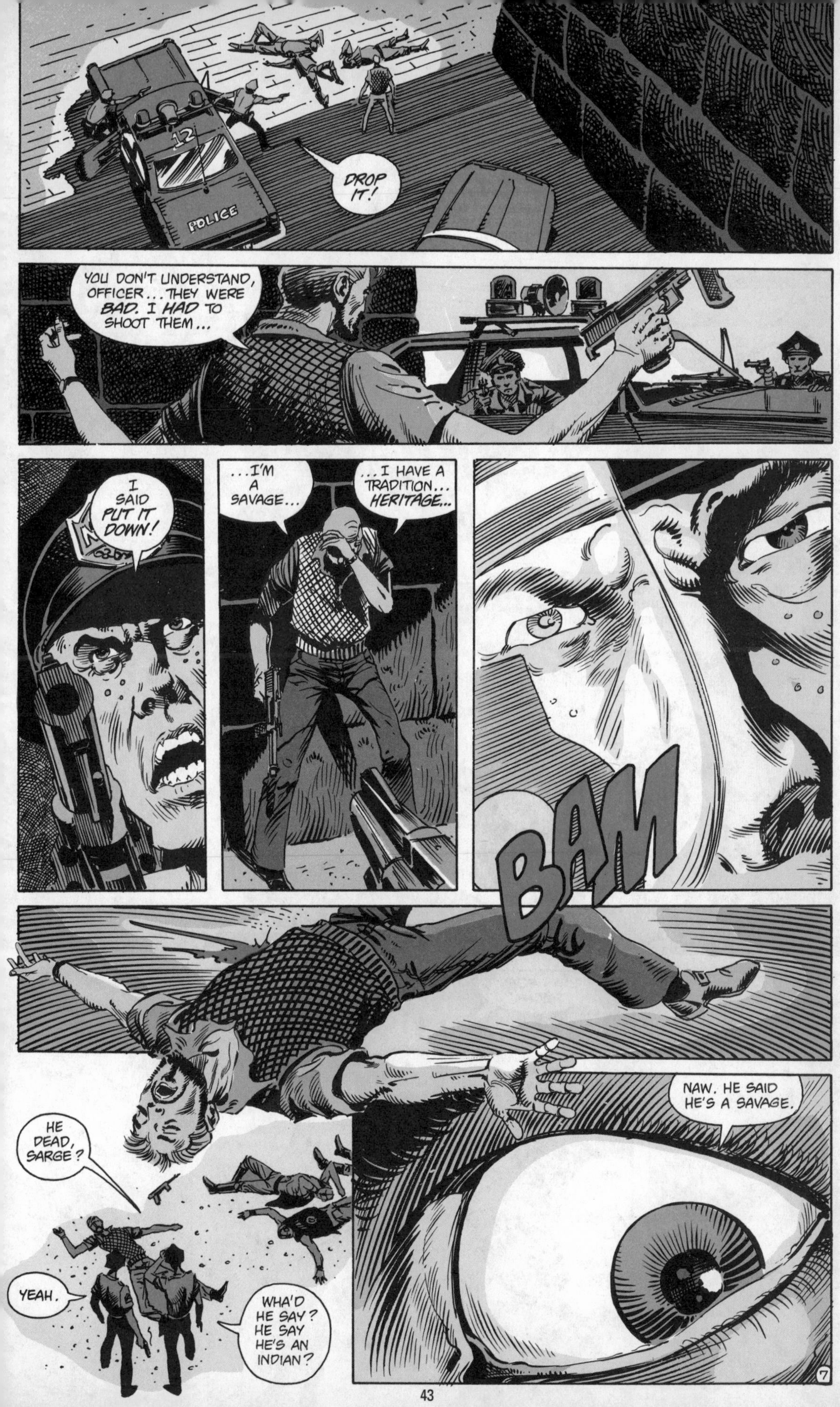
DROP IT!
YOU DON'T UNDERSTAND, OFFICER... THEY WERE BAD. I HAD TO SHOOT THEM...
I SAID PUT IT DOWN!
...I'M A SAVAGE...
...I HAVE A TRADITION... HERITAGE...
BAM
NAW. HE SAID HE'S A SAVAGE.
HE DEAD, SARGE?
YEAH.
WHA'D HE SAY? HE SAY HE'S AN INDIAN?
7

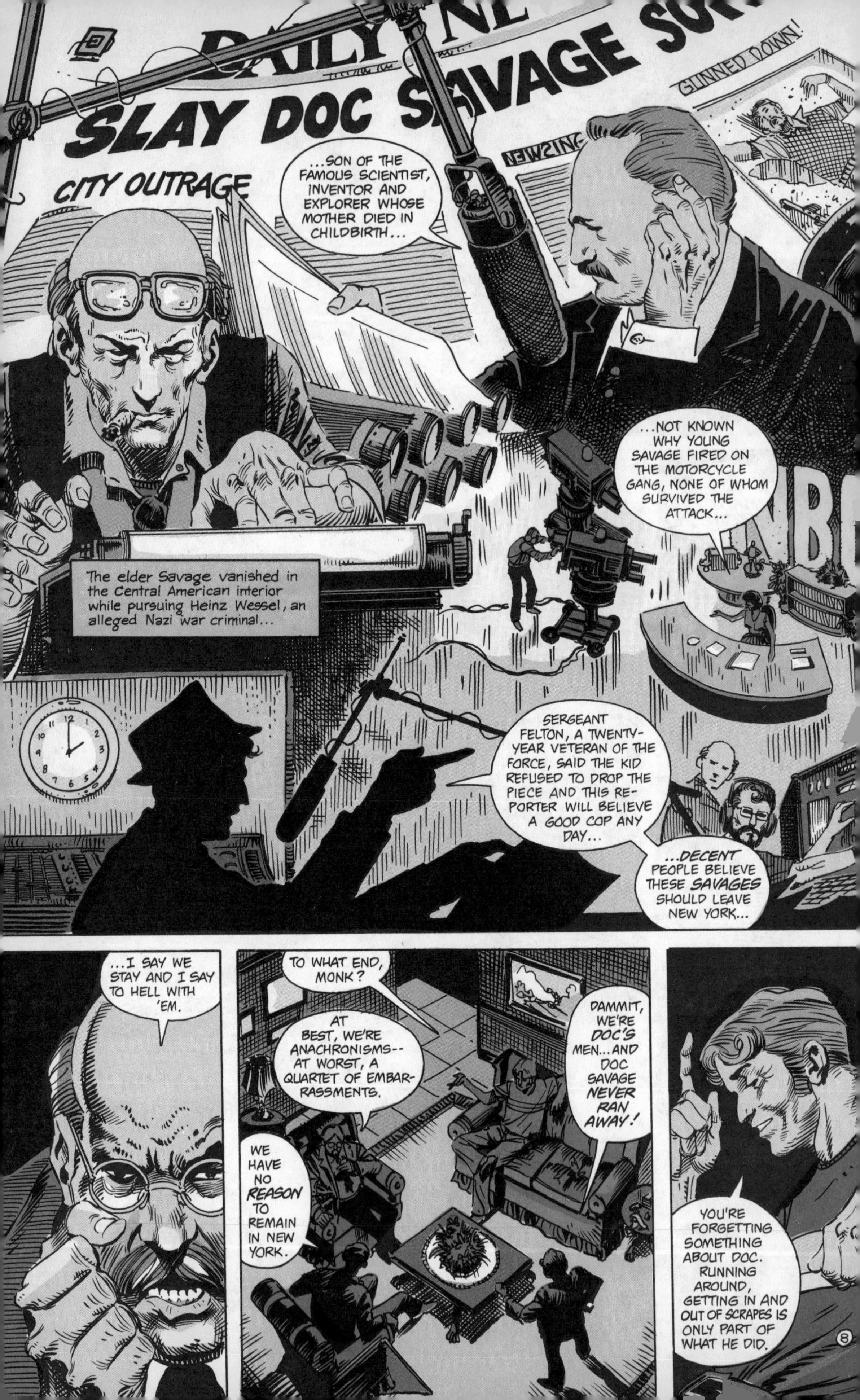
DAILY NE
SLAY DOC SAVAGE SON
GUNNED DOWN!
NEWSWEEK
CITY OUTRAGE
...SON OF THE FAMOUS SCIENTIST, INVENTOR AND EXPLORER WHOSE MOTHER DIED IN CHILDBIRTH...
...NOT KNOWN WHY YOUNG SAVAGE FIRED ON THE MOTORCYCLE GANG, NONE OF WHOM SURVIVED THE ATTACK...
The elder Savage vanished in the Central American interior while pursuing Heinz Wessel, an alleged Nazi war criminal...
SERGEANT FELTON, A TWENTY-YEAR VETERAN OF THE FORCE, SAID THE KID REFUSED TO DROP THE PIECE AND THIS REPORTER WILL BELIEVE A GOOD COP ANY DAY...
...DECENT PEOPLE BELIEVE THESE SAVAGES SHOULD LEAVE NEW YORK...
...I SAY WE STAY AND I SAY TO HELL WITH 'EM.
TO WHAT END, MONK?
AT BEST, WE'RE ANACHRONISMS--AT WORST, A QUARTET OF EMBARRASSMENTS.
WE HAVE NO REASON TO REMAIN IN NEW YORK.
DAMMIT, WE'RE DOC'S MEN...AND DOC SAVAGE NEVER RAN AWAY!
YOU'RE FORGETTING SOMETHING ABOUT DOC. RUNNING AROUND, GETTING IN AND OUT OF SCRAPES IS ONLY PART OF WHAT HE DID.

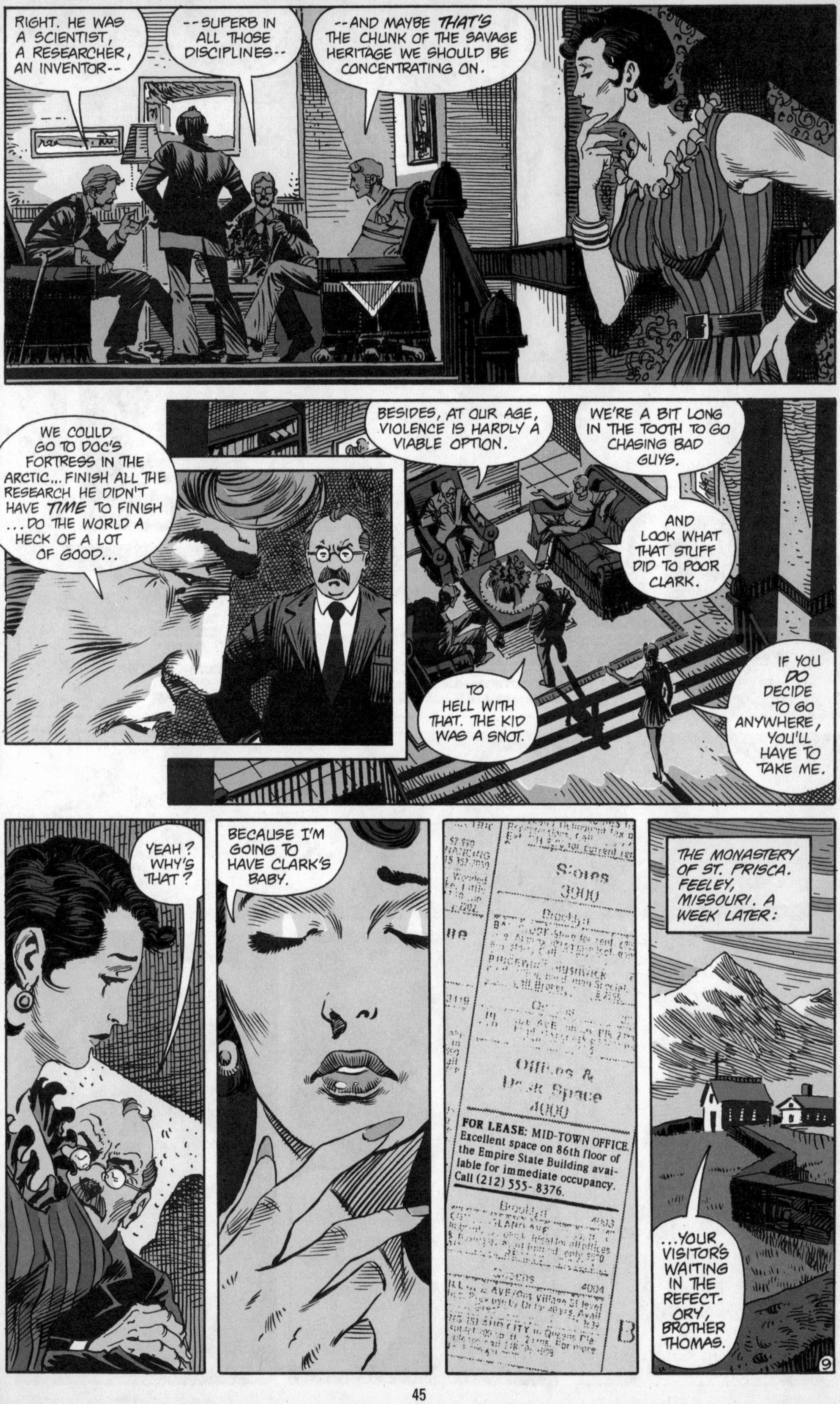

RIGHT. HE WAS A SCIENTIST, A RESEARCHER, AN INVENTOR--
--SUPERB IN ALL THOSE DISCIPLINES--
--AND MAYBE THAT'S THE CHUNK OF THE SAVAGE HERITAGE WE SHOULD BE CONCENTRATING ON.
WE COULD GO TO DOC'S FORTRESS IN THE ARCTIC... FINISH ALL THE RESEARCH HE DIDN'T HAVE TIME TO FINISH ...DO THE WORLD A HECK OF A LOT OF GOOD...
BESIDES, AT OUR AGE, VIOLENCE IS HARDLY A VIABLE OPTION.
WE'RE A BIT LONG IN THE TOOTH TO GO CHASING BAD GUYS.
AND LOOK WHAT THAT STUFF DID TO POOR CLARK.
TO HELL WITH THAT. THE KID WAS A SNOT.
IF YOU DO DECIDE TO GO ANYWHERE, YOU'LL HAVE TO TAKE ME.
YEAH? WHY'S THAT?
BECAUSE I'M GOING TO HAVE CLARK'S BABY.
Stores
3000
Offices &
Desk Space
4000
FOR LEASE: MID-TOWN OFFICE. Excellent space on 86th floor of the Empire State Building available for immediate occupancy. Call (212) 555-8376.
THE MONASTERY OF ST. PRISCA. FEELEY, MISSOURI. A WEEK LATER:
...YOUR VISITOR'S WAITING IN THE REFECTORY, BROTHER THOMAS.

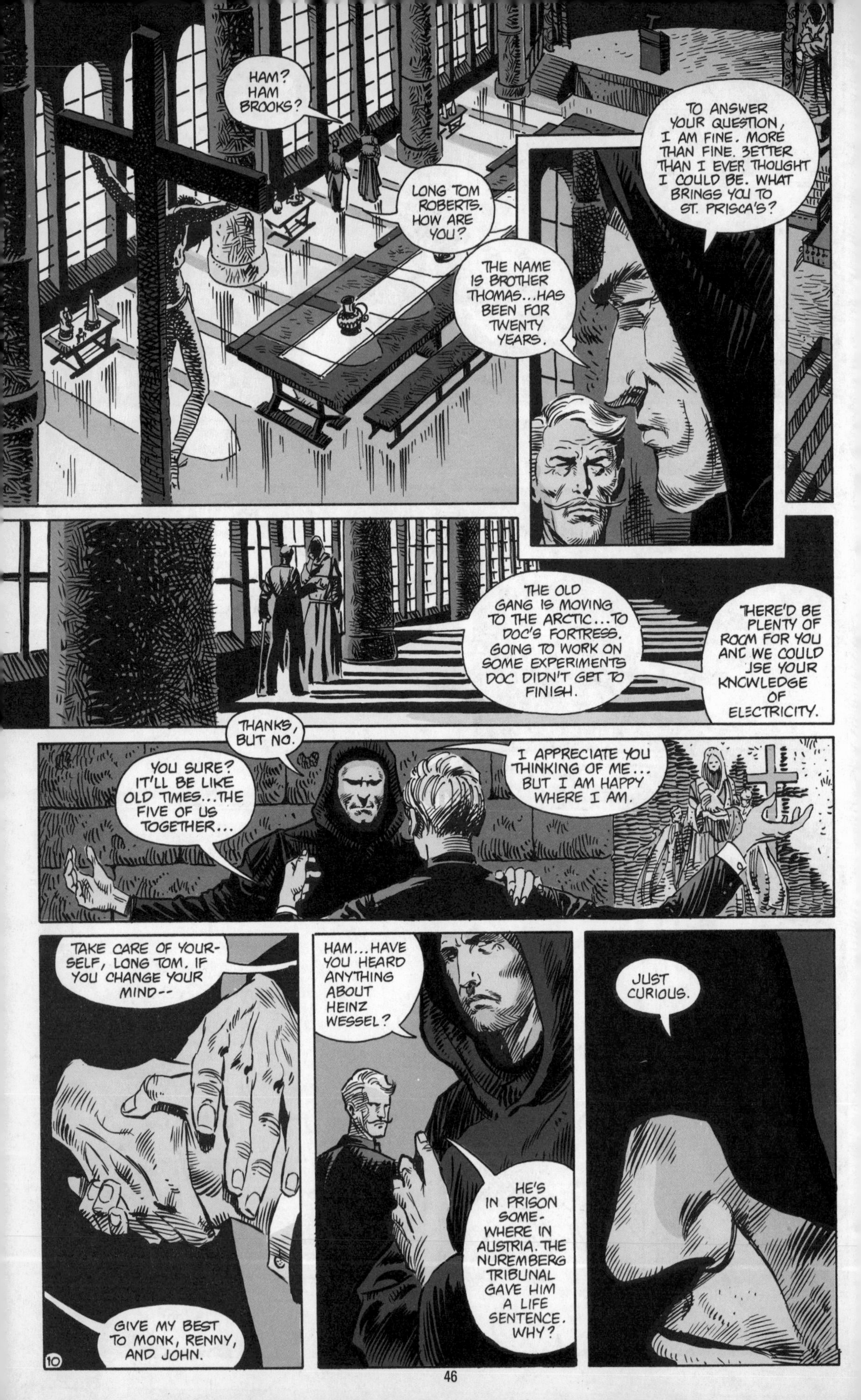
HAM? HAM BROOKS?
LONG TOM ROBERTS. HOW ARE YOU?
THE NAME IS BROTHER THOMAS...HAS BEEN FOR TWENTY YEARS.
TO ANSWER YOUR QUESTION, I AM FINE. MORE THAN FINE. BETTER THAN I EVER THOUGHT I COULD BE. WHAT BRINGS YOU TO ST. PRISCA'S?
THE OLD GANG IS MOVING TO THE ARCTIC...TO DOC'S FORTRESS. GOING TO WORK ON SOME EXPERIMENTS DOC DIDN'T GET TO FINISH.
THERE'D BE PLENTY OF ROOM FOR YOU AND WE COULD USE YOUR KNOWLEDGE OF ELECTRICITY.
THANKS, BUT NO.
YOU SURE? IT'LL BE LIKE OLD TIMES...THE FIVE OF US TOGETHER...
I APPRECIATE YOU THINKING OF ME... BUT I AM HAPPY WHERE I AM.
TAKE CARE OF YOURSELF, LONG TOM. IF YOU CHANGE YOUR MIND--
GIVE MY BEST TO MONK, RENNY, AND JOHN.
10
HAM...HAVE YOU HEARD ANYTHING ABOUT HEINZ WESSEL?
HE'S IN PRISON SOMEWHERE IN AUSTRIA. THE NUREMBERG TRIBUNAL GAVE HIM A LIFE SENTENCE. WHY?
JUST CURIOUS.

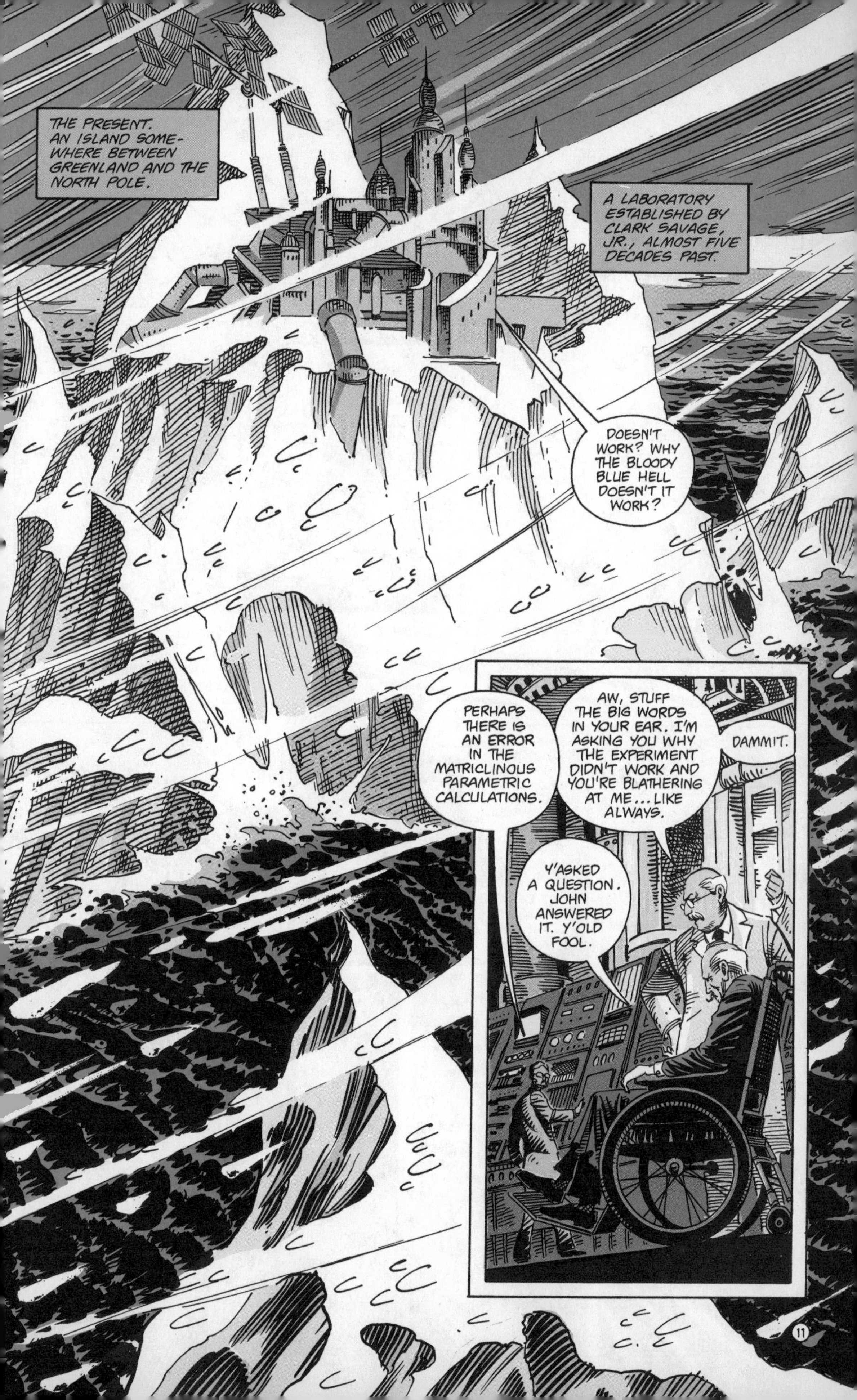
THE PRESENT. AN ISLAND SOMEWHERE BETWEEN GREENLAND AND THE NORTH POLE.
A LABORATORY ESTABLISHED BY CLARK SAVAGE, JR., ALMOST FIVE DECADES PAST.
DOESN'T WORK? WHY THE BLOODY BLUE HELL DOESN'T IT WORK?
PERHAPS THERE IS AN ERROR IN THE MATRICLINOUS PARAMETRIC CALCULATIONS.
AW, STUFF THE BIG WORDS IN YOUR EAR. I'M ASKING YOU WHY THE EXPERIMENT DIDN'T WORK AND YOU'RE BLATHERING AT ME... LIKE ALWAYS.
DAMMIT.
Y'ASKED A QUESTION. JOHN ANSWERED IT. Y'OLD FOOL.

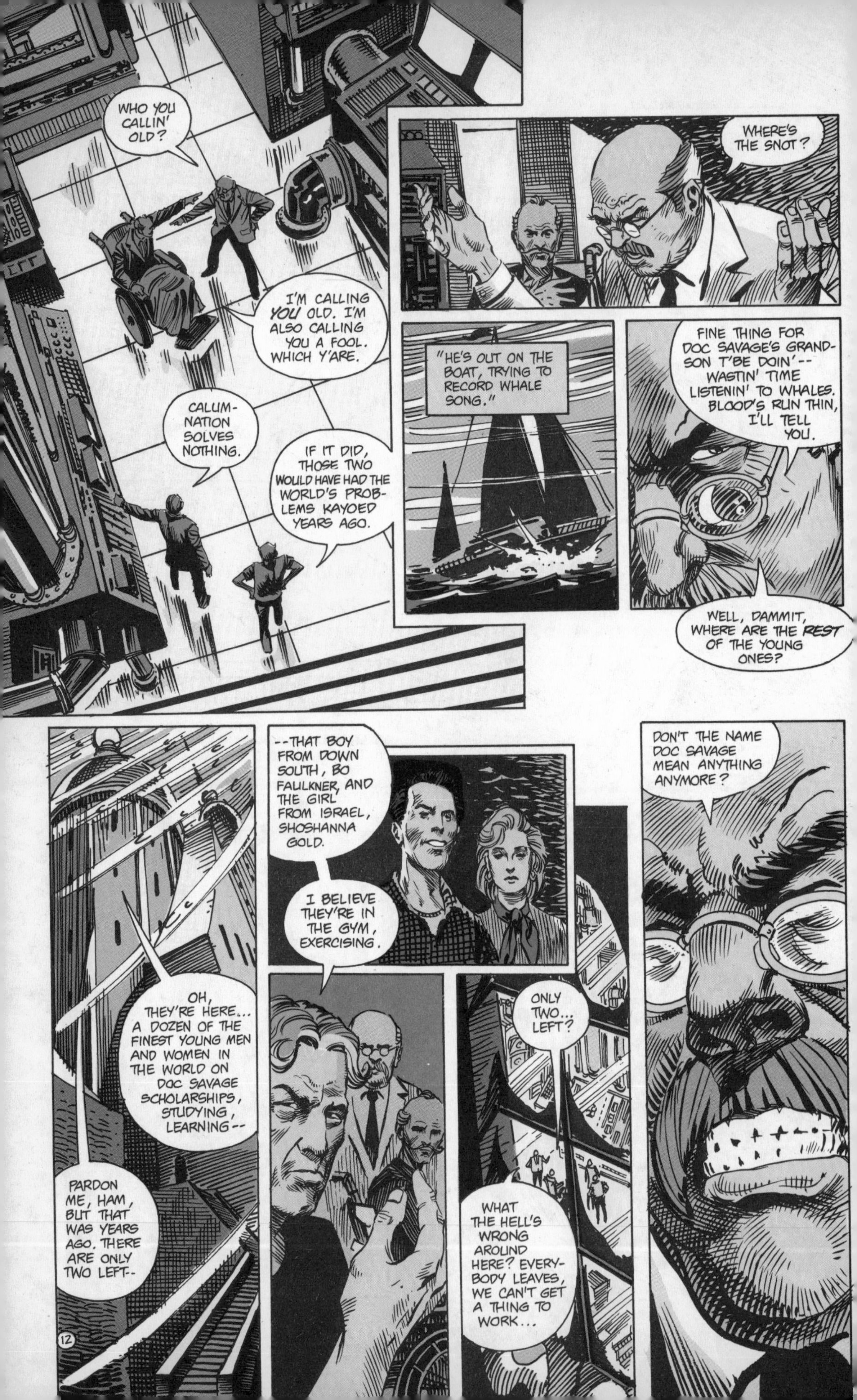
WHO YOU CALLIN' OLD?
I'M CALLING *YOU* OLD. I'M ALSO CALLING YOU A FOOL. WHICH Y'ARE.
CALUMNATION SOLVES NOTHING.
IF IT DID, THOSE TWO WOULD HAVE HAD THE WORLD'S PROBLEMS KAYOED YEARS AGO.
WHERE'S THE SNOT?
"HE'S OUT ON THE BOAT, TRYING TO RECORD WHALE SONG."
FINE THING FOR DOC SAVAGE'S GRANDSON T'BE DOIN'-- WASTIN' TIME LISTENIN' TO WHALES. BLOOD'S RUN THIN, I'LL TELL YOU.
WELL, DAMMIT, WHERE ARE THE *REST* OF THE YOUNG ONES?
OH, THEY'RE HERE... A DOZEN OF THE FINEST YOUNG MEN AND WOMEN IN THE WORLD ON DOC SAVAGE SCHOLARSHIPS, STUDYING, LEARNING--
PARDON ME, HAM, BUT THAT WAS YEARS AGO. THERE ARE ONLY TWO LEFT--
--THAT BOY FROM DOWN SOUTH, BO FAULKNER, AND THE GIRL FROM ISRAEL, SHOSHANNA GOLD.
I BELIEVE THEY'RE IN THE GYM, EXERCISING.
ONLY TWO... LEFT?
WHAT THE HELL'S WRONG AROUND HERE? EVERYBODY LEAVES, WE CAN'T GET A THING TO WORK...
DON'T THE NAME DOC SAVAGE MEAN ANYTHING ANYMORE?
12

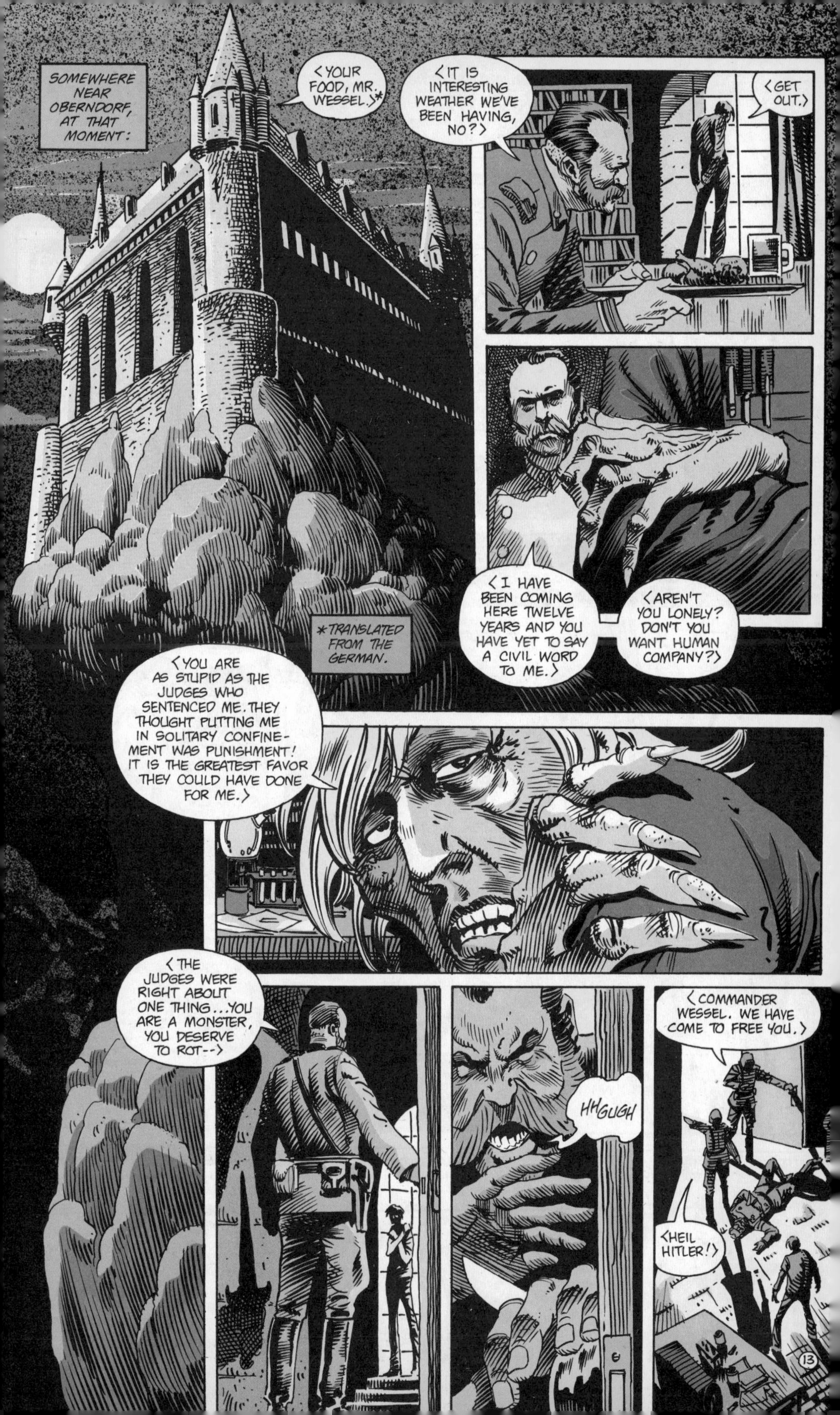
SOMEWHERE NEAR OBERNDORF, AT THAT MOMENT:
<YOUR FOOD, MR. WESSEL.>*
<IT IS INTERESTING WEATHER WE'VE BEEN HAVING, NO?>
<GET OUT.>
<I HAVE BEEN COMING HERE TWELVE YEARS AND YOU HAVE YET TO SAY A CIVIL WORD TO ME.>
<AREN'T YOU LONELY? DON'T YOU WANT HUMAN COMPANY?>
*TRANSLATED FROM THE GERMAN.
<YOU ARE AS STUPID AS THE JUDGES WHO SENTENCED ME. THEY THOUGHT PUTTING ME IN SOLITARY CONFINEMENT WAS PUNISHMENT! IT IS THE GREATEST FAVOR THEY COULD HAVE DONE FOR ME.>
<THE JUDGES WERE RIGHT ABOUT ONE THING... YOU ARE A MONSTER, YOU DESERVE TO ROT-->
HHGUGH
<COMMANDER WESSEL. WE HAVE COME TO FREE YOU.>
<HEIL HITLER!>

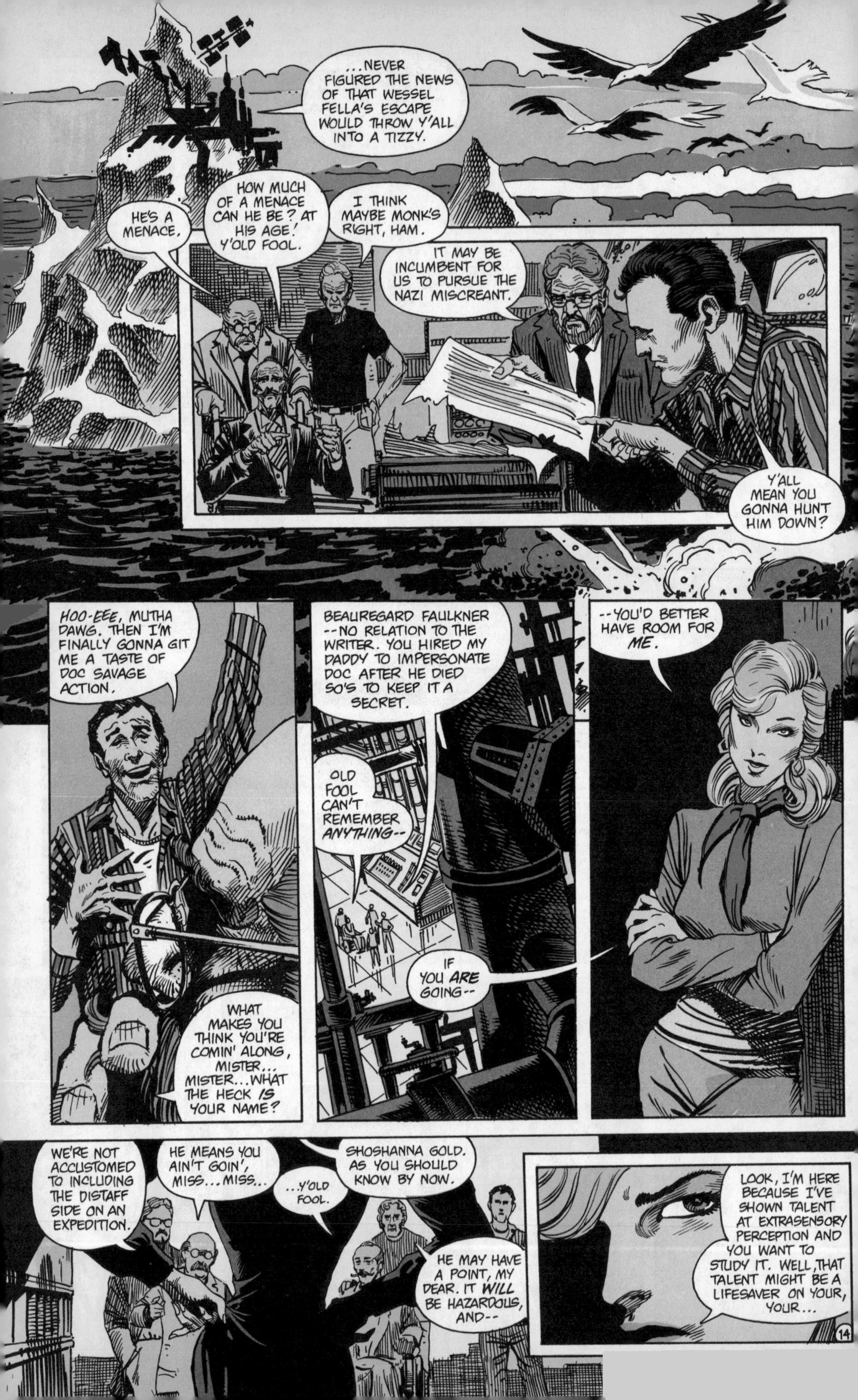
...NEVER FIGURED THE NEWS OF THAT WESSEL FELLA'S ESCAPE WOULD THROW Y'ALL INTO A TIZZY.
HE'S A MENACE.
HOW MUCH OF A MENACE CAN HE BE? AT HIS AGE! Y'OLD FOOL.
I THINK MAYBE MONK'S RIGHT, HAM.
IT MAY BE INCUMBENT FOR US TO PURSUE THE NAZI MISCREANT.
Y'ALL MEAN YOU GONNA HUNT HIM DOWN?
HOO-EEE, MUTHA DAWG. THEN I'M FINALLY GONNA GIT ME A TASTE OF DOC SAVAGE ACTION.
WHAT MAKES YOU THINK YOU'RE COMIN' ALONG, MISTER... MISTER...WHAT THE HECK IS YOUR NAME?
BEAUREGARD FAULKNER --NO RELATION TO THE WRITER. YOU HIRED MY DADDY TO IMPERSONATE DOC AFTER HE DIED SO'S TO KEEP IT A SECRET.
OLD FOOL CAN'T REMEMBER ANYTHING--
IF YOU ARE GOING--
--YOU'D BETTER HAVE ROOM FOR ME.
WE'RE NOT ACCUSTOMED TO INCLUDING THE DISTAFF SIDE ON AN EXPEDITION.
HE MEANS YOU AIN'T GOIN', MISS...MISS...
...Y'OLD FOOL.
SHOSHANNA GOLD. AS YOU SHOULD KNOW BY NOW.
HE MAY HAVE A POINT, MY DEAR. IT WILL BE HAZARDOUS, AND--
LOOK, I'M HERE BECAUSE I'VE SHOWN TALENT AT EXTRASENSORY PERCEPTION AND YOU WANT TO STUDY IT. WELL, THAT TALENT MIGHT BE A LIFESAVER ON YOUR, YOUR...
14

...EXPEDITION.

WHAT-EVER.

SHE HAS A POINT.

SHE'S A **WOMAN.** DAMMIT.

SHE'S ALSO A GOOD RIFLE SHOT, NEAR EXPERT WITH A HANDGUN AND SHE HAS MORE ENERGY THAN A TORNADO. I SAY SHE GOES.

I'M CONVINCED.

I DON'T KNOW IF I GOT A VOTE... BUT I'M CASTIN' IT *FOR* HER.

THE OLD FOOL'S OUTVOTED.

YOU'LL ALL BE SORRY.

I ACCEDE ALSO.

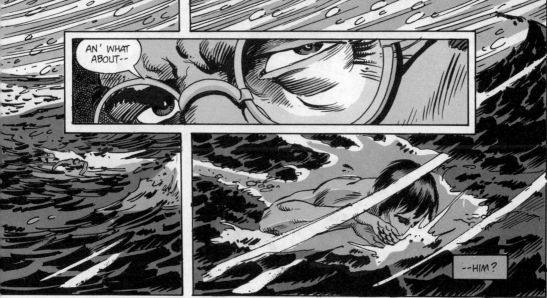

AN' WHAT ABOUT--

--HIM?

HIS PACIFIS-C CON-ICTIONS--

I SEE NO POINT--

I KINDA DOUBT--

NOT TERRIBLY LIKELY HE'D--

I THINK WE ALL AGREE--

--DOC SAVAGE'S GRANDSON WON'T BE COMING ALONG.

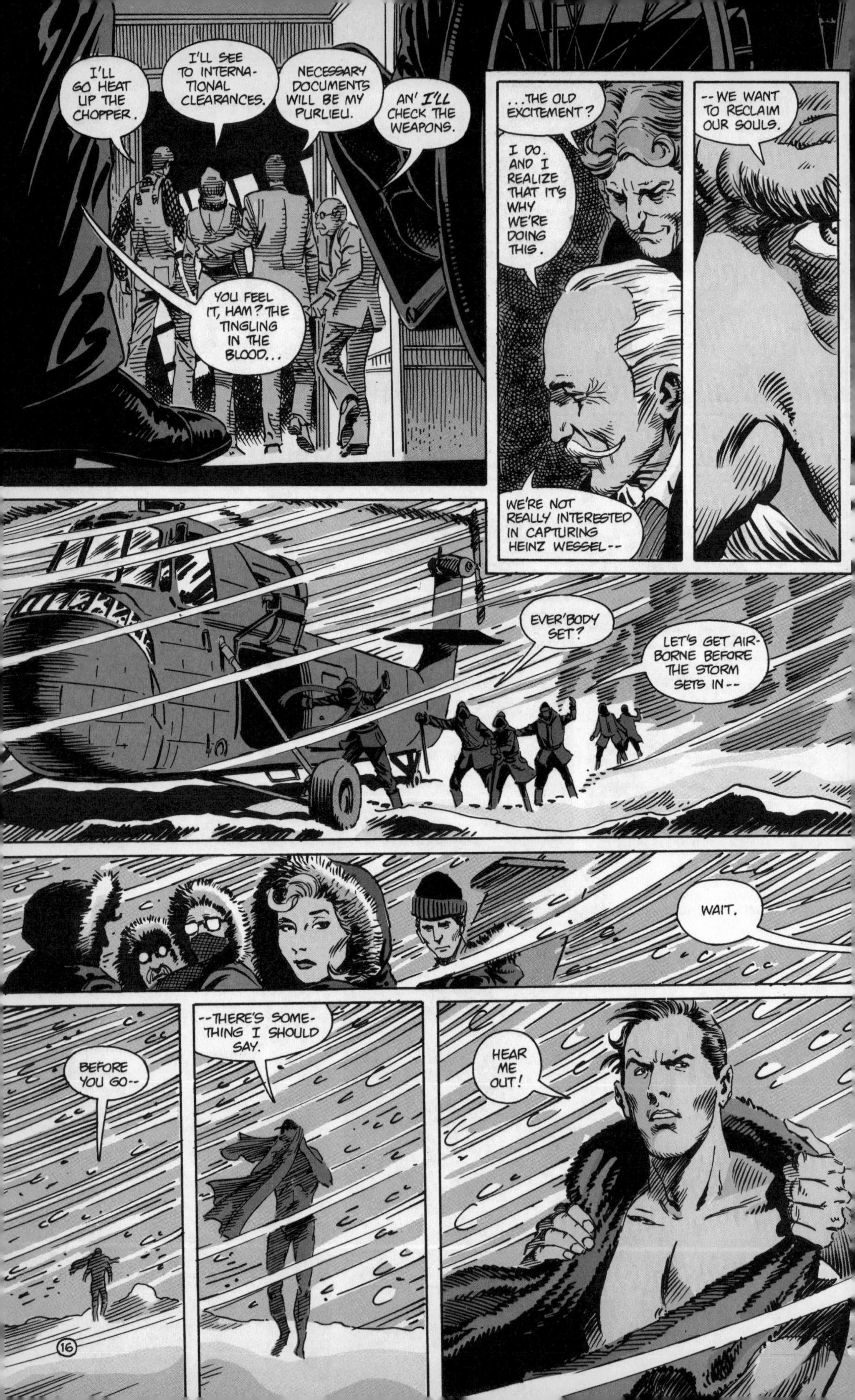

I'LL GO HEAT UP THE CHOPPER.
I'LL SEE TO INTERNA-TIONAL CLEARANCES.
NECESSARY DOCUMENTS WILL BE MY PURLIEU.
AN' I'LL CHECK THE WEAPONS.
YOU FEEL IT, HAM? THE TINGLING IN THE BLOOD...
...THE OLD EXCITEMENT?
I DO. AND I REALIZE THAT IT'S WHY WE'RE DOING THIS.
WE'RE NOT REALLY INTERESTED IN CAPTURING HEINZ WESSEL--
--WE WANT TO RECLAIM OUR SOULS.
EVER'BODY SET?
LET'S GET AIR-BORNE BEFORE THE STORM SETS IN--
WAIT.
BEFORE YOU GO--
--THERE'S SOME-THING I SHOULD SAY.
HEAR ME OUT!

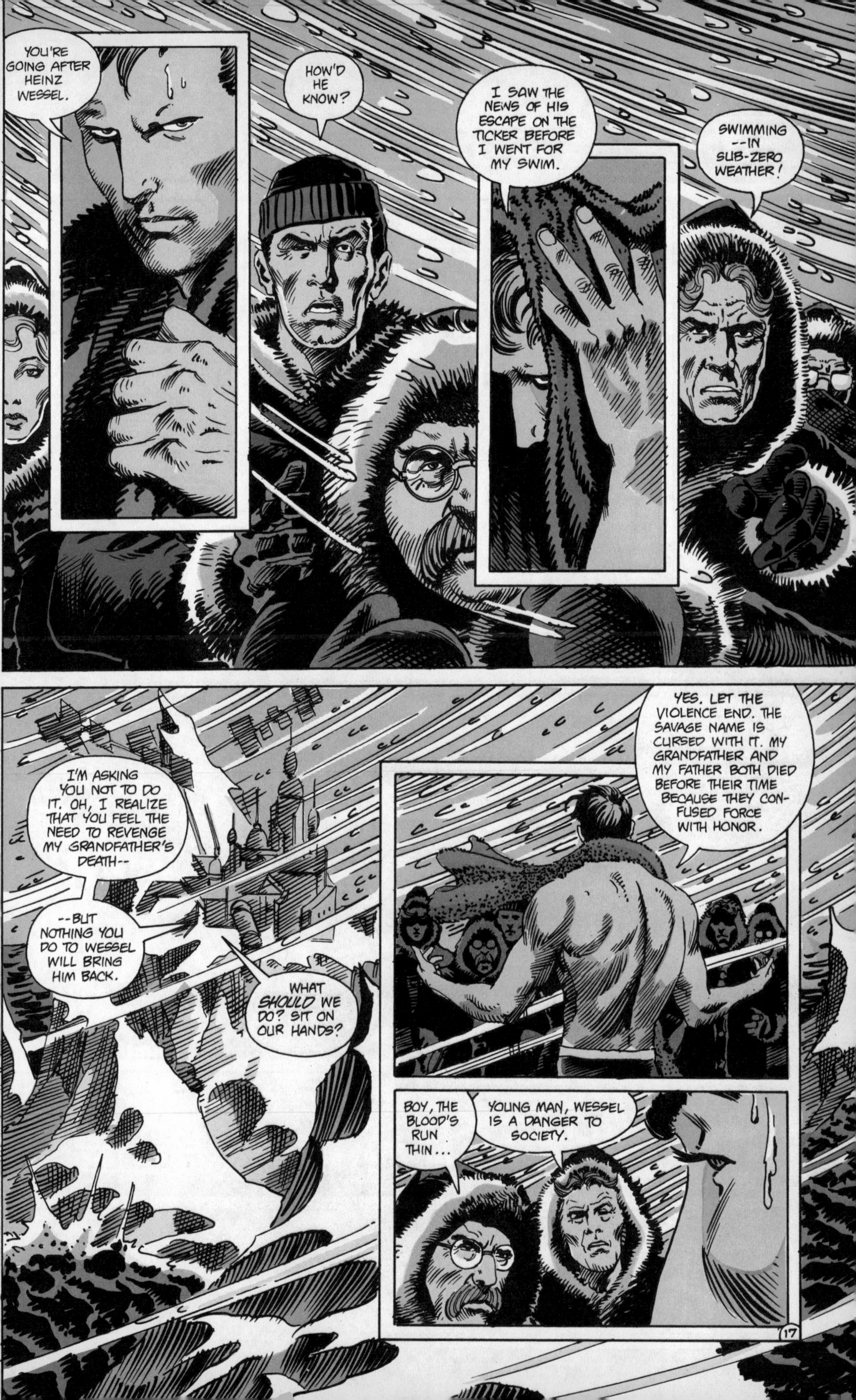
YOU'RE GOING AFTER HEINZ WESSEL.
HOW'D HE KNOW?
I SAW THE NEWS OF HIS ESCAPE ON THE TICKER BEFORE I WENT FOR MY SWIM.
SWIMMING --IN SUB-ZERO WEATHER!
I'M ASKING YOU NOT TO DO IT. OH, I REALIZE THAT YOU FEEL THE NEED TO REVENGE MY GRANDFATHER'S DEATH--
--BUT NOTHING YOU DO TO WESSEL WILL BRING HIM BACK.
WHAT SHOULD WE DO? SIT ON OUR HANDS?
YES. LET THE VIOLENCE END. THE SAVAGE NAME IS CURSED WITH IT. MY GRANDFATHER AND MY FATHER BOTH DIED BEFORE THEIR TIME BECAUSE THEY CONFUSED FORCE WITH HONOR.
BOY, THE BLOOD'S RUN THIN...
YOUNG MAN, WESSEL IS A DANGER TO SOCIETY.
17

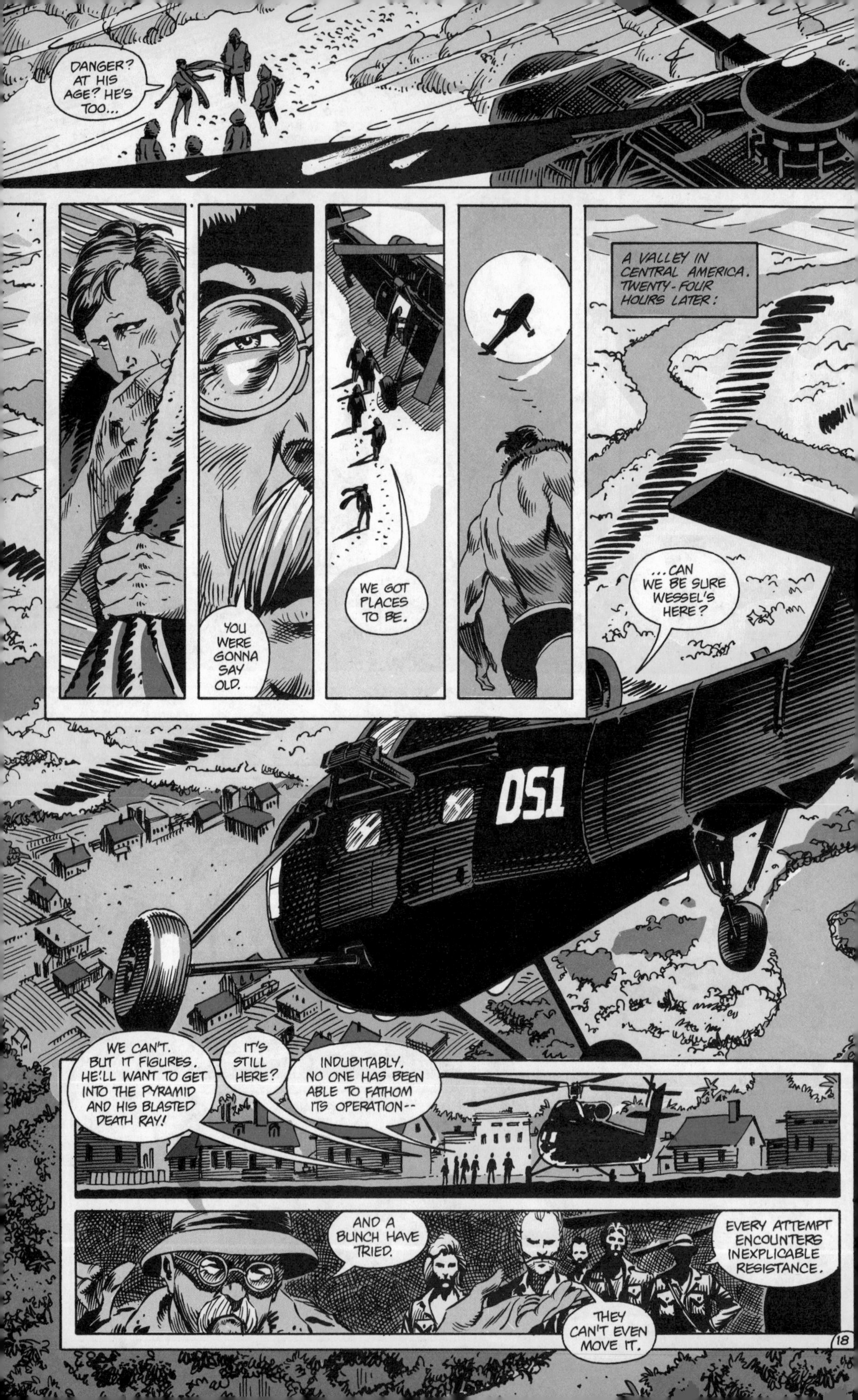
DANGER? AT HIS AGE? HE'S TOO...
YOU WERE GONNA SAY OLD.
WE GOT PLACES TO BE.
A VALLEY IN CENTRAL AMERICA. TWENTY-FOUR HOURS LATER:
...CAN WE BE SURE WESSEL'S HERE?
DS1
WE CAN'T. BUT IT FIGURES. HE'LL WANT TO GET INTO THE PYRAMID AND HIS BLASTED DEATH RAY!
IT'S STILL HERE?
INDUBITABLY. NO ONE HAS BEEN ABLE TO FATHOM ITS OPERATION--
AND A BUNCH HAVE TRIED.
EVERY ATTEMPT ENCOUNTERS INEXPLICABLE RESISTANCE.
THEY CAN'T EVEN MOVE IT.

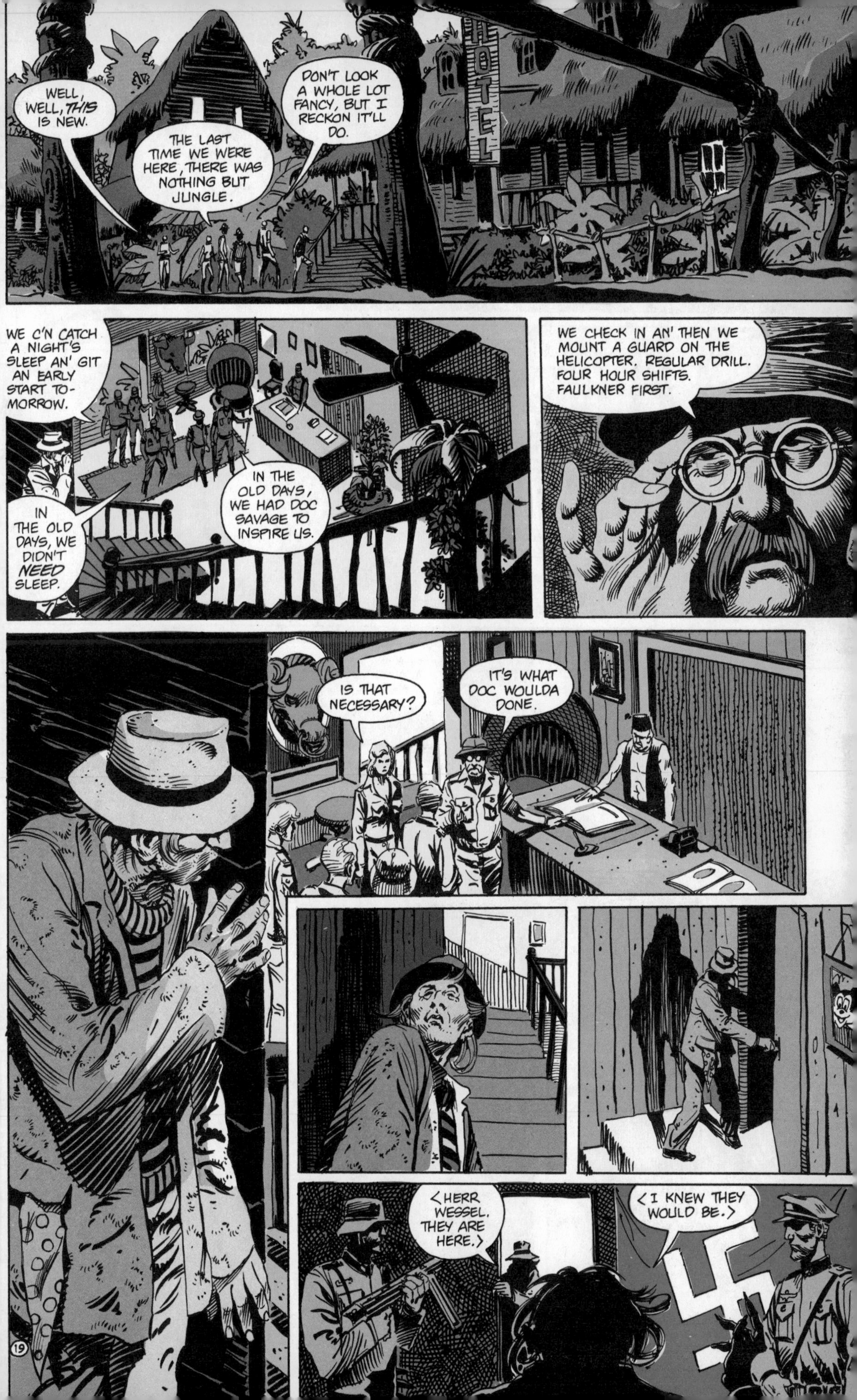
WELL, WELL, THIS IS NEW.
THE LAST TIME WE WERE HERE, THERE WAS NOTHING BUT JUNGLE.
DON'T LOOK A WHOLE LOT FANCY, BUT I RECKON IT'LL DO.
HOTEL
WE C'N CATCH A NIGHT'S SLEEP AN' GIT AN EARLY START TO-MORROW.
IN THE OLD DAYS, WE HAD DOC SAVAGE TO INSPIRE US.
IN THE OLD DAYS, WE DIDN'T NEED SLEEP.
WE CHECK IN AN' THEN WE MOUNT A GUARD ON THE HELICOPTER. REGULAR DRILL. FOUR HOUR SHIFTS. FAULKNER FIRST.
IS THAT NECESSARY?
IT'S WHAT DOC WOULDA DONE.
<HERR WESSEL. THEY ARE HERE.>
<I KNEW THEY WOULD BE.>

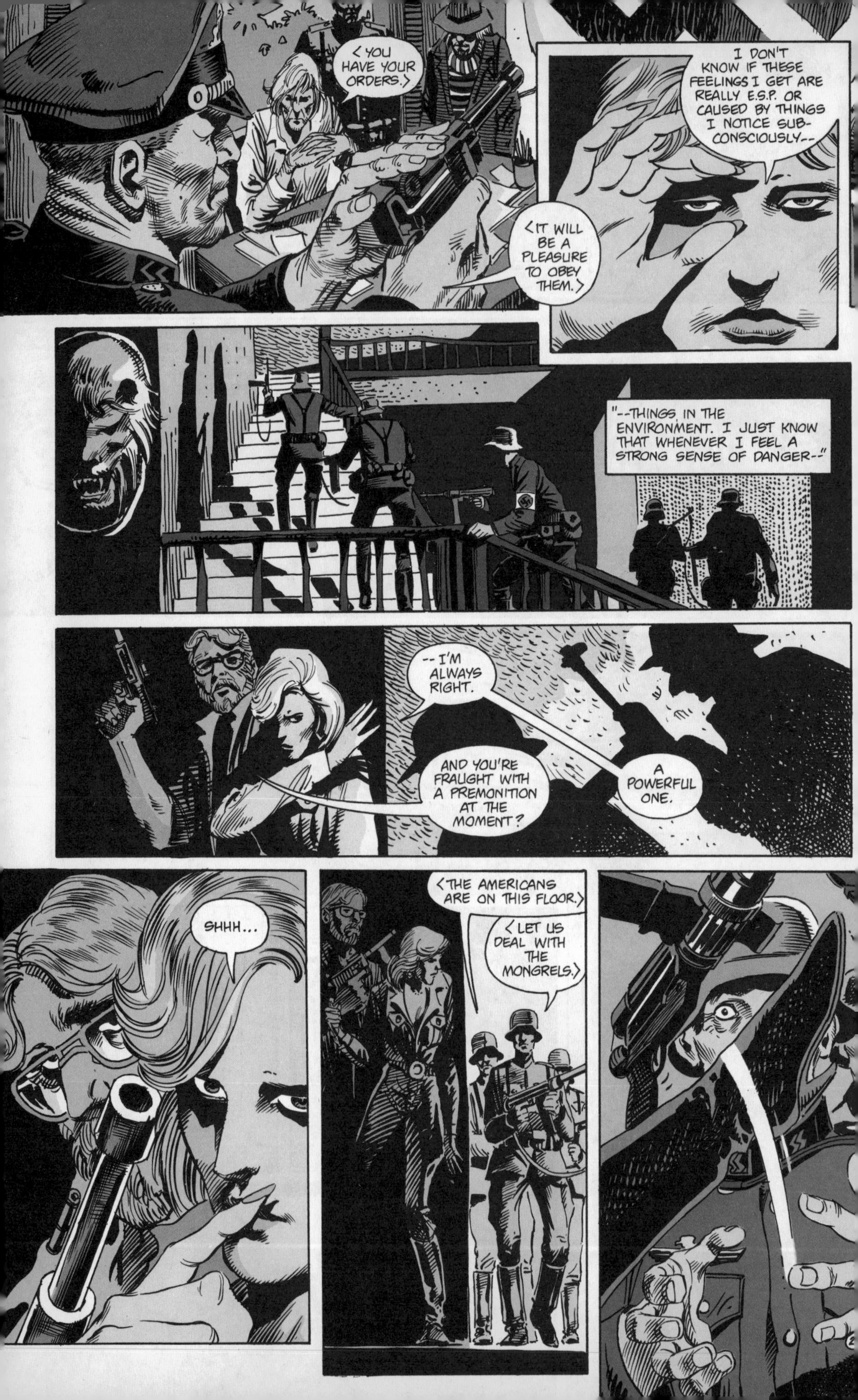
<YOU HAVE YOUR ORDERS.>
I DON'T KNOW IF THESE FEELINGS I GET ARE REALLY E.S.P. OR CAUSED BY THINGS I NOTICE SUB-CONSCIOUSLY--
<IT WILL BE A PLEASURE TO OBEY THEM.>
"--THINGS IN THE ENVIRONMENT. I JUST KNOW THAT WHENEVER I FEEL A STRONG SENSE OF DANGER--"
--I'M ALWAYS RIGHT.
AND YOU'RE FRAUGHT WITH A PREMONITION AT THE MOMENT?
A POWERFUL ONE.
SHHH...
<THE AMERICANS ARE ON THIS FLOOR.>
<LET US DEAL WITH THE MONGRELS.>

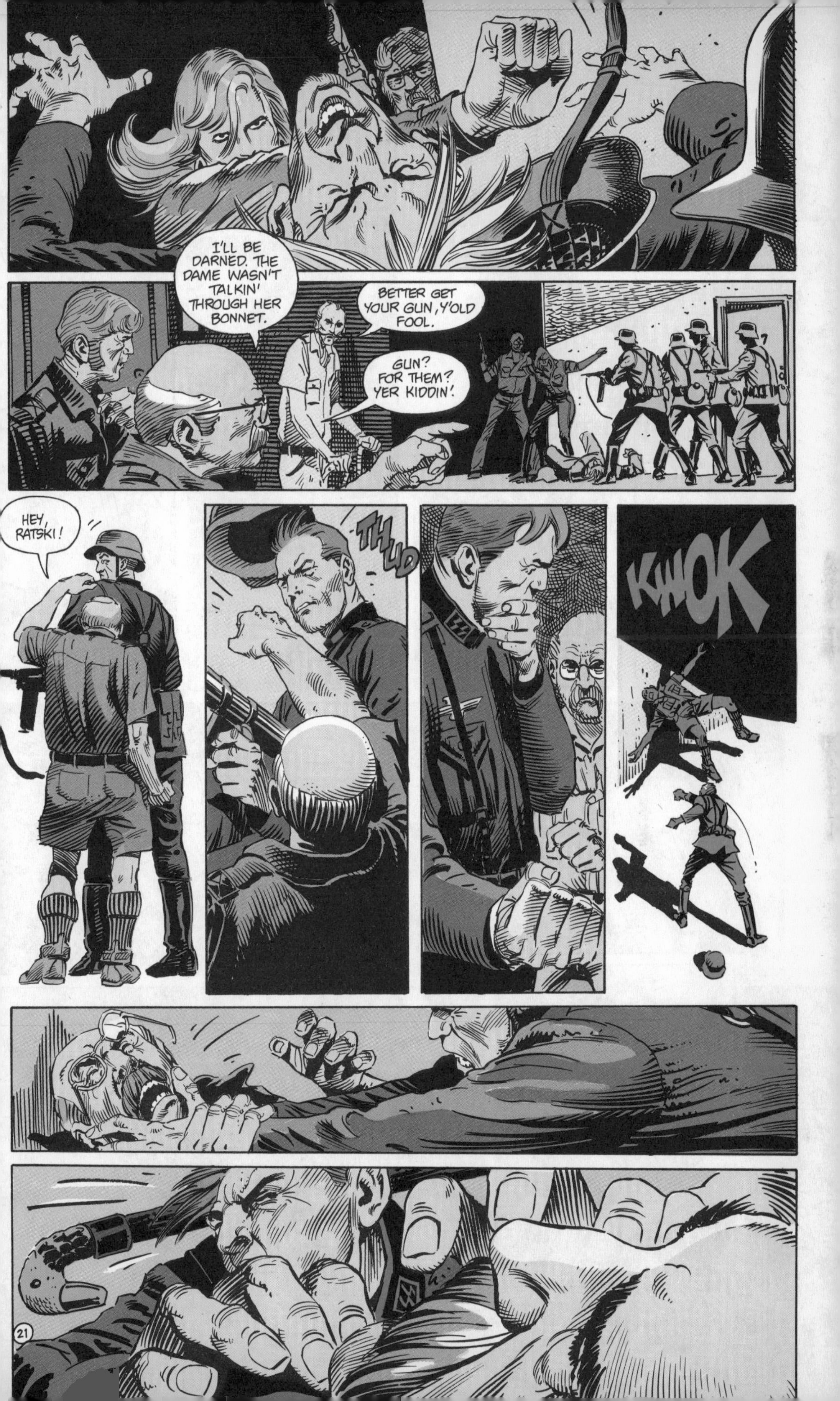
I'LL BE DARNED. THE DAME WASN'T TALKIN' THROUGH HER BONNET.
BETTER GET YOUR GUN, Y'OLD FOOL.
GUN? FOR THEM? YER KIDDIN'.
HEY, RATSKI!
THUD
KHOK
21

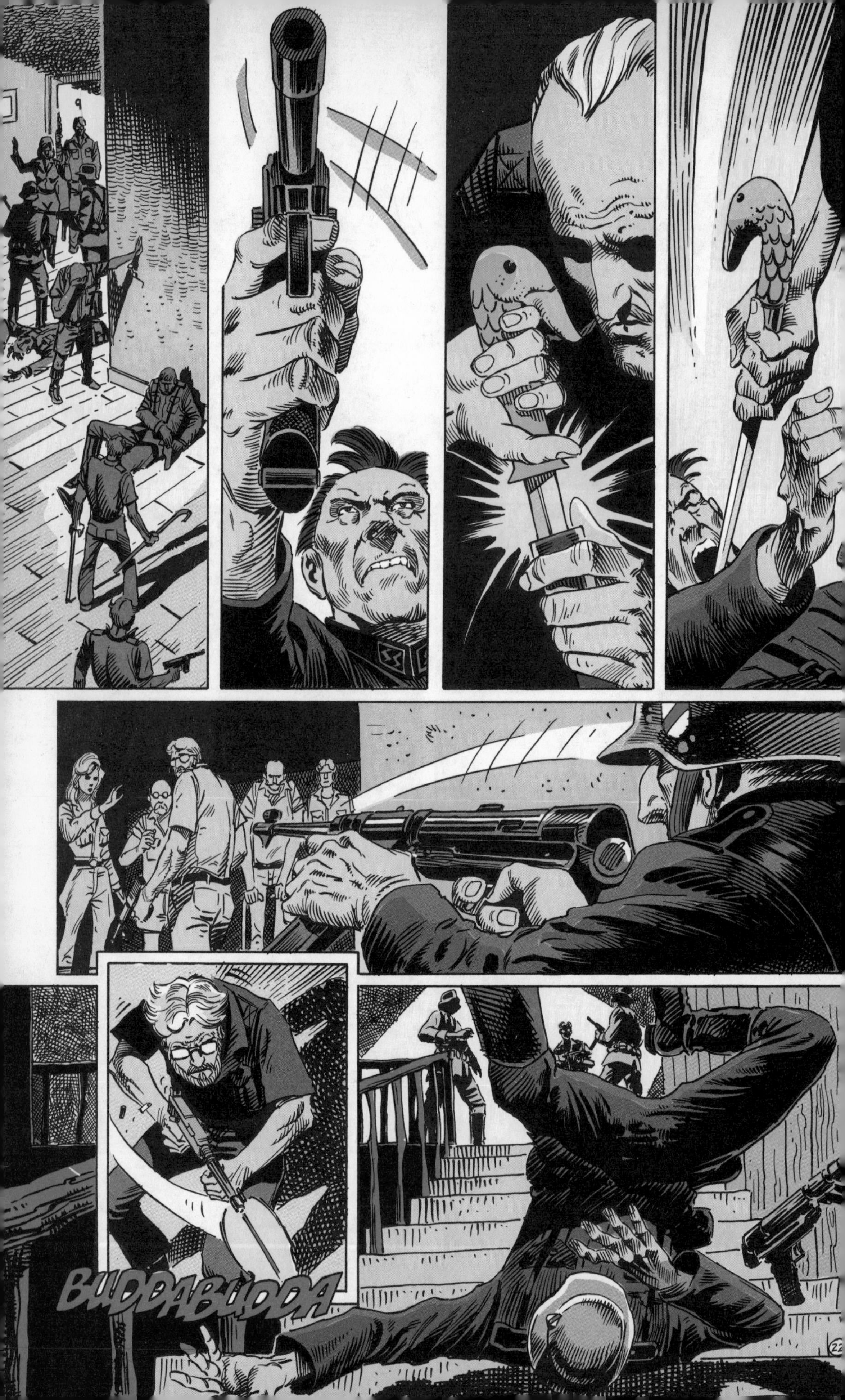
BUDDABUDDA

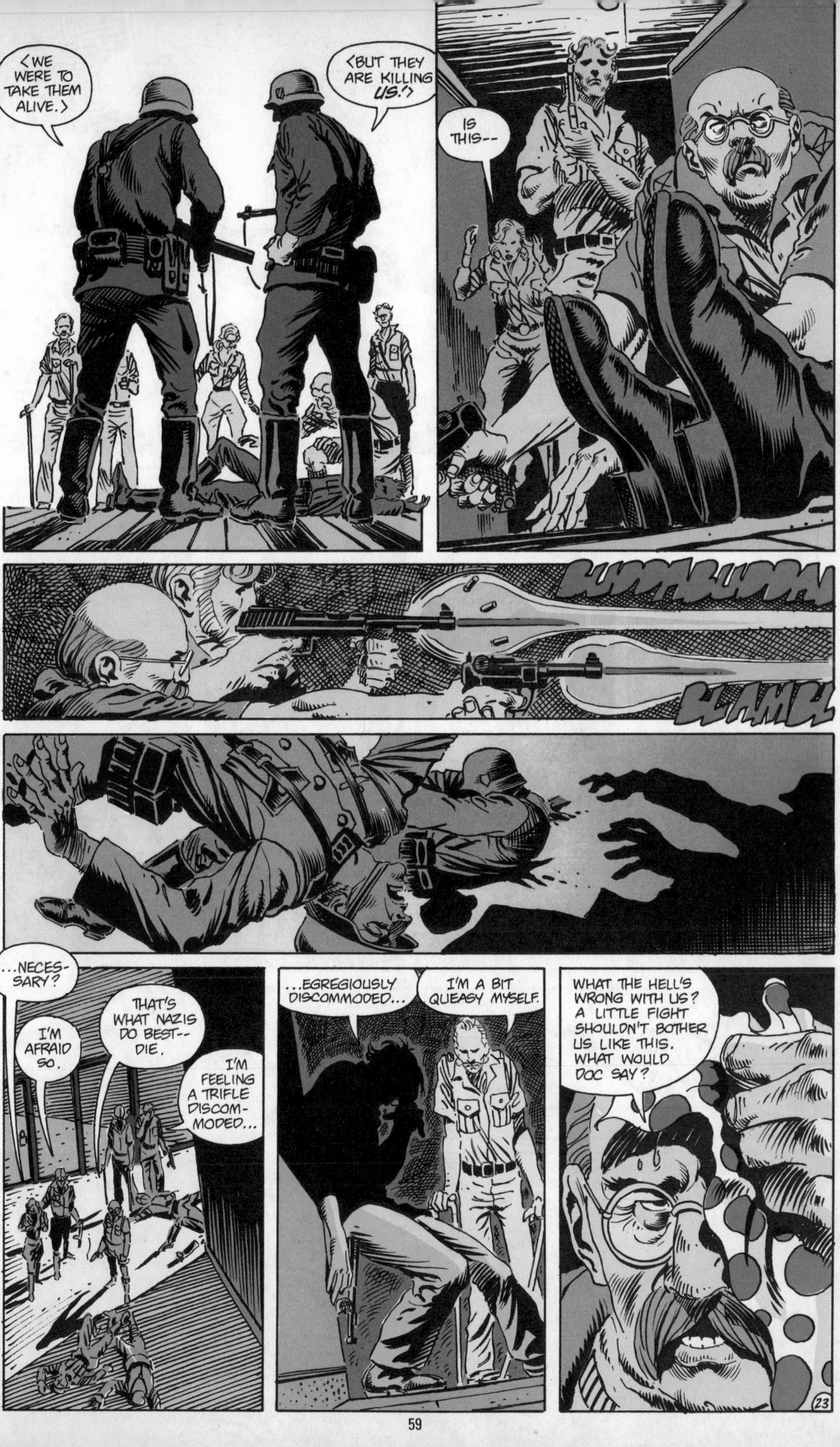

<WE WERE TO TAKE THEM ALIVE.>
<BUT THEY ARE KILLING US!>
IS THIS--
...NECESSARY?
I'M AFRAID SO.
THAT'S WHAT NAZIS DO BEST--DIE.
I'M FEELING A TRIFLE DISCOMMODED...
...EGREGIOUSLY DISCOMMODED...
I'M A BIT QUEASY MYSELF.
WHAT THE HELL'S WRONG WITH US? A LITTLE FIGHT SHOULDN'T BOTHER US LIKE THIS. WHAT WOULD DOC SAY?
23

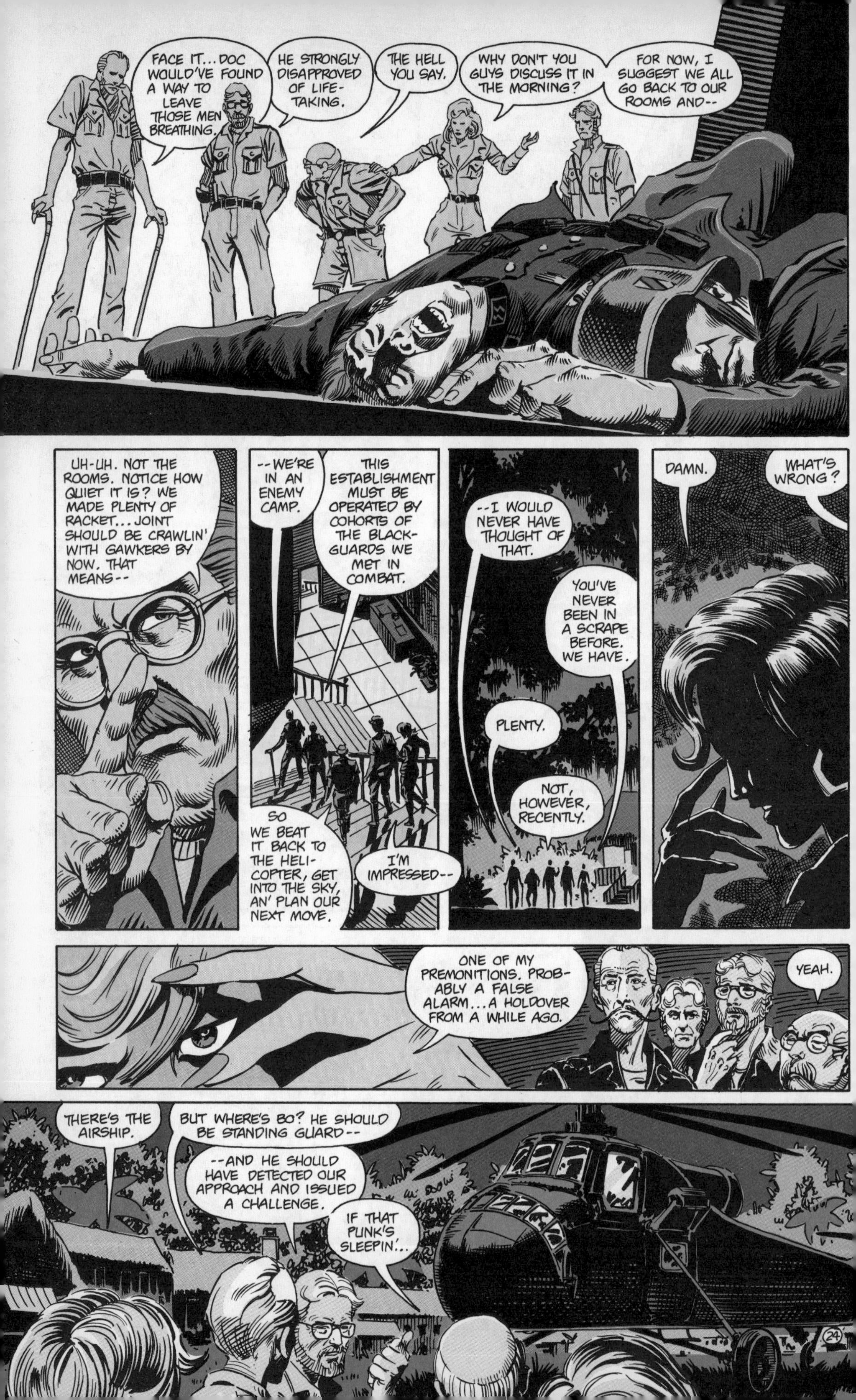
FACE IT... DOC WOULD'VE FOUND A WAY TO LEAVE THOSE MEN BREATHING.
HE STRONGLY DISAPPROVED OF LIFE-TAKING.
THE HELL YOU SAY.
WHY DON'T YOU GUYS DISCUSS IT IN THE MORNING?
FOR NOW, I SUGGEST WE ALL GO BACK TO OUR ROOMS AND--
UH-UH. NOT THE ROOMS. NOTICE HOW QUIET IT IS? WE MADE PLENTY OF RACKET... JOINT SHOULD BE CRAWLIN' WITH GAWKERS BY NOW. THAT MEANS--
--WE'RE IN AN ENEMY CAMP.
THIS ESTABLISHMENT MUST BE OPERATED BY COHORTS OF THE BLACK-GUARDS WE MET IN COMBAT.
SO WE BEAT IT BACK TO THE HELI-COPTER, GET INTO THE SKY, AN' PLAN OUR NEXT MOVE.
I'M IMPRESSED--
--I WOULD NEVER HAVE THOUGHT OF THAT.
YOU'VE NEVER BEEN IN A SCRAPE BEFORE. WE HAVE.
PLENTY.
NOT, HOWEVER, RECENTLY.
DAMN.
WHAT'S WRONG?
ONE OF MY PREMONITIONS. PROB-ABLY A FALSE ALARM... A HOLDOVER FROM A WHILE AGO.
YEAH.
THERE'S THE AIRSHIP.
BUT WHERE'S BO? HE SHOULD BE STANDING GUARD--
--AND HE SHOULD HAVE DETECTED OUR APPROACH AND ISSUED A CHALLENGE.
IF THAT PUNK'S SLEEPIN'...
24

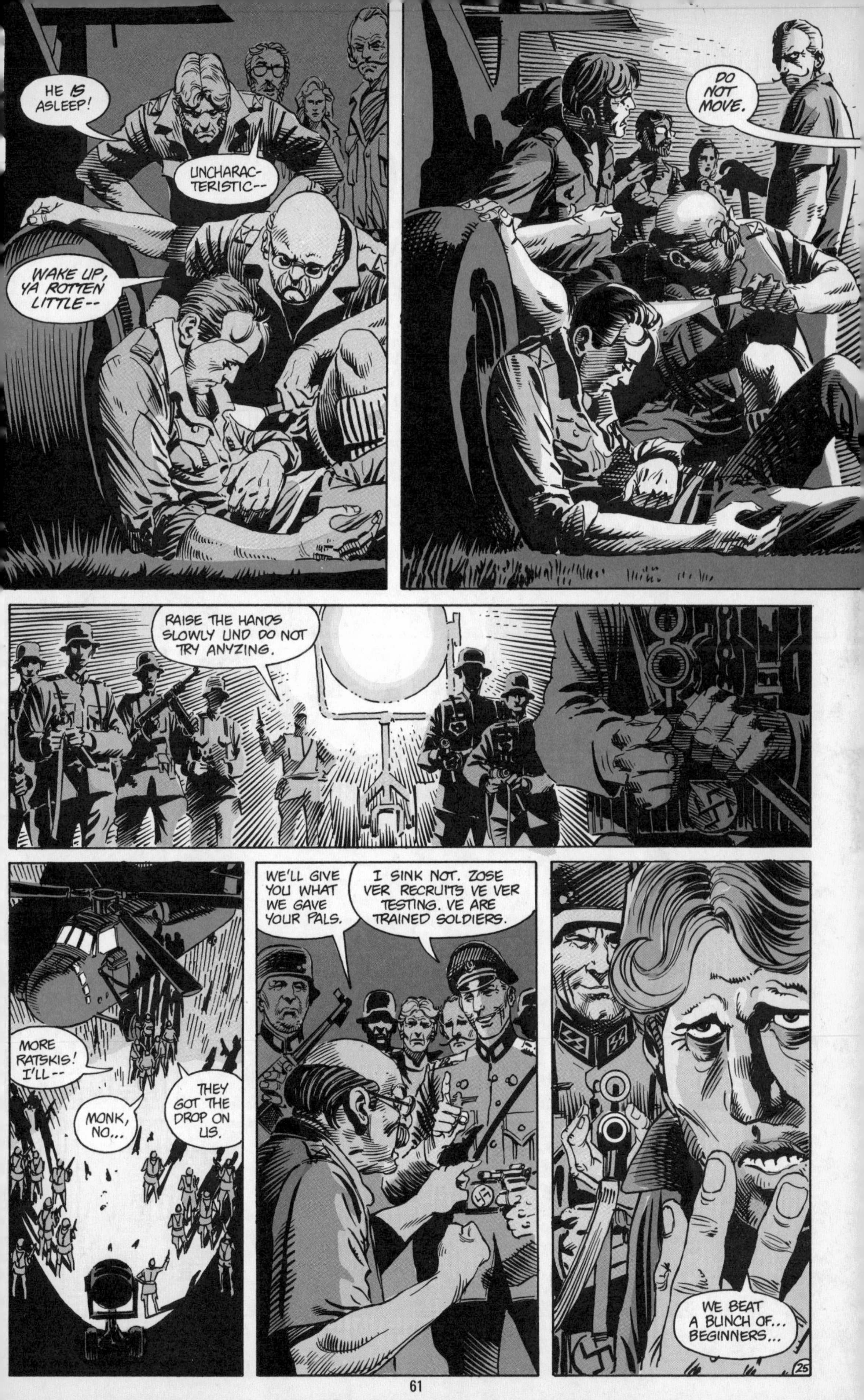
HE IS ASLEEP!
UNCHARAC-TERISTIC--
WAKE UP, YA ROTTEN LITTLE--
DO NOT MOVE.
RAISE THE HANDS SLOWLY UND DO NOT TRY ANYZING.
MORE RATSKIS! I'LL--
MONK, NO...
THEY GOT THE DROP ON US.
WE'LL GIVE YOU WHAT WE GAVE YOUR PALS.
I SINK NOT. ZOSE VER RECRUITS VE VER TESTING. VE ARE TRAINED SOLDIERS.
WE BEAT A BUNCH OF... BEGINNERS...
25

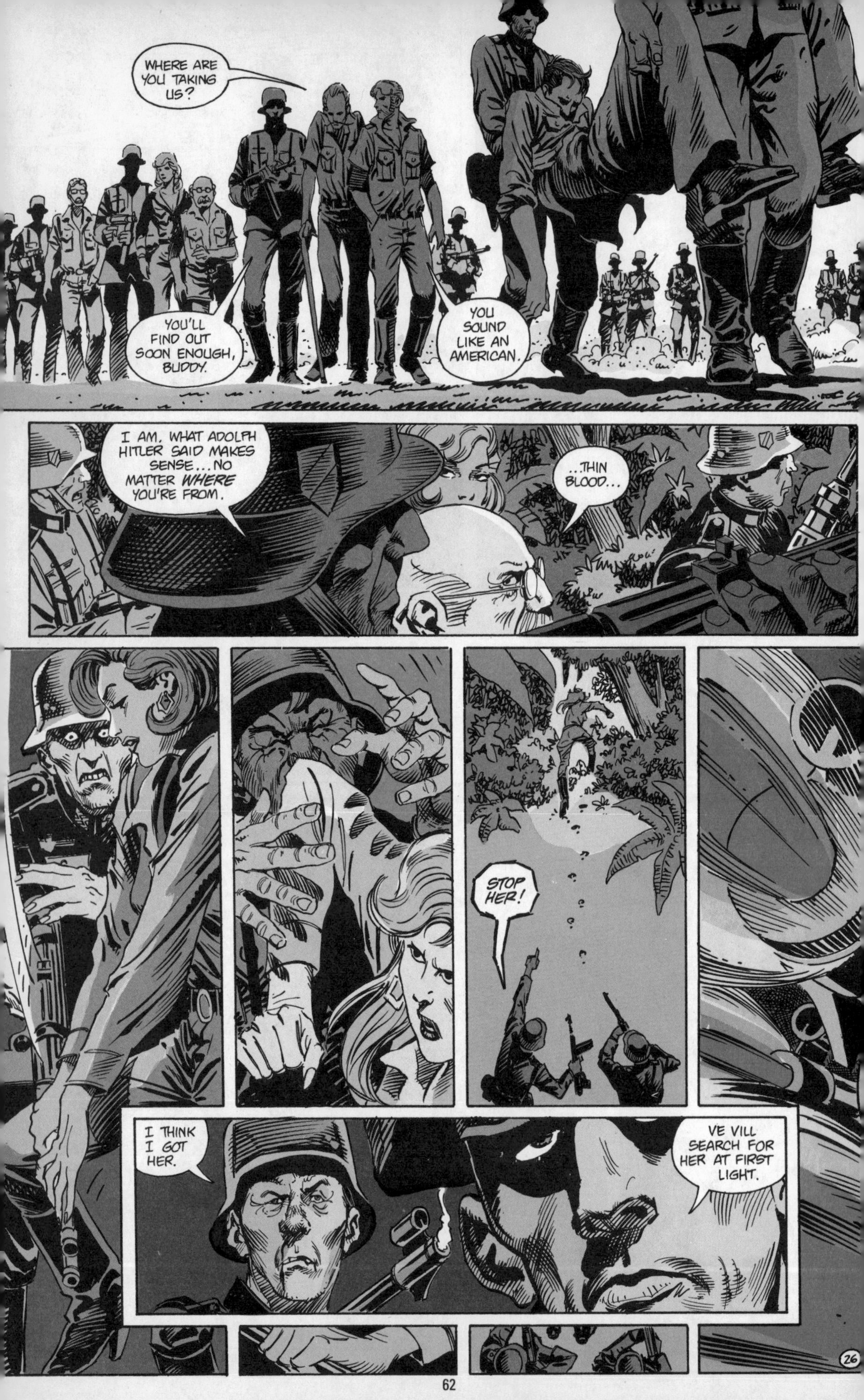
WHERE ARE YOU TAKING US?
YOU'LL FIND OUT SOON ENOUGH, BUDDY.
YOU SOUND LIKE AN AMERICAN.
I AM. WHAT ADOLPH HITLER SAID MAKES SENSE... NO MATTER *WHERE* YOU'RE FROM.
...THIN BLOOD...
STOP HER!
I THINK I GOT HER.
VE VILL SEARCH FOR HER AT FIRST LIGHT.
26

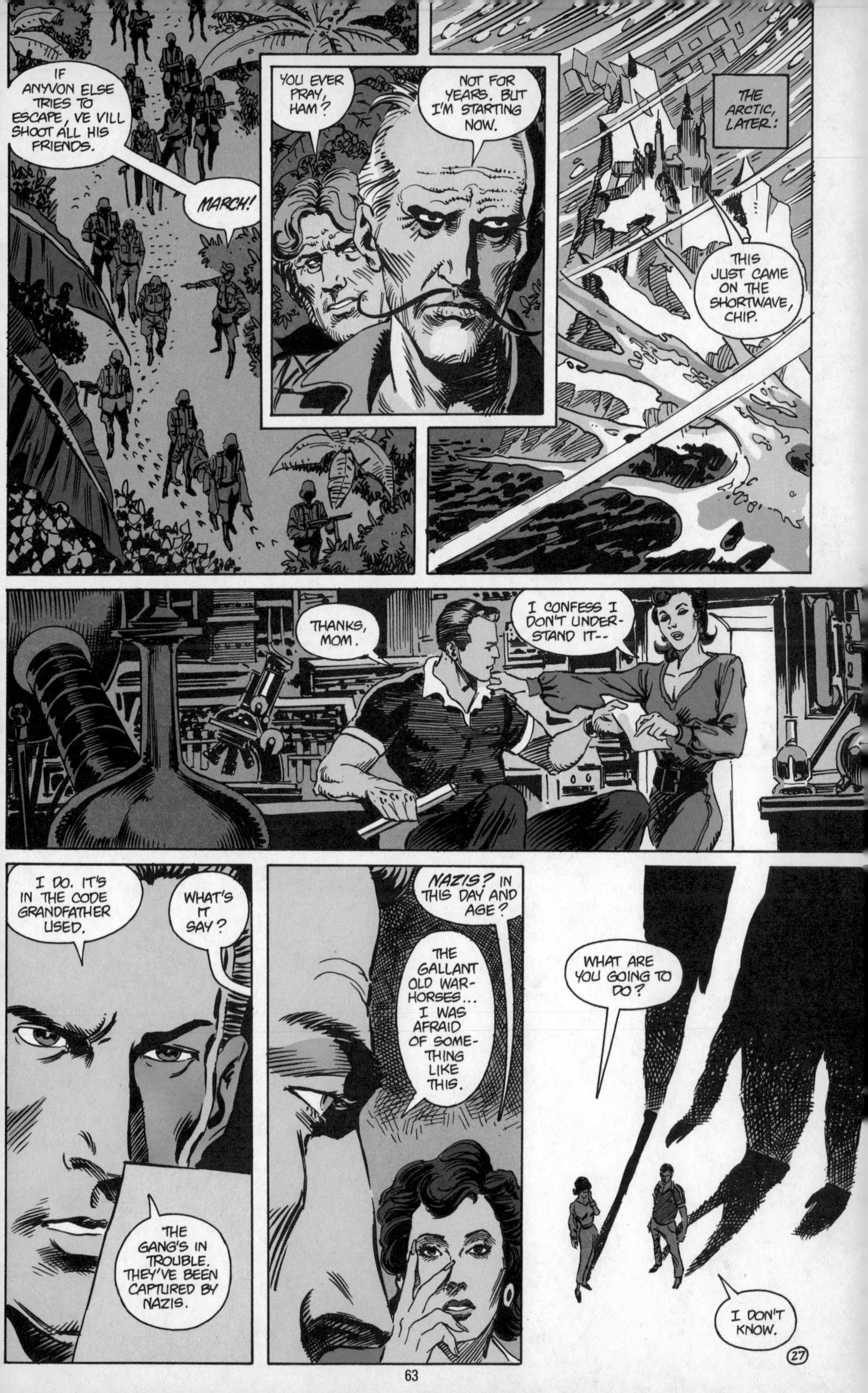
IF ANYVON ELSE TRIES TO ESCAPE, VE VILL SHOOT ALL HIS FRIENDS.
MARCH!
YOU EVER PRAY, HAM?
NOT FOR YEARS. BUT I'M STARTING NOW.
THE ARCTIC, LATER:
THIS JUST CAME ON THE SHORTWAVE, CHIP.
THANKS, MOM.
I CONFESS I DON'T UNDERSTAND IT--
I DO. IT'S IN THE CODE GRANDFATHER USED.
WHAT'S IT SAY?
THE GANG'S IN TROUBLE. THEY'VE BEEN CAPTURED BY NAZIS.
NAZIS? IN THIS DAY AND AGE?
THE GALLANT OLD WAR-HORSES... I WAS AFRAID OF SOMETHING LIKE THIS.
WHAT ARE YOU GOING TO DO?
I DON'T KNOW.
27

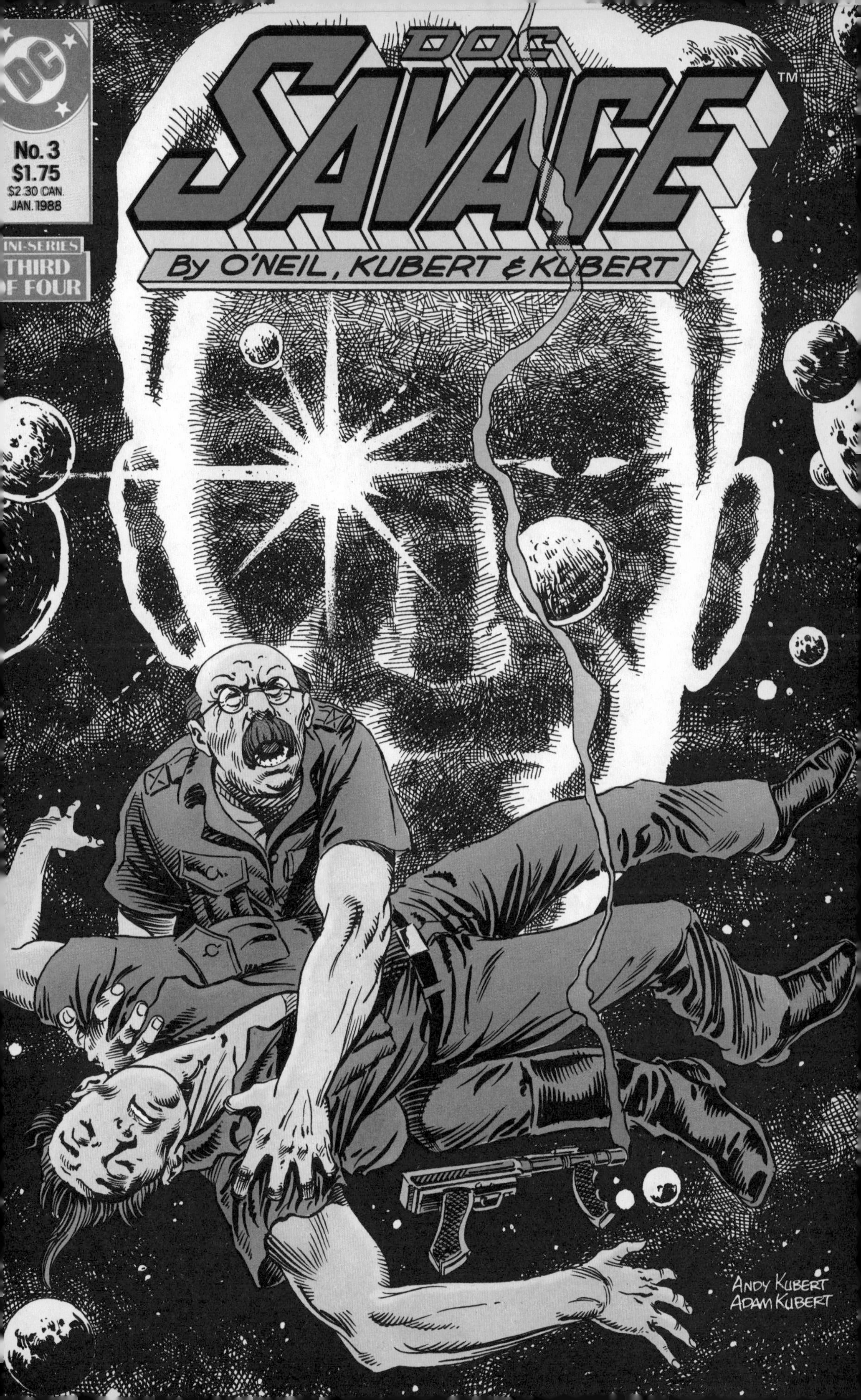
DOC SAVAGE™
No. 3
$1.75
$2.30 CAN.
JAN. 1988
INI-SERIES
THIRD
F FOUR
By O'NEIL, KUBERT & KUBERT
ANDY KUBERT
ADAM KUBERT

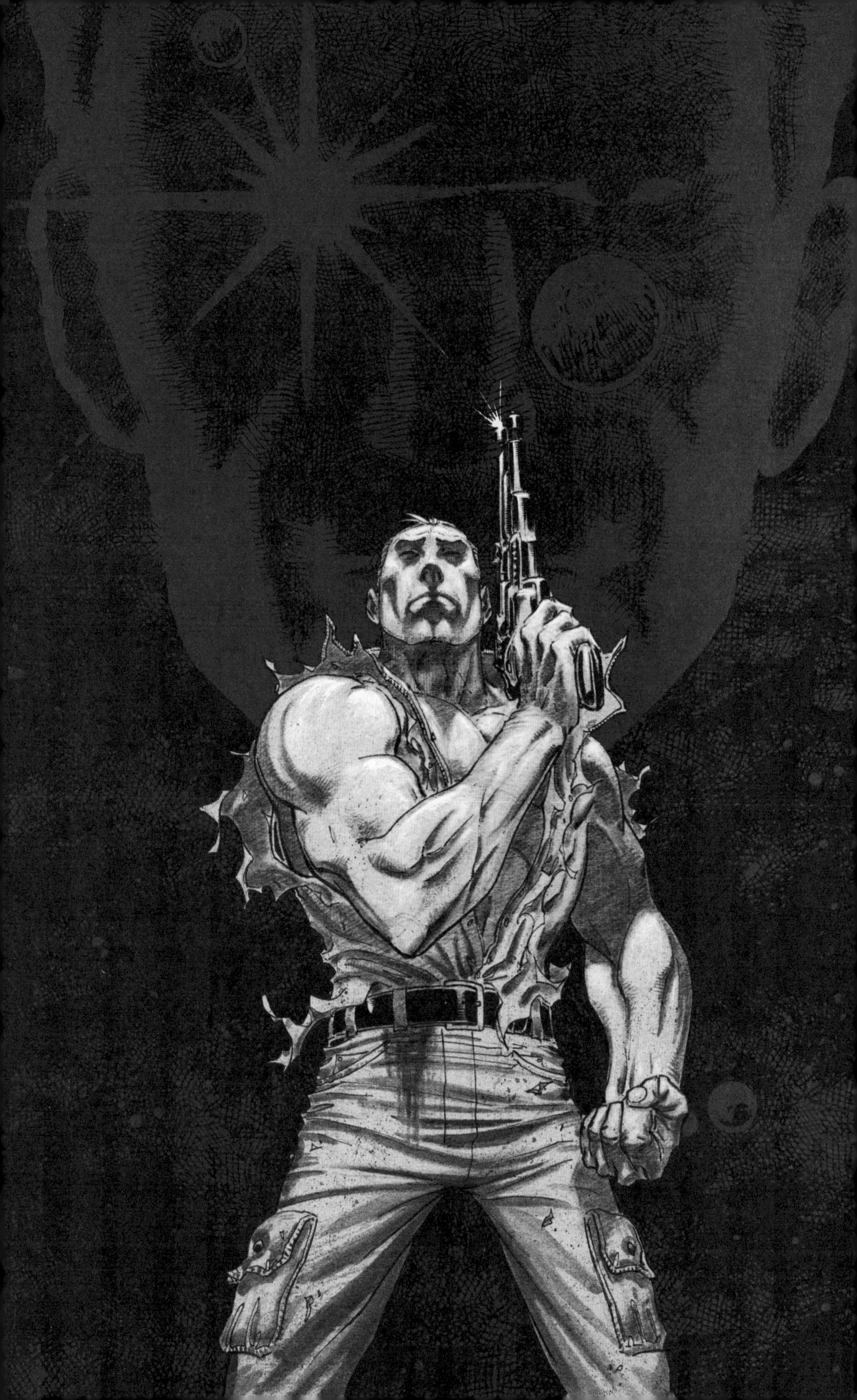

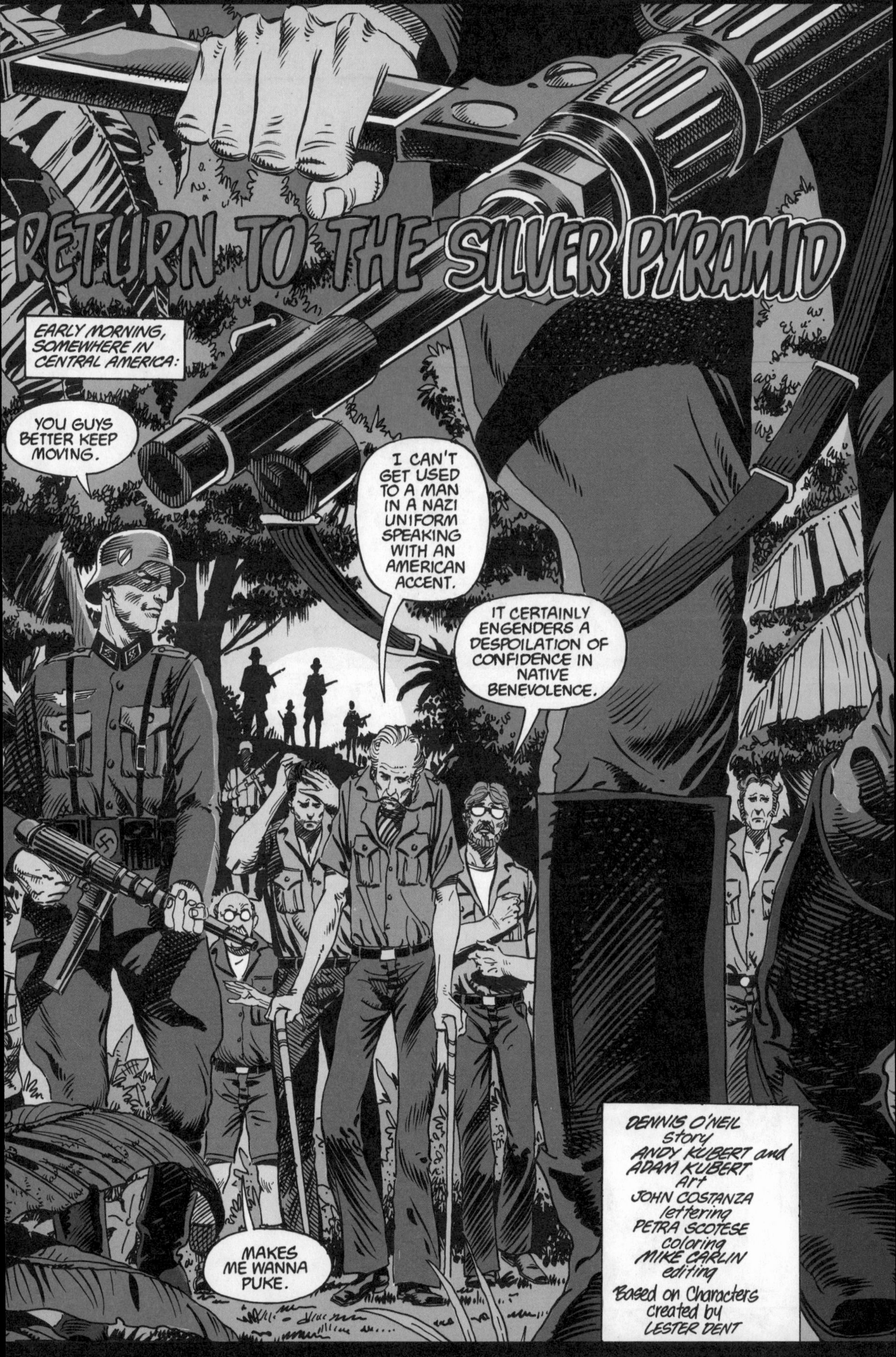
RETURN TO THE SILVER PYRAMID
EARLY MORNING, SOMEWHERE IN CENTRAL AMERICA:
YOU GUYS BETTER KEEP MOVING.
I CAN'T GET USED TO A MAN IN A NAZI UNIFORM SPEAKING WITH AN AMERICAN ACCENT.
IT CERTAINLY ENGENDERS A DESPOILATION OF CONFIDENCE IN NATIVE BENEVOLENCE.
MAKES ME WANNA PUKE.
DENNIS O'NEIL Story
ANDY KUBERT and ADAM KUBERT Art
JOHN COSTANZA lettering
PETRA SCOTESE coloring
MIKE CARLIN editing
Based on Characters created by LESTER DENT

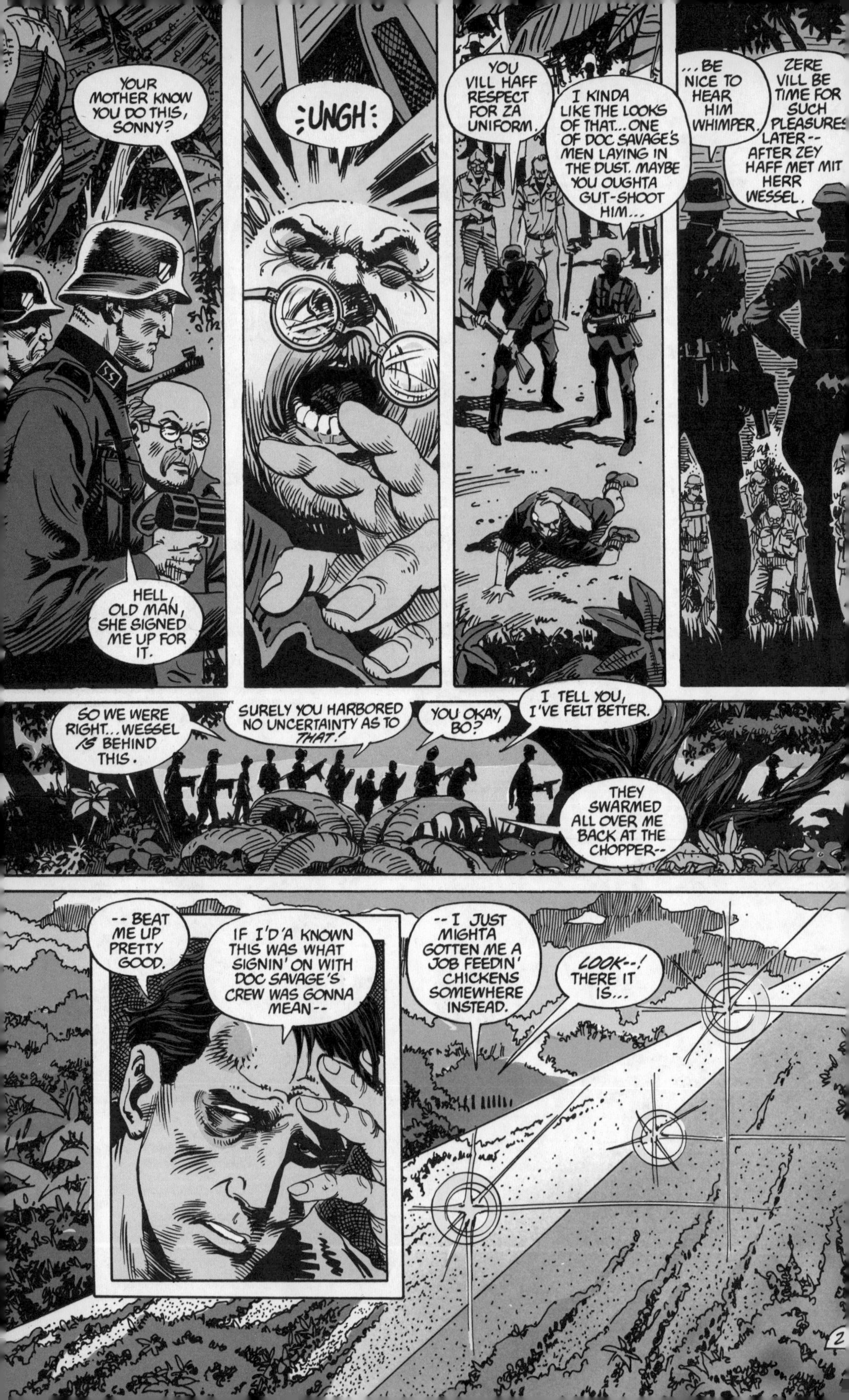
YOUR MOTHER KNOW YOU DO THIS, SONNY?
HELL OLD MAN, SHE SIGNED ME UP FOR IT.
UNGH
YOU VILL HAFF RESPECT FOR ZA UNIFORM.
I KINDA LIKE THE LOOKS OF THAT... ONE OF DOC SAVAGE'S MEN LAYING IN THE DUST. MAYBE YOU OUGHTA GUT-SHOOT HIM...
...BE NICE TO HEAR HIM WHIMPER.
ZERE VILL BE TIME FOR SUCH PLEASURES LATER -- AFTER ZEY HAFF MET MIT HERR WESSEL.
SO WE WERE RIGHT... WESSEL IS BEHIND THIS.
SURELY YOU HARBORED NO UNCERTAINTY AS TO THAT!
YOU OKAY, BO?
I TELL YOU, I'VE FELT BETTER.
THEY SWARMED ALL OVER ME BACK AT THE CHOPPER--
-- BEAT ME UP PRETTY GOOD.
IF I'D'A KNOWN THIS WAS WHAT SIGNIN' ON WITH DOC SAVAGE'S CREW WAS GONNA MEAN--
-- I JUST MIGHTA GOTTEN ME A JOB FEEDIN' CHICKENS SOMEWHERE INSTEAD.
LOOK--! THERE IT IS...

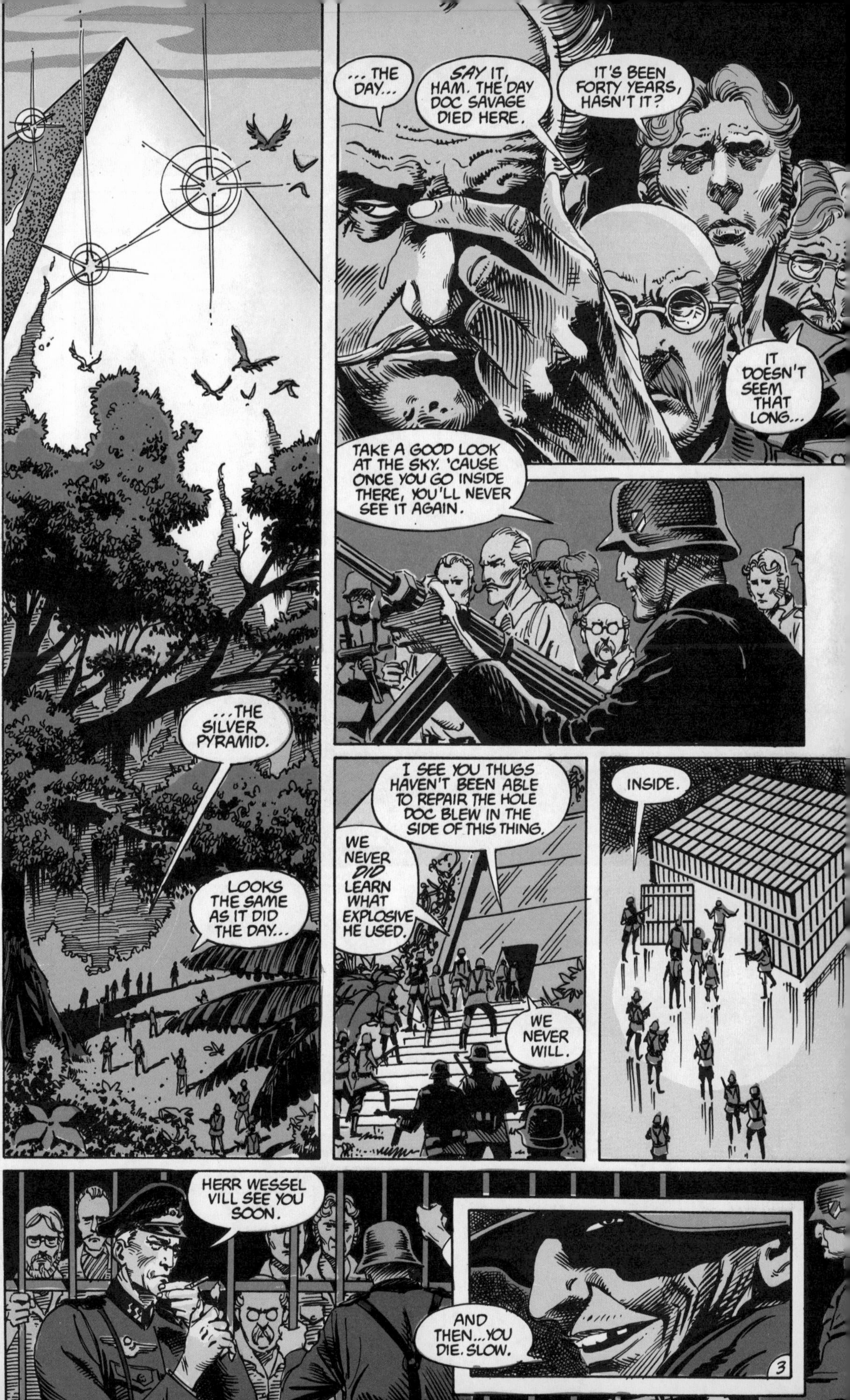
...THE SILVER PYRAMID.
LOOKS THE SAME AS IT DID THE DAY...
...THE DAY...
SAY IT, HAM. THE DAY DOC SAVAGE DIED HERE.
IT'S BEEN FORTY YEARS, HASN'T IT?
IT DOESN'T SEEM THAT LONG...
TAKE A GOOD LOOK AT THE SKY. 'CAUSE ONCE YOU GO INSIDE THERE, YOU'LL NEVER SEE IT AGAIN.
I SEE YOU THUGS HAVEN'T BEEN ABLE TO REPAIR THE HOLE DOC BLEW IN THE SIDE OF THIS THING.
WE NEVER DID LEARN WHAT EXPLOSIVE HE USED.
WE NEVER WILL.
INSIDE.
HERR WESSEL VILL SEE YOU SOON.
AND THEN...YOU DIE. SLOW.
3

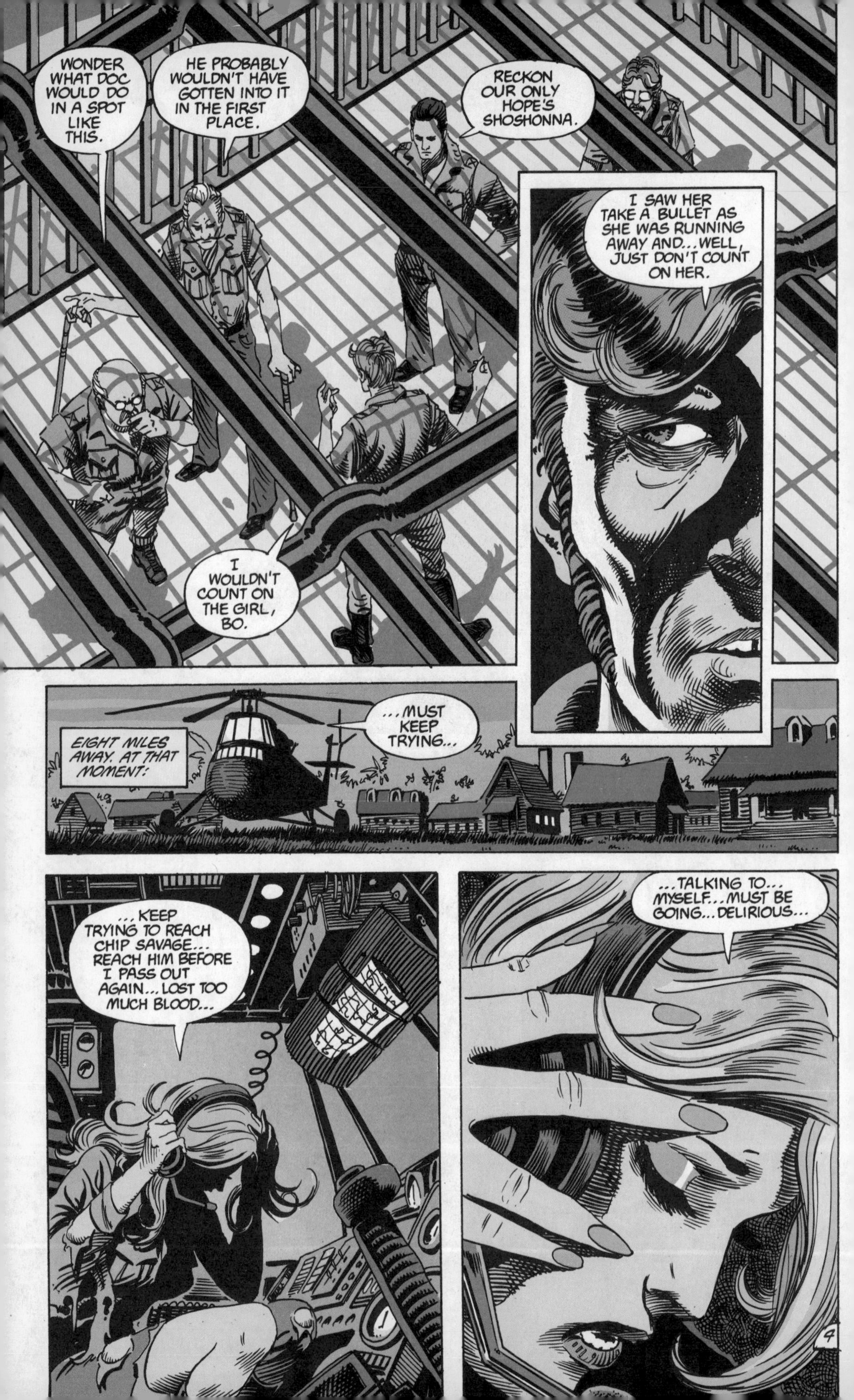
WONDER WHAT DOC WOULD DO IN A SPOT LIKE THIS.
HE PROBABLY WOULDN'T HAVE GOTTEN INTO IT IN THE FIRST PLACE.
RECKON OUR ONLY HOPE'S SHOSHONNA.
I WOULDN'T COUNT ON THE GIRL, BO.
I SAW HER TAKE A BULLET AS SHE WAS RUNNING AWAY AND...WELL, JUST DON'T COUNT ON HER.
EIGHT MILES AWAY. AT THAT MOMENT:
...MUST KEEP TRYING...
...KEEP TRYING TO REACH CHIP SAVAGE... REACH HIM BEFORE I PASS OUT AGAIN...LOST TOO MUCH BLOOD...
...TALKING TO... MYSELF...MUST BE GOING...DELIRIOUS...
4

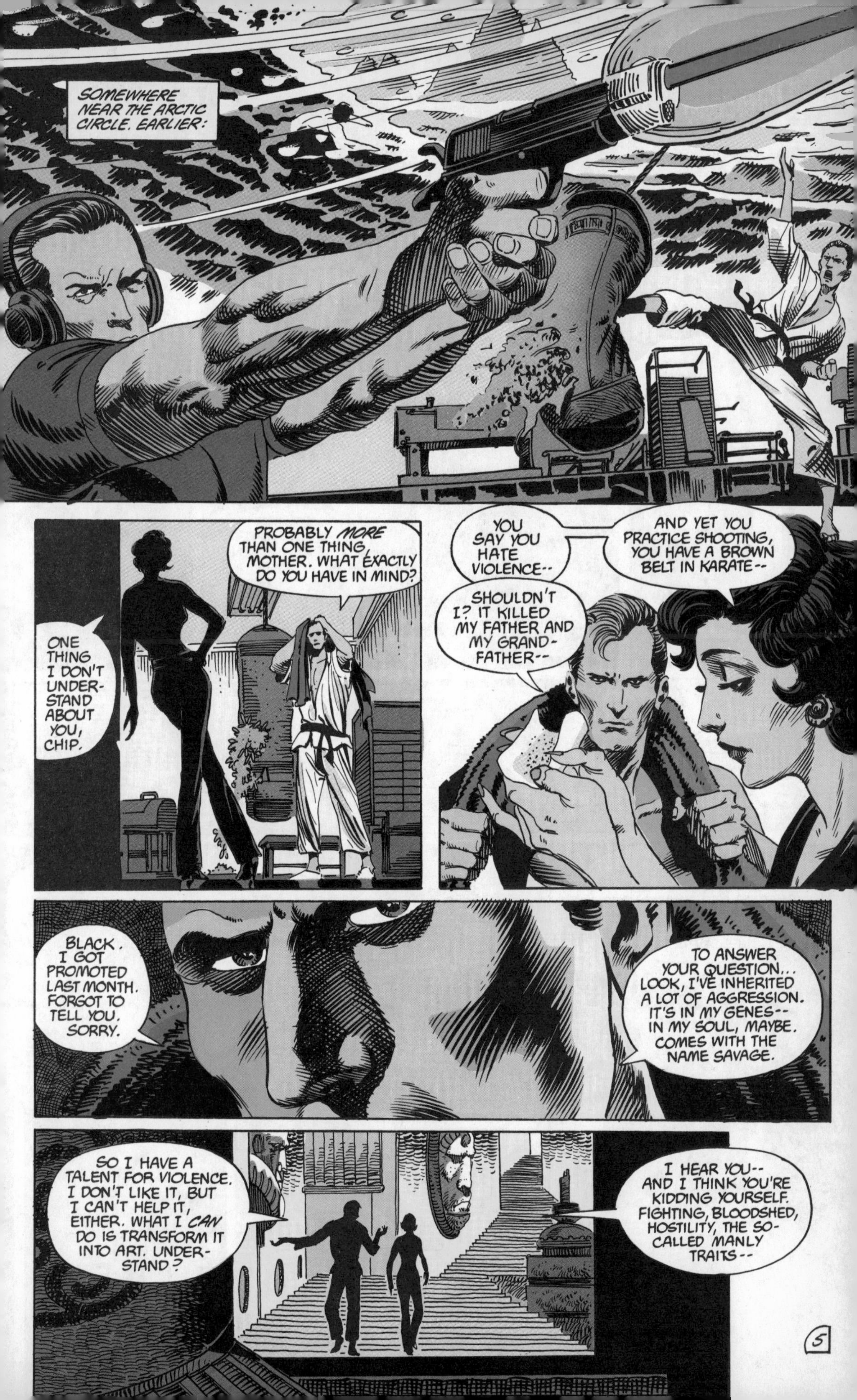

SOMEWHERE NEAR THE ARCTIC CIRCLE. EARLIER:
ONE THING I DON'T UNDERSTAND ABOUT YOU, CHIP.
PROBABLY MORE THAN ONE THING, MOTHER. WHAT EXACTLY DO YOU HAVE IN MIND?
YOU SAY YOU HATE VIOLENCE--
AND YET YOU PRACTICE SHOOTING, YOU HAVE A BROWN BELT IN KARATE--
SHOULDN'T I? IT KILLED MY FATHER AND MY GRANDFATHER--
BLACK. I GOT PROMOTED LAST MONTH. FORGOT TO TELL YOU. SORRY.
TO ANSWER YOUR QUESTION... LOOK, I'VE INHERITED A LOT OF AGGRESSION. IT'S IN MY GENES--IN MY SOUL, MAYBE. COMES WITH THE NAME SAVAGE.
SO I HAVE A TALENT FOR VIOLENCE. I DON'T LIKE IT, BUT I CAN'T HELP IT, EITHER. WHAT I CAN DO IS TRANSFORM IT INTO ART. UNDERSTAND?
I HEAR YOU--AND I THINK YOU'RE KIDDING YOURSELF. FIGHTING, BLOODSHED, HOSTILITY, THE SO-CALLED MANLY TRAITS--
5

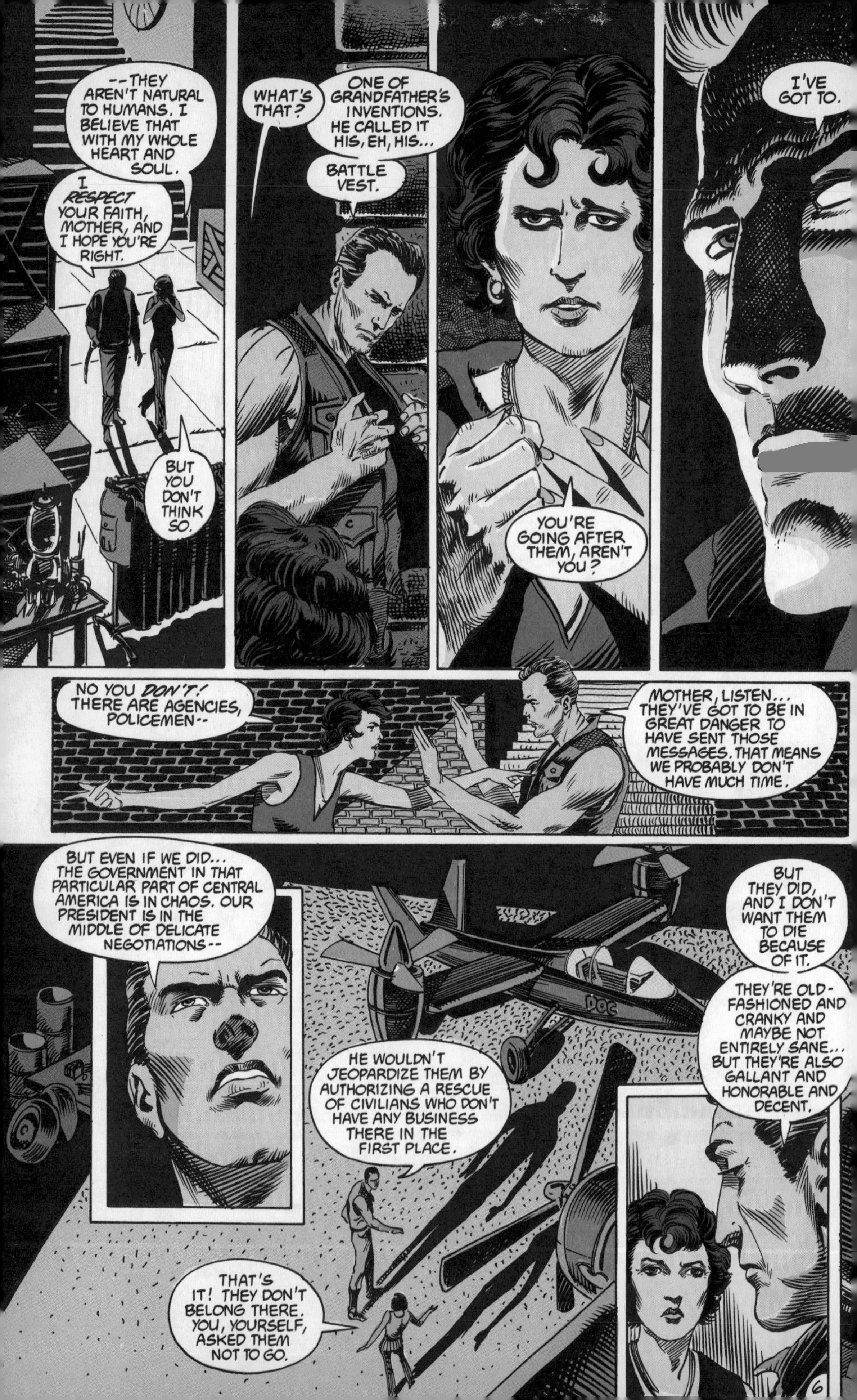
--THEY AREN'T NATURAL TO HUMANS. I BELIEVE THAT WITH MY WHOLE HEART AND SOUL.
I RESPECT YOUR FAITH, MOTHER, AND I HOPE YOU'RE RIGHT.
BUT YOU DON'T THINK SO.
WHAT'S THAT?
ONE OF GRANDFATHER'S INVENTIONS. HE CALLED IT HIS, EH, HIS...
BATTLE VEST.
YOU'RE GOING AFTER THEM, AREN'T YOU?
I'VE GOT TO.
NO YOU DON'T! THERE ARE AGENCIES, POLICEMEN--
MOTHER, LISTEN... THEY'VE GOT TO BE IN GREAT DANGER TO HAVE SENT THOSE MESSAGES. THAT MEANS WE PROBABLY DON'T HAVE MUCH TIME.
BUT EVEN IF WE DID... THE GOVERNMENT IN THAT PARTICULAR PART OF CENTRAL AMERICA IS IN CHAOS. OUR PRESIDENT IS IN THE MIDDLE OF DELICATE NEGOTIATIONS--
HE WOULDN'T JEOPARDIZE THEM BY AUTHORIZING A RESCUE OF CIVILIANS WHO DON'T HAVE ANY BUSINESS THERE IN THE FIRST PLACE.
THAT'S IT! THEY DON'T BELONG THERE. YOU, YOURSELF, ASKED THEM NOT TO GO.
BUT THEY DID, AND I DON'T WANT THEM TO DIE BECAUSE OF IT.
THEY'RE OLD-FASHIONED AND CRANKY AND MAYBE NOT ENTIRELY SANE... BUT THEY'RE ALSO GALLANT AND HONORABLE AND DECENT.
DOC
6

AND APART FROM YOU, THEY'RE ALL THE FAMILY I'VE GOT.

TAKE CARE, MOTHER. I'LL SEE YOU IN A FEW DAYS.

COME BACK TO ME, SON, PLEASE...

NEXT STOP CENTRAL AMERICA.

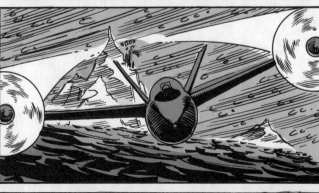

7

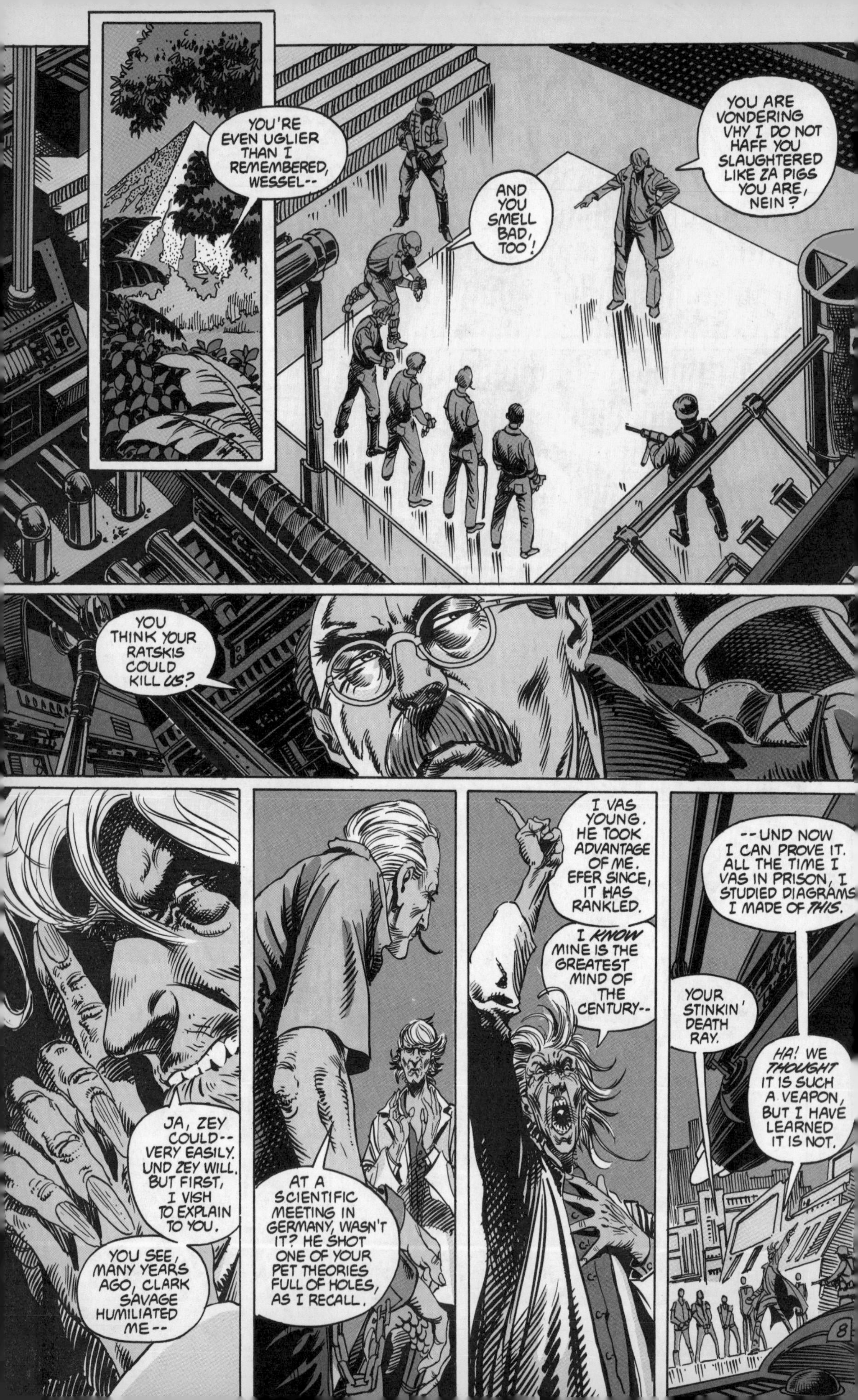

YOU'RE EVEN UGLIER THAN I REMEMBERED, WESSEL--
AND YOU SMELL BAD, TOO!
YOU ARE VONDERING VHY I DO NOT HAFF YOU SLAUGHTERED LIKE ZA PIGS YOU ARE, NEIN?
YOU THINK YOUR RATSKIS COULD KILL US?
JA, ZEY COULD-- VERY EASILY. UND ZEY WILL. BUT FIRST, I VISH TO EXPLAIN TO YOU.
YOU SEE, MANY YEARS AGO, CLARK SAVAGE HUMILIATED ME--
AT A SCIENTIFIC MEETING IN GERMANY, WASN'T IT? HE SHOT ONE OF YOUR PET THEORIES FULL OF HOLES, AS I RECALL.
I VAS YOUNG. HE TOOK ADVANTAGE OF ME. EFER SINCE, IT HAS RANKLED.
I KNOW MINE IS THE GREATEST MIND OF THE CENTURY--
--UND NOW I CAN PROVE IT. ALL THE TIME I VAS IN PRISON, I STUDIED DIAGRAMS I MADE OF THIS.
YOUR STINKIN' DEATH RAY.
HA! WE THOUGHT IT IS SUCH A VEAPON, BUT I HAVE LEARNED IT IS NOT.

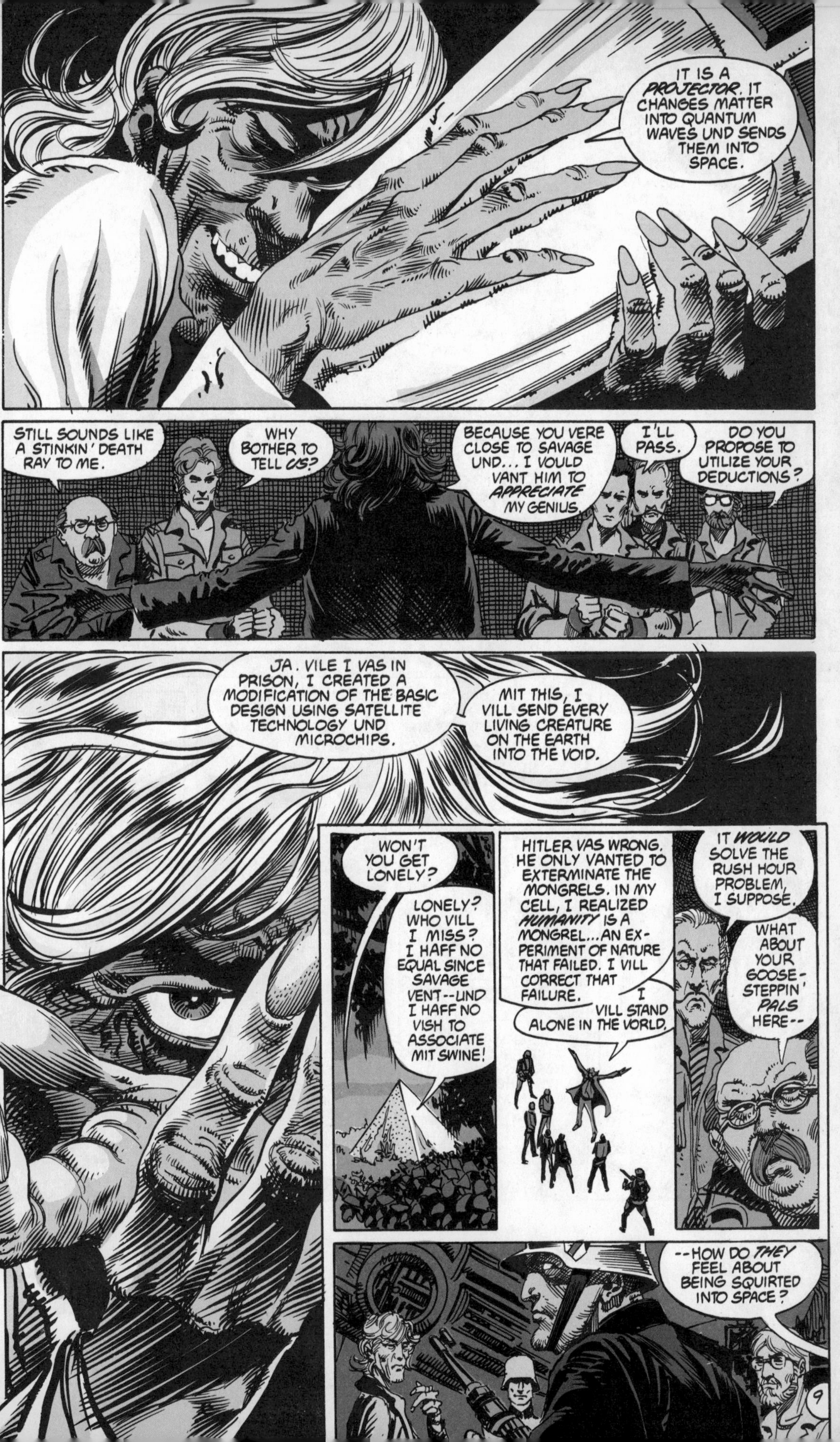
IT IS A PROJECTOR. IT CHANGES MATTER INTO QUANTUM WAVES UND SENDS THEM INTO SPACE.
STILL SOUNDS LIKE A STINKIN' DEATH RAY TO ME.
WHY BOTHER TO TELL US?
BECAUSE YOU VERE CLOSE TO SAVAGE UND... I VOULD VANT HIM TO APPRECIATE MY GENIUS.
I'LL PASS.
DO YOU PROPOSE TO UTILIZE YOUR DEDUCTIONS?
JA. VILE I VAS IN PRISON, I CREATED A MODIFICATION OF THE BASIC DESIGN USING SATELLITE TECHNOLOGY UND MICROCHIPS.
MIT THIS, I VILL SEND EVERY LIVING CREATURE ON THE EARTH INTO THE VOID.
WON'T YOU GET LONELY?
LONELY? WHO VILL I MISS? I HAFF NO EQUAL SINCE SAVAGE VENT--UND I HAFF NO VISH TO ASSOCIATE MIT SWINE!
HITLER VAS WRONG. HE ONLY VANTED TO EXTERMINATE THE MONGRELS. IN MY CELL, I REALIZED HUMANITY IS A MONGREL...AN EXPERIMENT OF NATURE THAT FAILED. I VILL CORRECT THAT FAILURE.
I VILL STAND ALONE IN THE VORLD.
IT WOULD SOLVE THE RUSH HOUR PROBLEM, I SUPPOSE.
WHAT ABOUT YOUR GOOSE-STEPPIN' PALS HERE--
--HOW DO THEY FEEL ABOUT BEING SQUIRTED INTO SPACE?
9

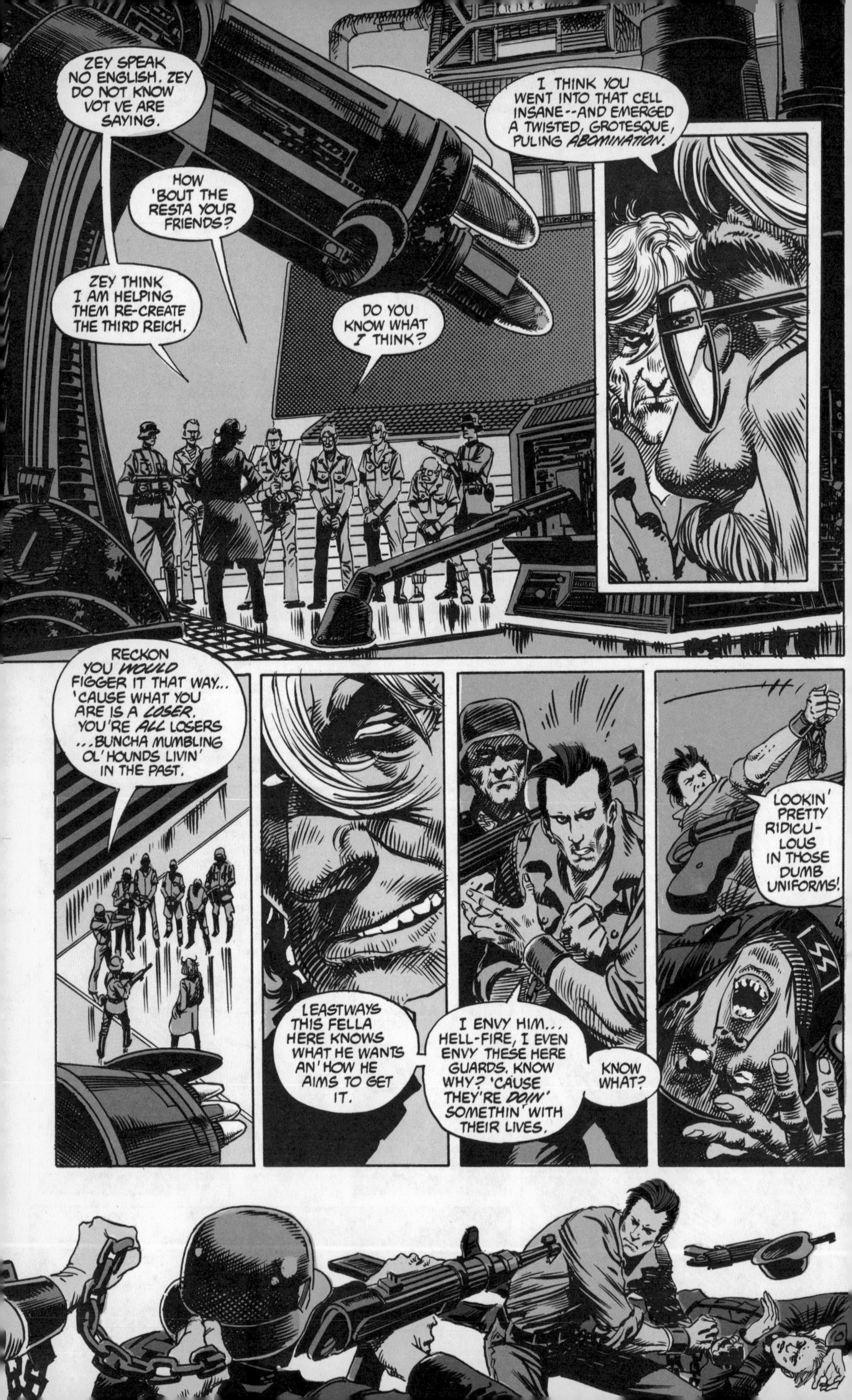
ZEY SPEAK NO ENGLISH. ZEY DO NOT KNOW VOT VE ARE SAYING.
HOW 'BOUT THE RESTA YOUR FRIENDS?
ZEY THINK I AM HELPING THEM RE-CREATE THE THIRD REICH.
DO YOU KNOW WHAT *I* THINK?
I THINK YOU WENT INTO THAT CELL INSANE--AND EMERGED A TWISTED, GROTESQUE, PULING *ABOMINATION*.
RECKON YOU *WOULD* FIGGER IT THAT WAY... 'CAUSE WHAT YOU ARE IS A *LOSER*. YOU'RE *ALL* LOSERS ...BUNCHA MUMBLING OL' HOUNDS LIVIN' IN THE PAST.
LEASTWAYS THIS FELLA HERE KNOWS WHAT HE WANTS AN' HOW HE AIMS TO GET IT.
I ENVY HIM... HELL-FIRE, I EVEN ENVY THESE HERE GUARDS. KNOW WHY? 'CAUSE THEY'RE *DOIN'* SOMETHIN' WITH THEIR LIVES.
KNOW WHAT?
LOOKIN' PRETTY RIDICU-LOUS IN THOSE DUMB UNIFORMS!

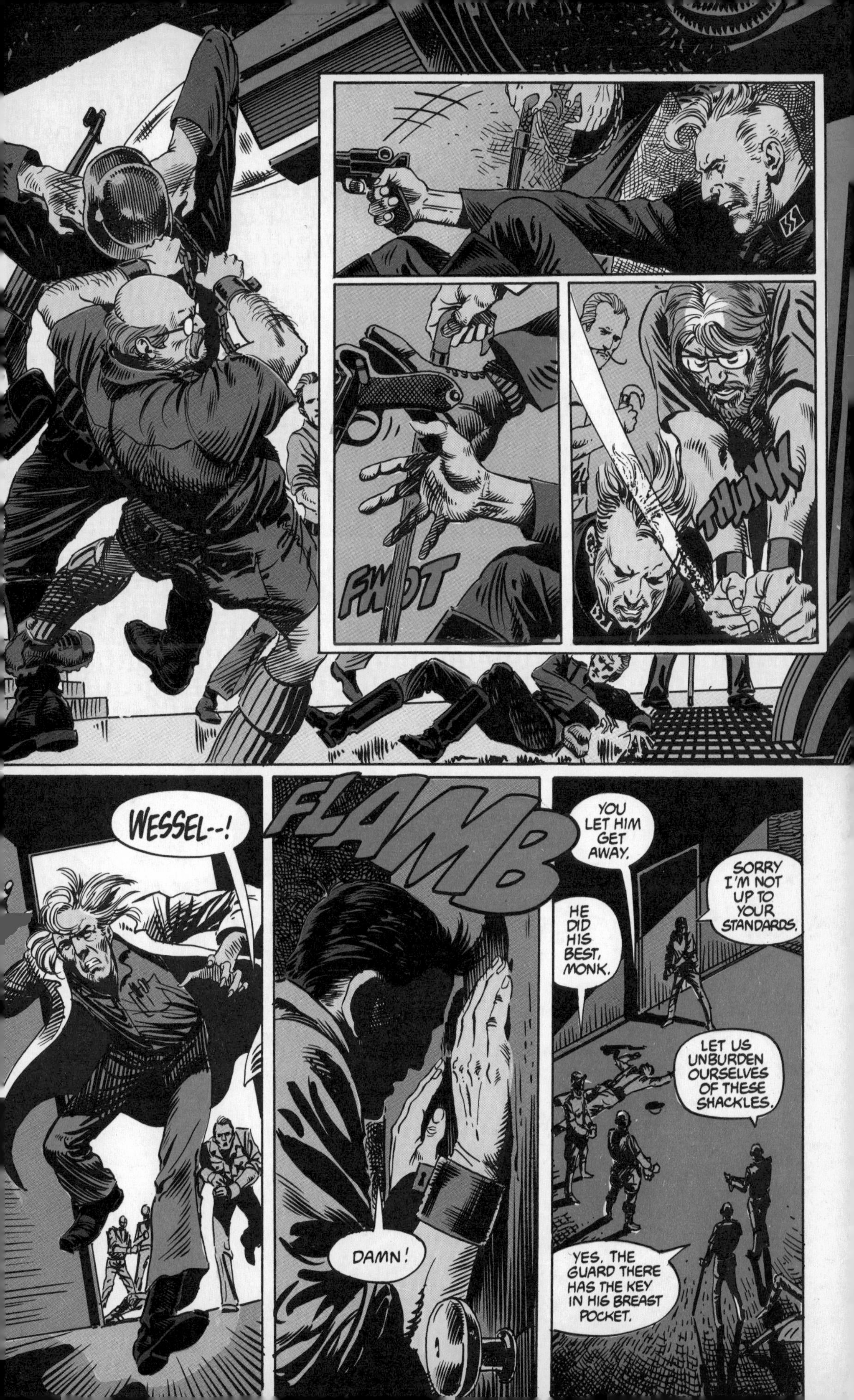
FWOT
THUNK
WESSEL--!
FLAMB
DAMN!
YOU LET HIM GET AWAY.
HE DID HIS BEST, MONK.
SORRY I'M NOT UP TO YOUR STANDARDS.
LET US UNBURDEN OURSELVES OF THESE SHACKLES.
YES. THE GUARD THERE HAS THE KEY IN HIS BREAST POCKET.

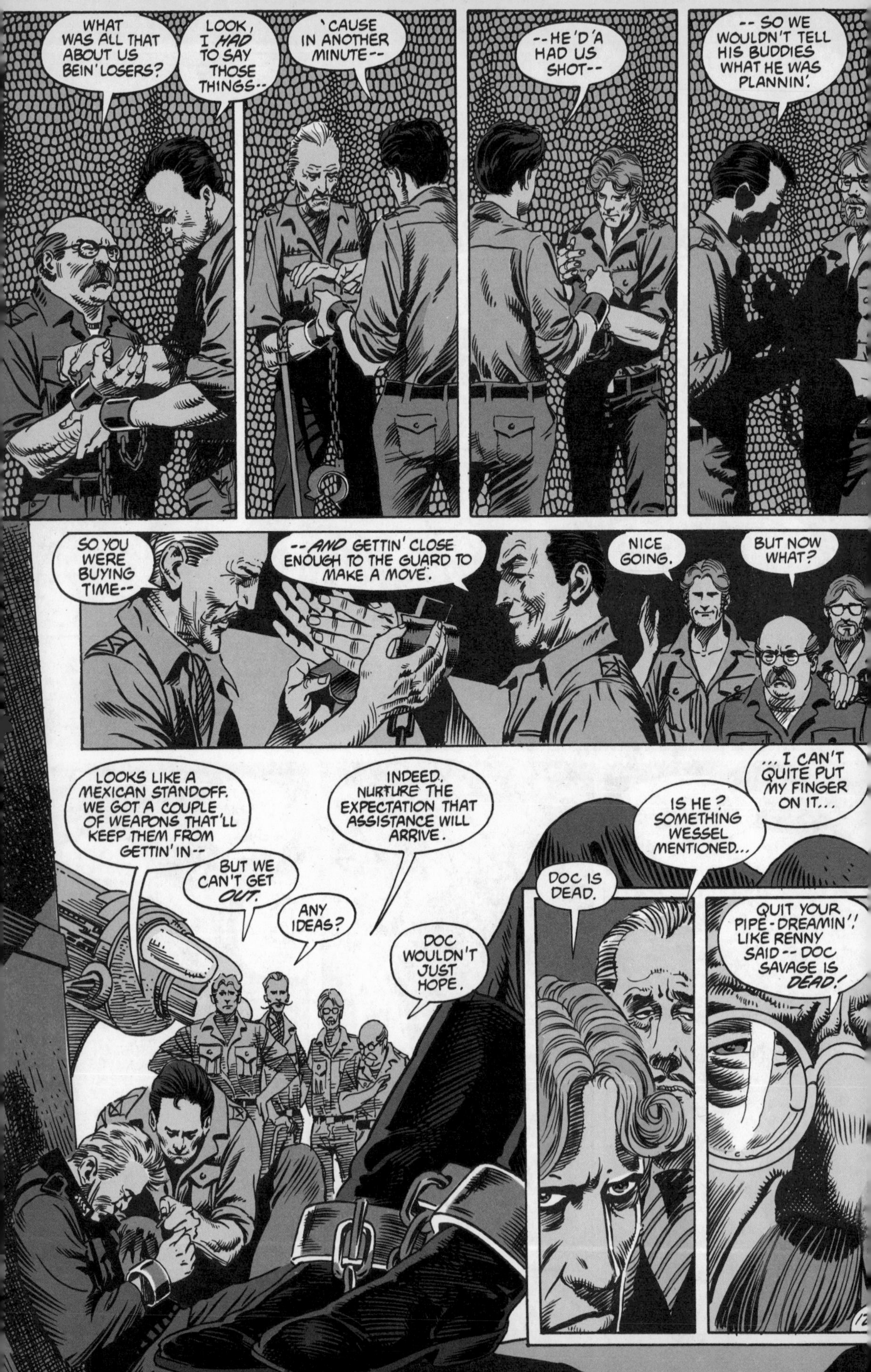
WHAT WAS ALL THAT ABOUT US BEIN' LOSERS?
LOOK, I HAD TO SAY THOSE THINGS--
'CAUSE IN ANOTHER MINUTE--
--HE'D'A HAD US SHOT--
--SO WE WOULDN'T TELL HIS BUDDIES WHAT HE WAS PLANNIN'.
SO YOU WERE BUYING TIME--
--AND GETTIN' CLOSE ENOUGH TO THE GUARD TO MAKE A MOVE.
NICE GOING.
BUT NOW WHAT?
LOOKS LIKE A MEXICAN STANDOFF. WE GOT A COUPLE OF WEAPONS THAT'LL KEEP THEM FROM GETTIN' IN--
BUT WE CAN'T GET OUT.
ANY IDEAS?
INDEED. NURTURE THE EXPECTATION THAT ASSISTANCE WILL ARRIVE.
DOC WOULDN'T JUST HOPE.
DOC IS DEAD.
IS HE? SOMETHING WESSEL MENTIONED...
...I CAN'T QUITE PUT MY FINGER ON IT...
QUIT YOUR PIPE-DREAMIN'! LIKE RENNY SAID--DOC SAVAGE IS DEAD!
12

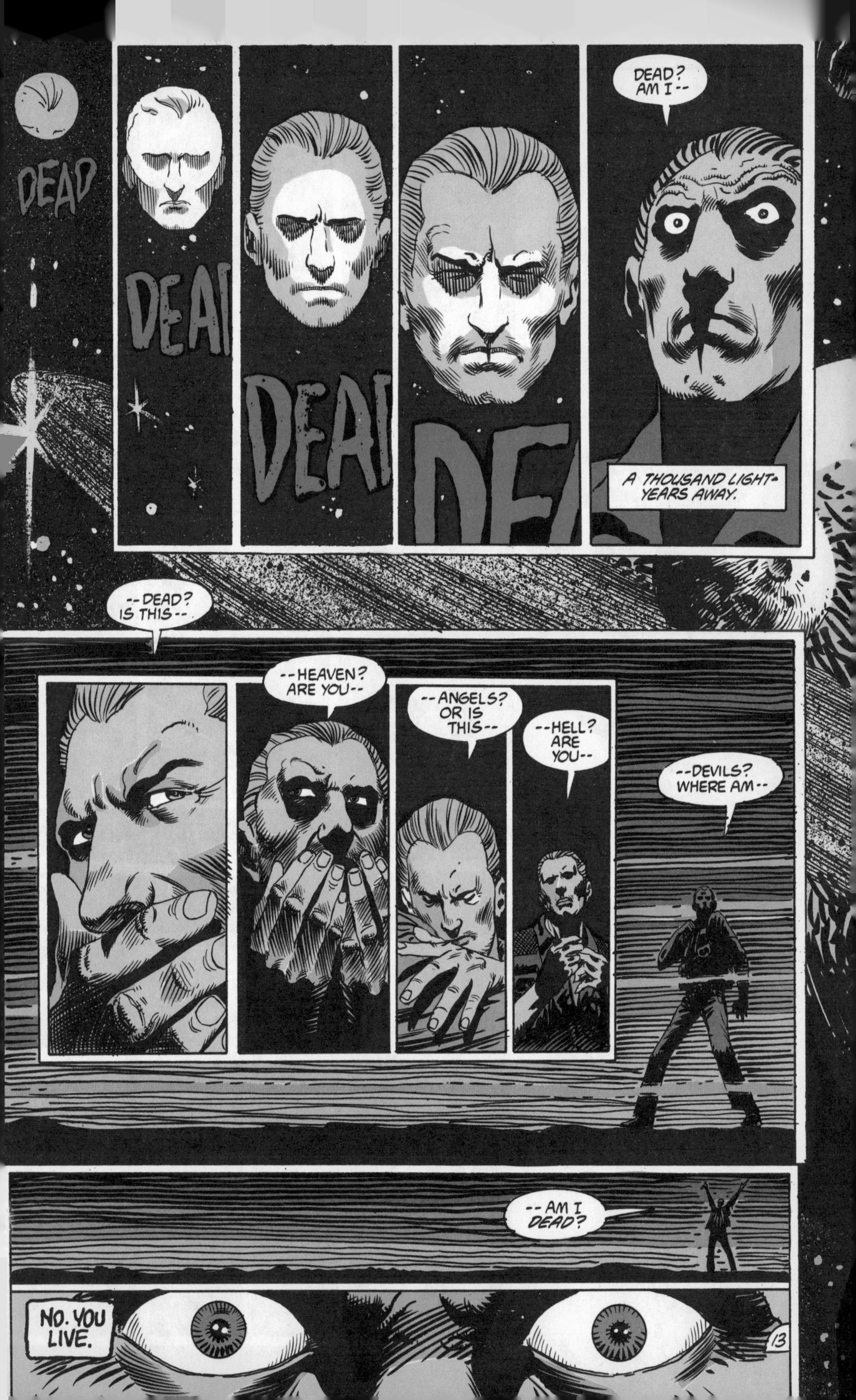
DEAD
DEAD
DEAD
DEA
DEAD? AM I--
A THOUSAND LIGHT-YEARS AWAY.
--DEAD? IS THIS--
--HEAVEN? ARE YOU--
--ANGELS? OR IS THIS--
--HELL? ARE YOU--
--DEVILS? WHERE AM--
--AM I DEAD?
NO. YOU LIVE.
13

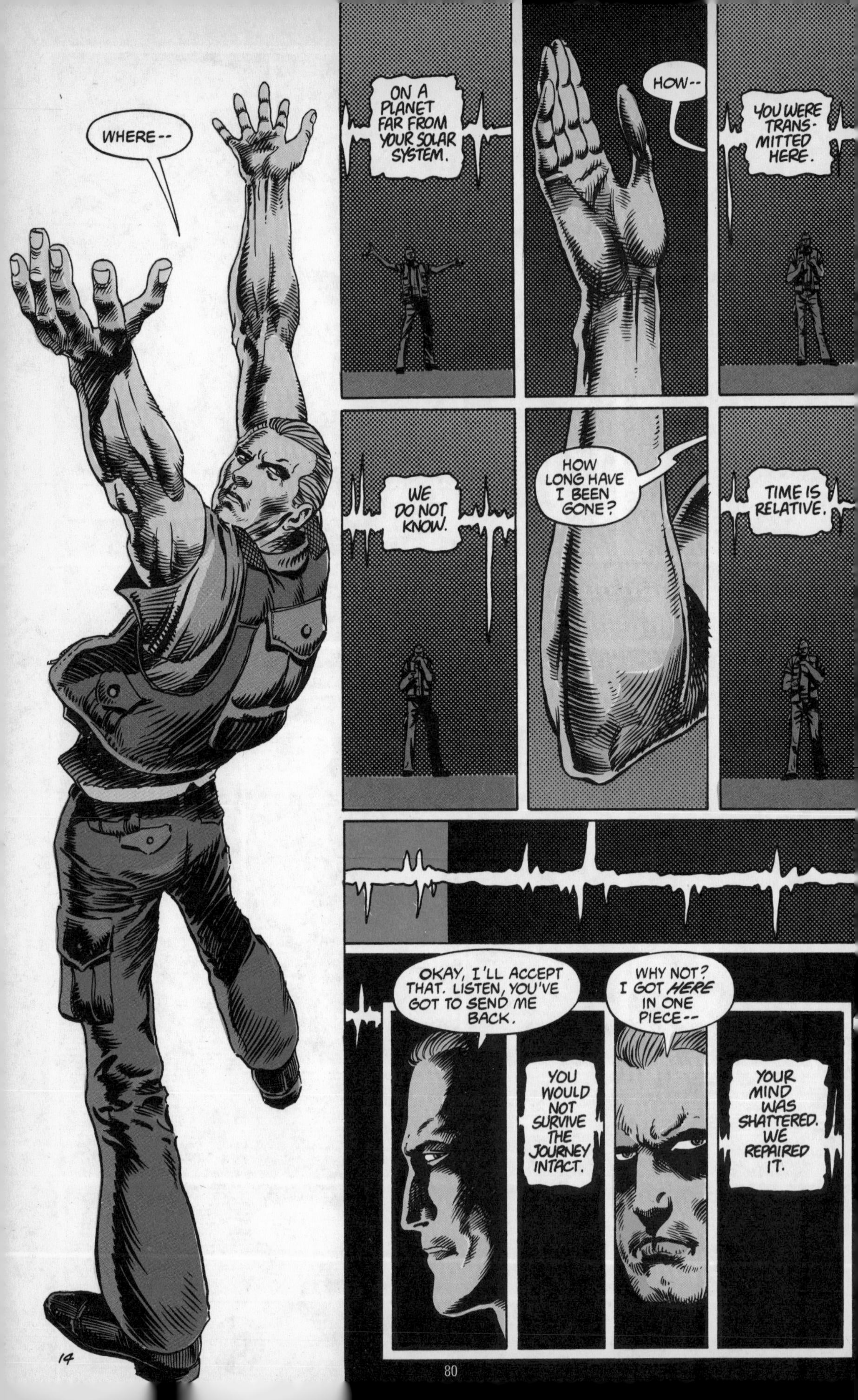

WHERE--
ON A PLANET FAR FROM YOUR SOLAR SYSTEM.
HOW--
YOU WERE TRANS-MITTED HERE.
WE DO NOT KNOW.
HOW LONG HAVE I BEEN GONE?
TIME IS RELATIVE.
OKAY, I'LL ACCEPT THAT. LISTEN, YOU'VE GOT TO SEND ME BACK.
YOU WOULD NOT SURVIVE THE JOURNEY INTACT.
WHY NOT? I GOT *HERE* IN ONE PIECE--
YOUR MIND WAS SHATTERED. WE REPAIRED IT.
14

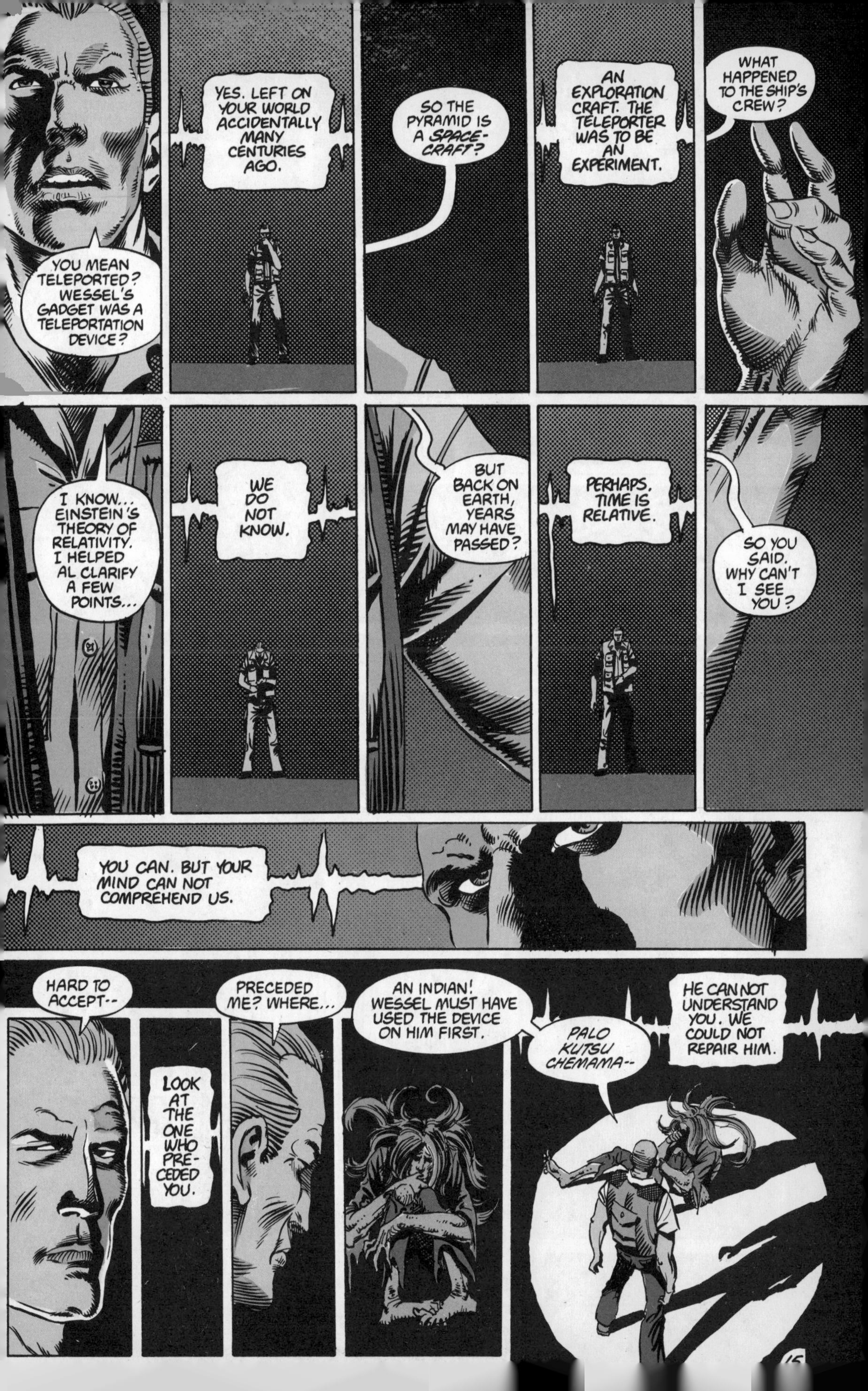
YOU MEAN TELEPORTED? WESSEL'S GADGET WAS A TELEPORTATION DEVICE?
YES. LEFT ON YOUR WORLD ACCIDENTALLY MANY CENTURIES AGO.
SO THE PYRAMID IS A SPACE-CRAFT?
AN EXPLORATION CRAFT. THE TELEPORTER WAS TO BE AN EXPERIMENT.
WHAT HAPPENED TO THE SHIP'S CREW?
WE DO NOT KNOW.
BUT BACK ON EARTH, YEARS MAY HAVE PASSED?
PERHAPS. TIME IS RELATIVE.
I KNOW... EINSTEIN'S THEORY OF RELATIVITY. I HELPED AL CLARIFY A FEW POINTS...
SO YOU SAID. WHY CAN'T I SEE YOU?
YOU CAN. BUT YOUR MIND CAN NOT COMPREHEND US.
HARD TO ACCEPT--
LOOK AT THE ONE WHO PRE-CEDED YOU.
PRECEDED ME? WHERE...
AN INDIAN! WESSEL MUST HAVE USED THE DEVICE ON HIM FIRST.
PALO KUTSU CHEMAMA--
HE CAN NOT UNDERSTAND YOU. WE COULD NOT REPAIR HIM.
15

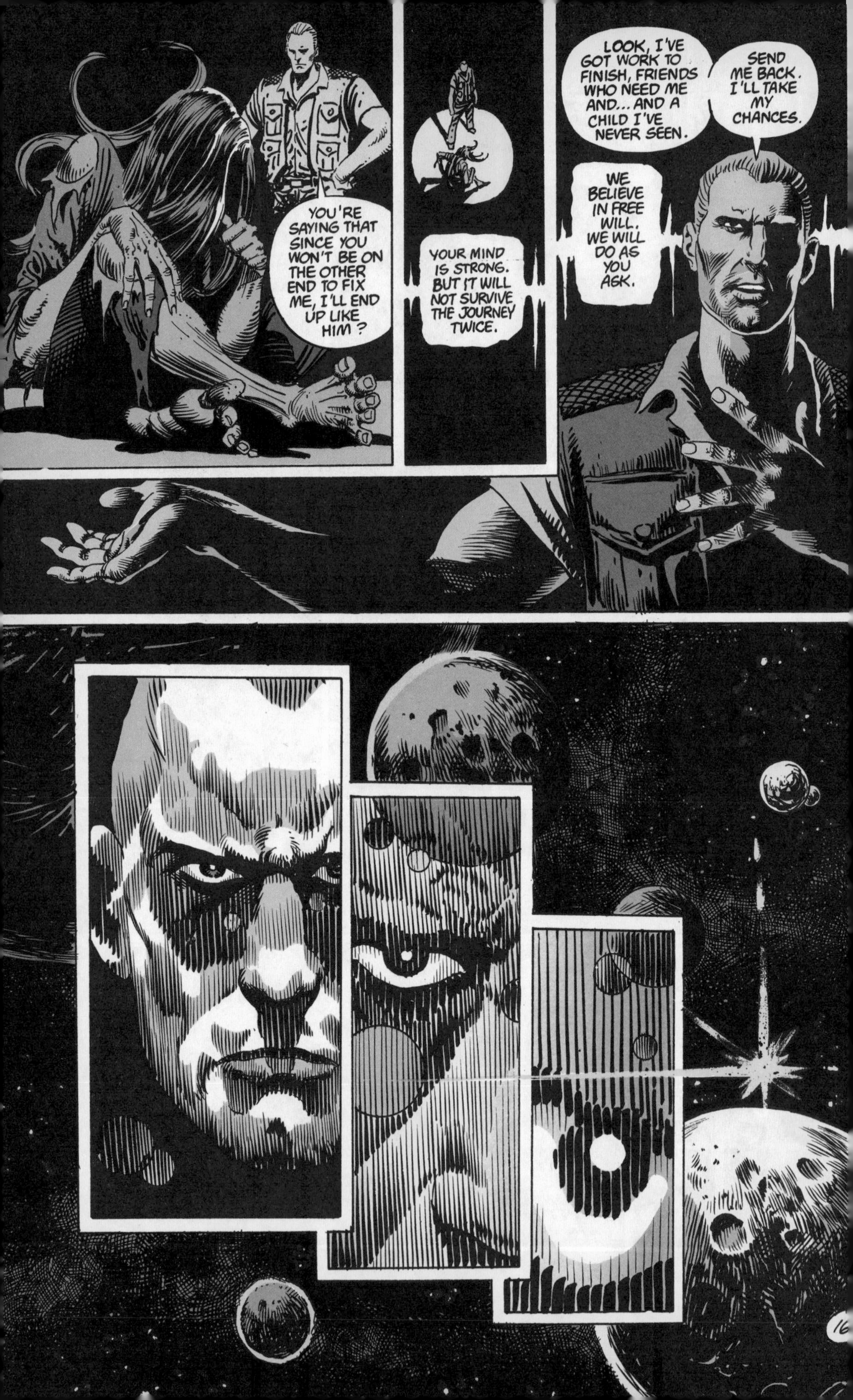
YOU'RE SAYING THAT SINCE YOU WON'T BE ON THE OTHER END TO FIX ME, I'LL END UP LIKE HIM ?
YOUR MIND IS STRONG. BUT IT WILL NOT SURVIVE THE JOURNEY TWICE.
LOOK, I'VE GOT WORK TO FINISH, FRIENDS WHO NEED ME AND... AND A CHILD I'VE NEVER SEEN.
SEND ME BACK. I'LL TAKE MY CHANCES.
WE BELIEVE IN FREE WILL. WE WILL DO AS YOU ASK.
16

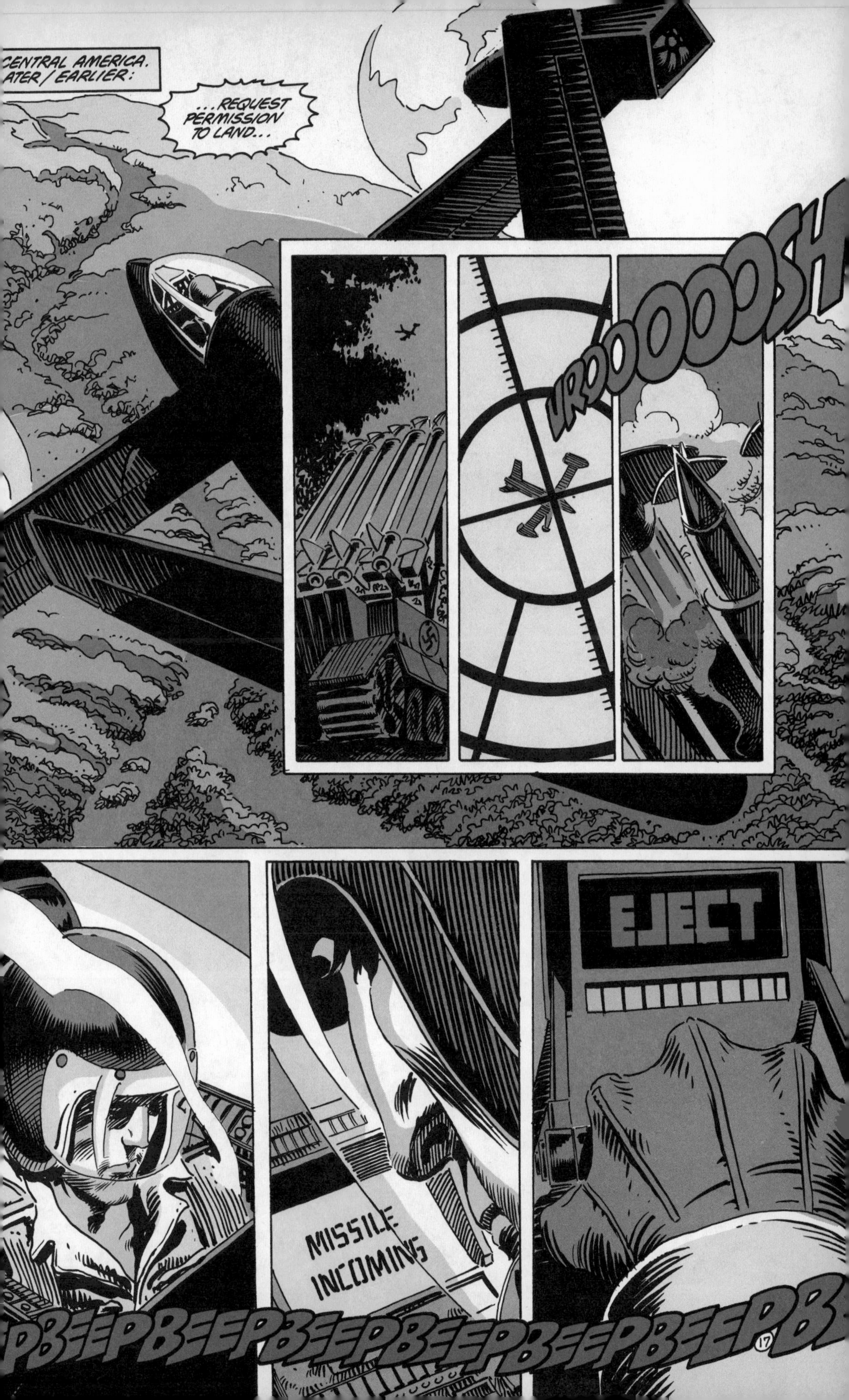
CENTRAL AMERICA.
LATER / EARLIER:
...REQUEST PERMISSION TO LAND...
VROOOOOOSH
EJECT
MISSILE INCOMING
BEEPBEEPBEEPBEEPBEEPBEEPB

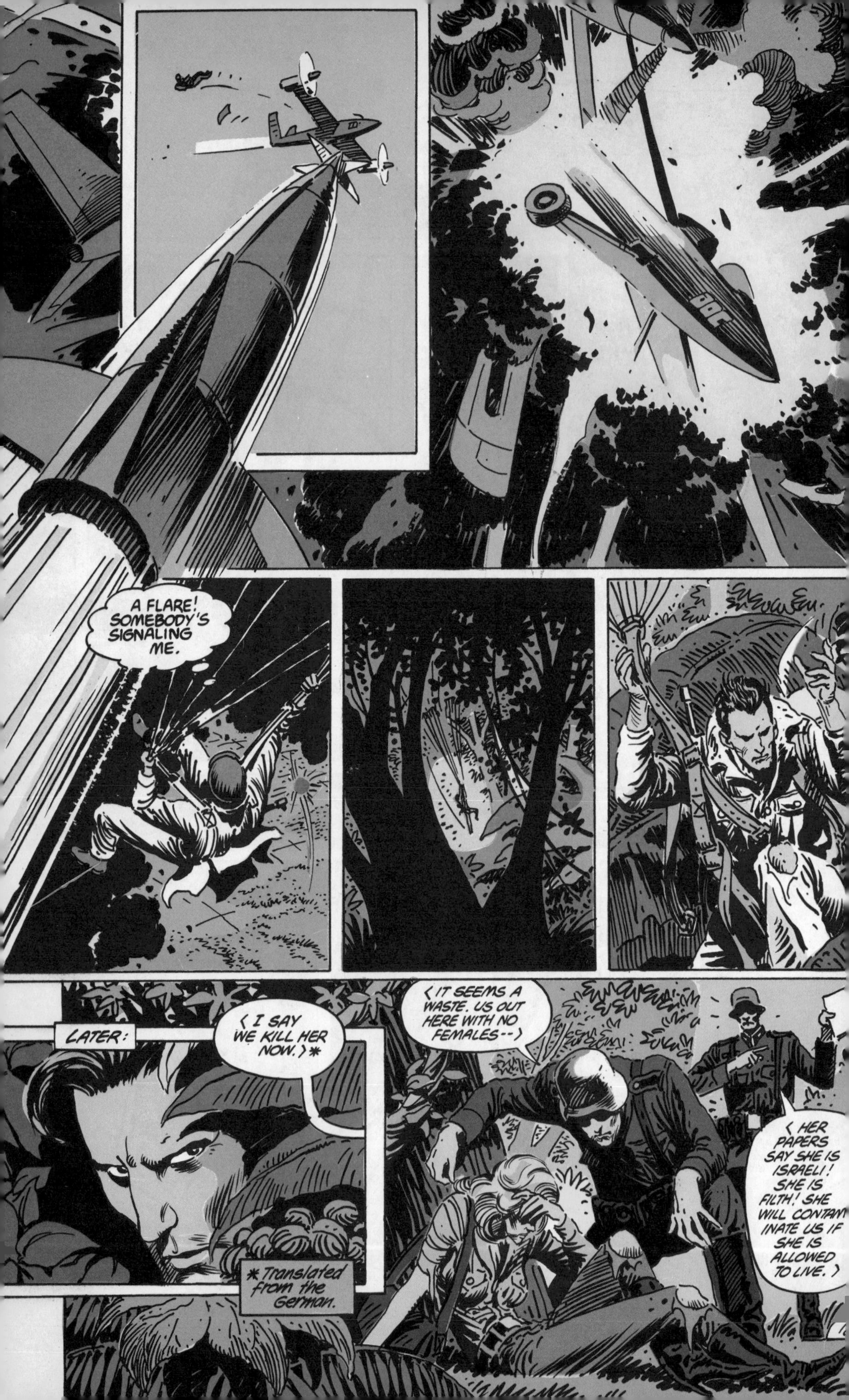
A FLARE! SOMEBODY'S SIGNALING ME.
LATER:
⟨ I SAY WE KILL HER NOW. ⟩*
⟨ IT SEEMS A WASTE. US OUT HERE WITH NO FEMALES-- ⟩
⟨ HER PAPERS SAY SHE IS ISRAELI! SHE IS FILTH! SHE WILL CONTAMINATE US IF SHE IS ALLOWED TO LIVE. ⟩
*Translated from the German.

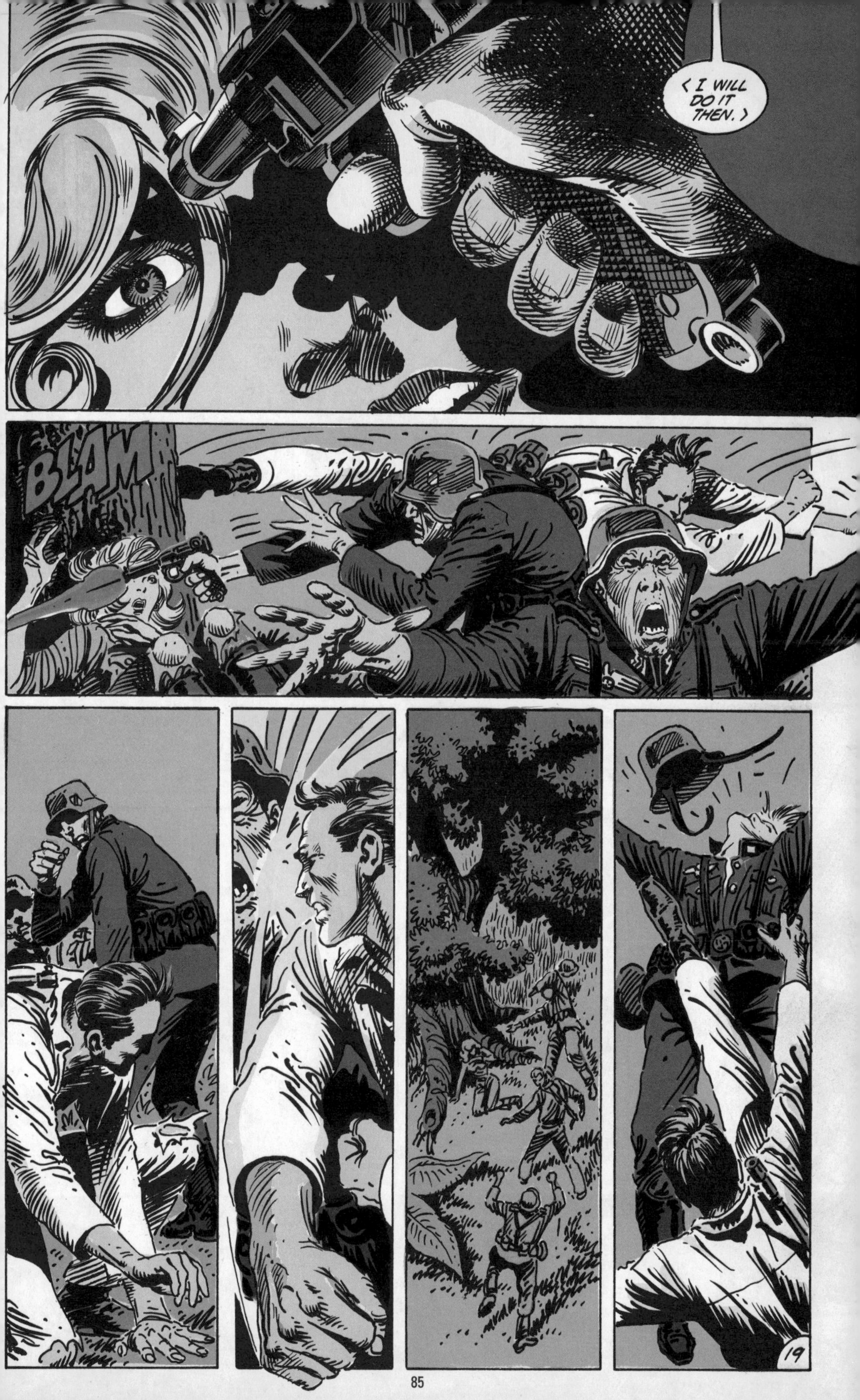

< I WILL DO IT THEN. >
BLAM
19

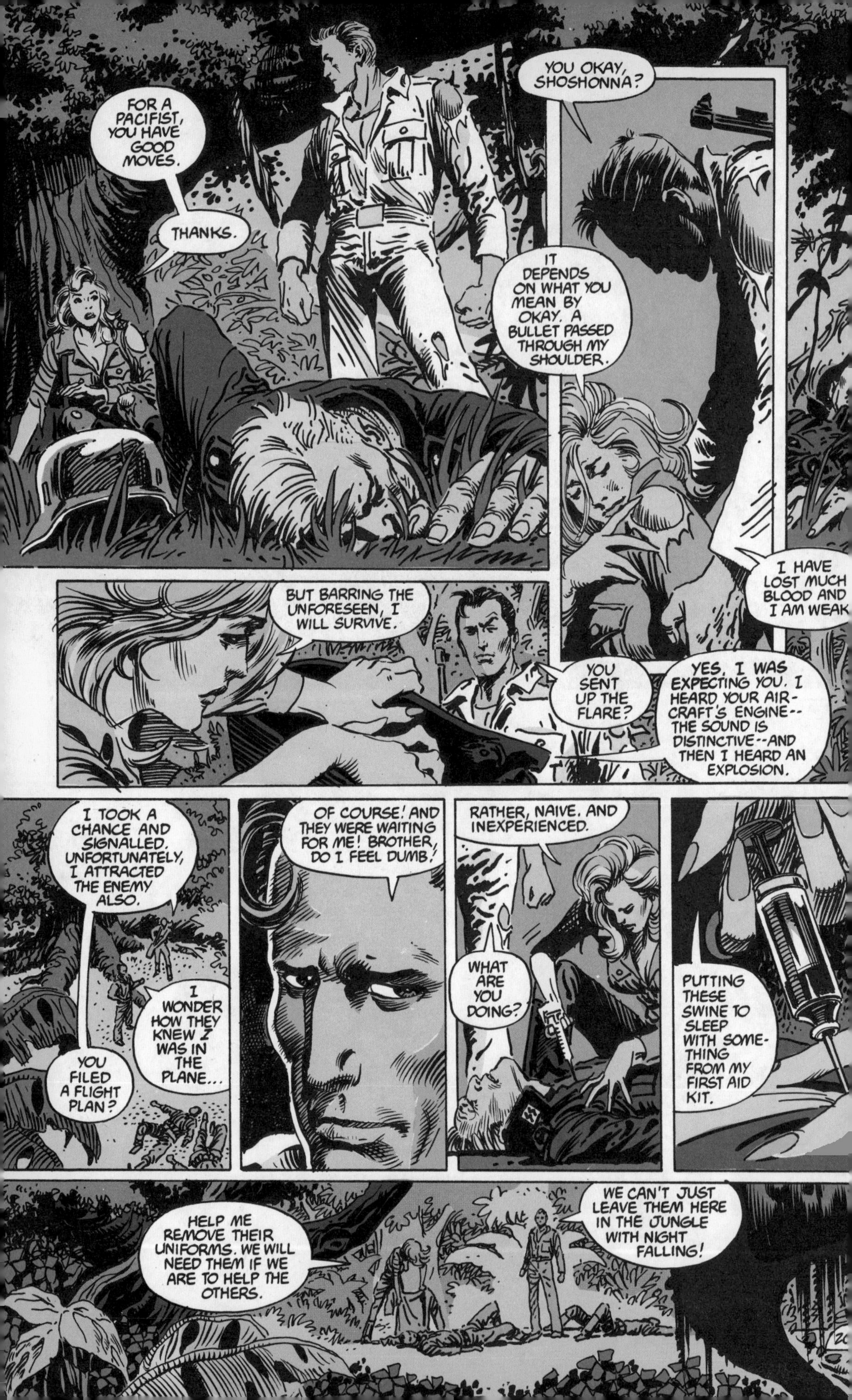
FOR A PACIFIST, YOU HAVE GOOD MOVES.
THANKS.
YOU OKAY, SHOSHONNA?
IT DEPENDS ON WHAT YOU MEAN BY OKAY. A BULLET PASSED THROUGH MY SHOULDER.
I HAVE LOST MUCH BLOOD AND I AM WEAK
BUT BARRING THE UNFORESEEN, I WILL SURVIVE.
YOU SENT UP THE FLARE?
YES. I WAS EXPECTING YOU. I HEARD YOUR AIRCRAFT'S ENGINE-- THE SOUND IS DISTINCTIVE--AND THEN I HEARD AN EXPLOSION.
I TOOK A CHANCE AND SIGNALLED. UNFORTUNATELY, I ATTRACTED THE ENEMY ALSO.
I WONDER HOW THEY KNEW I WAS IN THE PLANE...
YOU FILED A FLIGHT PLAN?
OF COURSE! AND THEY WERE WAITING FOR ME! BROTHER, DO I FEEL DUMB!
RATHER, NAIVE. AND INEXPERIENCED.
WHAT ARE YOU DOING?
PUTTING THESE SWINE TO SLEEP WITH SOMETHING FROM MY FIRST AID KIT.
HELP ME REMOVE THEIR UNIFORMS. WE WILL NEED THEM IF WE ARE TO HELP THE OTHERS.
WE CAN'T JUST LEAVE THEM HERE IN THE JUNGLE WITH NIGHT FALLING!
20

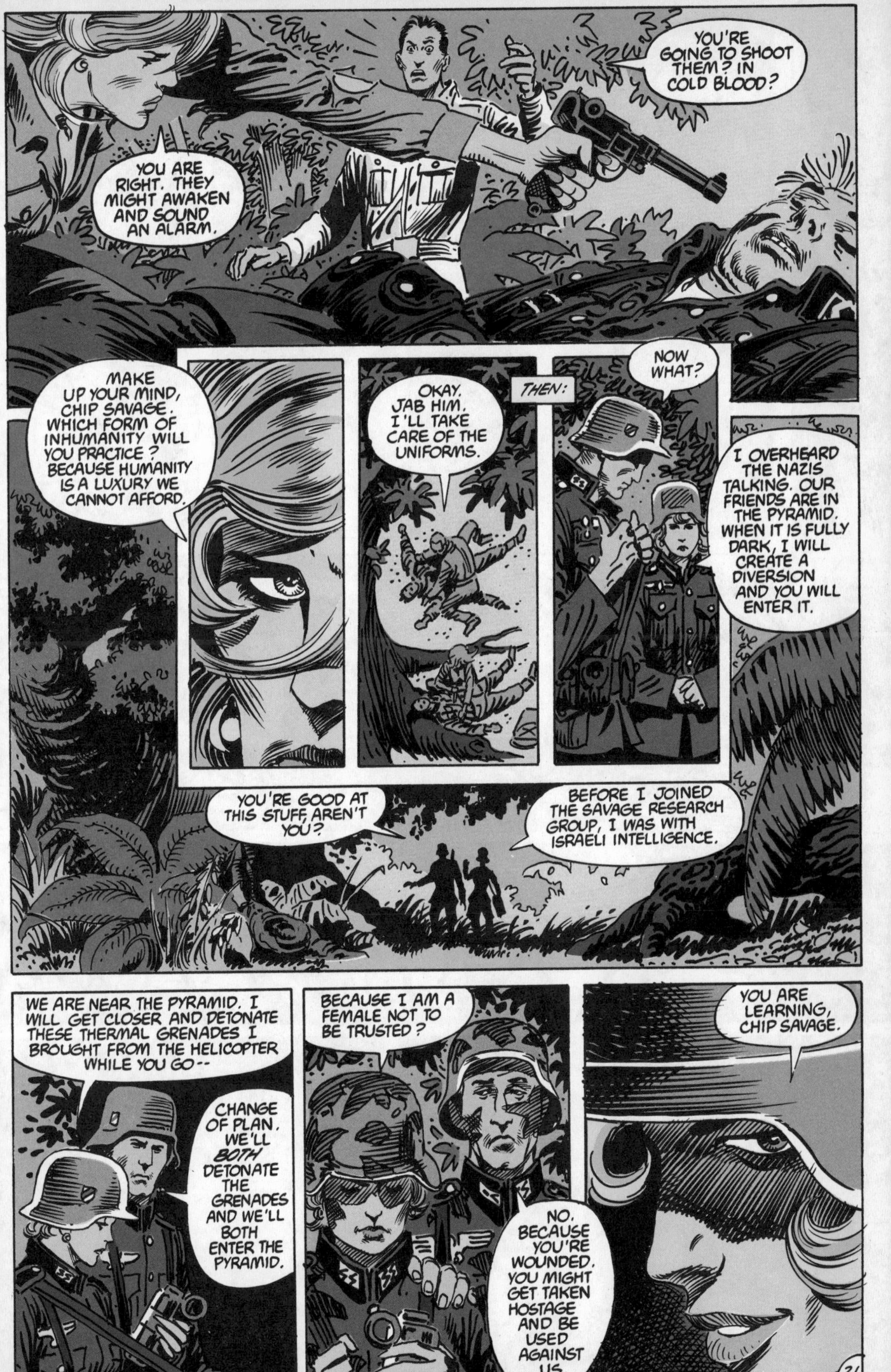
YOU'RE GOING TO SHOOT THEM? IN COLD BLOOD?
YOU ARE RIGHT. THEY MIGHT AWAKEN AND SOUND AN ALARM.
MAKE UP YOUR MIND, CHIP SAVAGE. WHICH FORM OF INHUMANITY WILL YOU PRACTICE? BECAUSE HUMANITY IS A LUXURY WE CANNOT AFFORD.
OKAY. JAB HIM. I'LL TAKE CARE OF THE UNIFORMS.
THEN:
NOW WHAT?
I OVERHEARD THE NAZIS TALKING. OUR FRIENDS ARE IN THE PYRAMID. WHEN IT IS FULLY DARK, I WILL CREATE A DIVERSION AND YOU WILL ENTER IT.
YOU'RE GOOD AT THIS STUFF, AREN'T YOU?
BEFORE I JOINED THE SAVAGE RESEARCH GROUP, I WAS WITH ISRAELI INTELLIGENCE.
WE ARE NEAR THE PYRAMID. I WILL GET CLOSER AND DETONATE THESE THERMAL GRENADES I BROUGHT FROM THE HELICOPTER WHILE YOU GO--
CHANGE OF PLAN. WE'LL BOTH DETONATE THE GRENADES AND WE'LL BOTH ENTER THE PYRAMID.
BECAUSE I AM A FEMALE NOT TO BE TRUSTED?
NO. BECAUSE YOU'RE WOUNDED. YOU MIGHT GET TAKEN HOSTAGE AND BE USED AGAINST US.
YOU ARE LEARNING, CHIP SAVAGE.
21

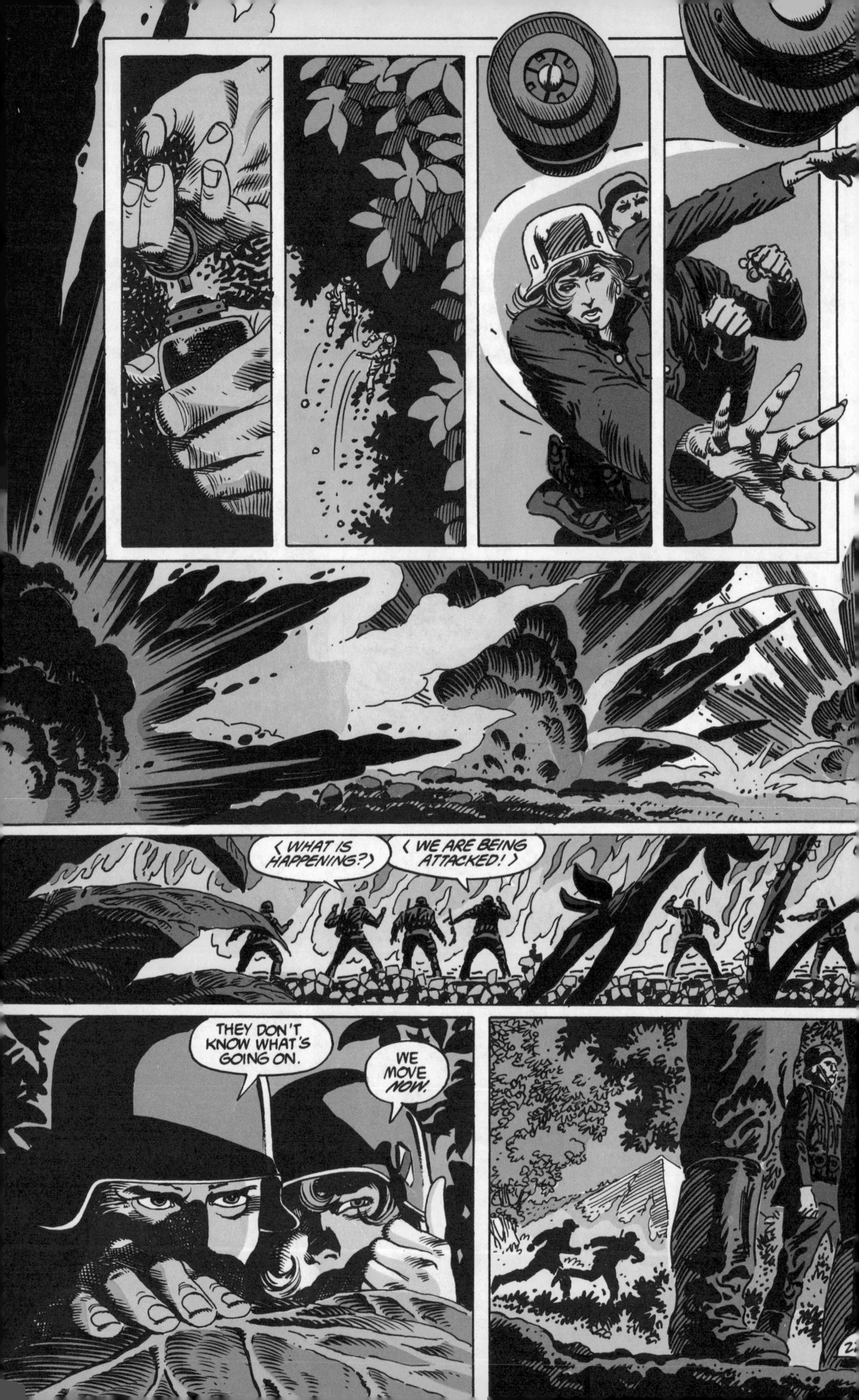
‹ WHAT IS HAPPENING? ›
‹ WE ARE BEING ATTACKED! ›
THEY DON'T KNOW WHAT'S GOING ON.
WE MOVE *NOW*.

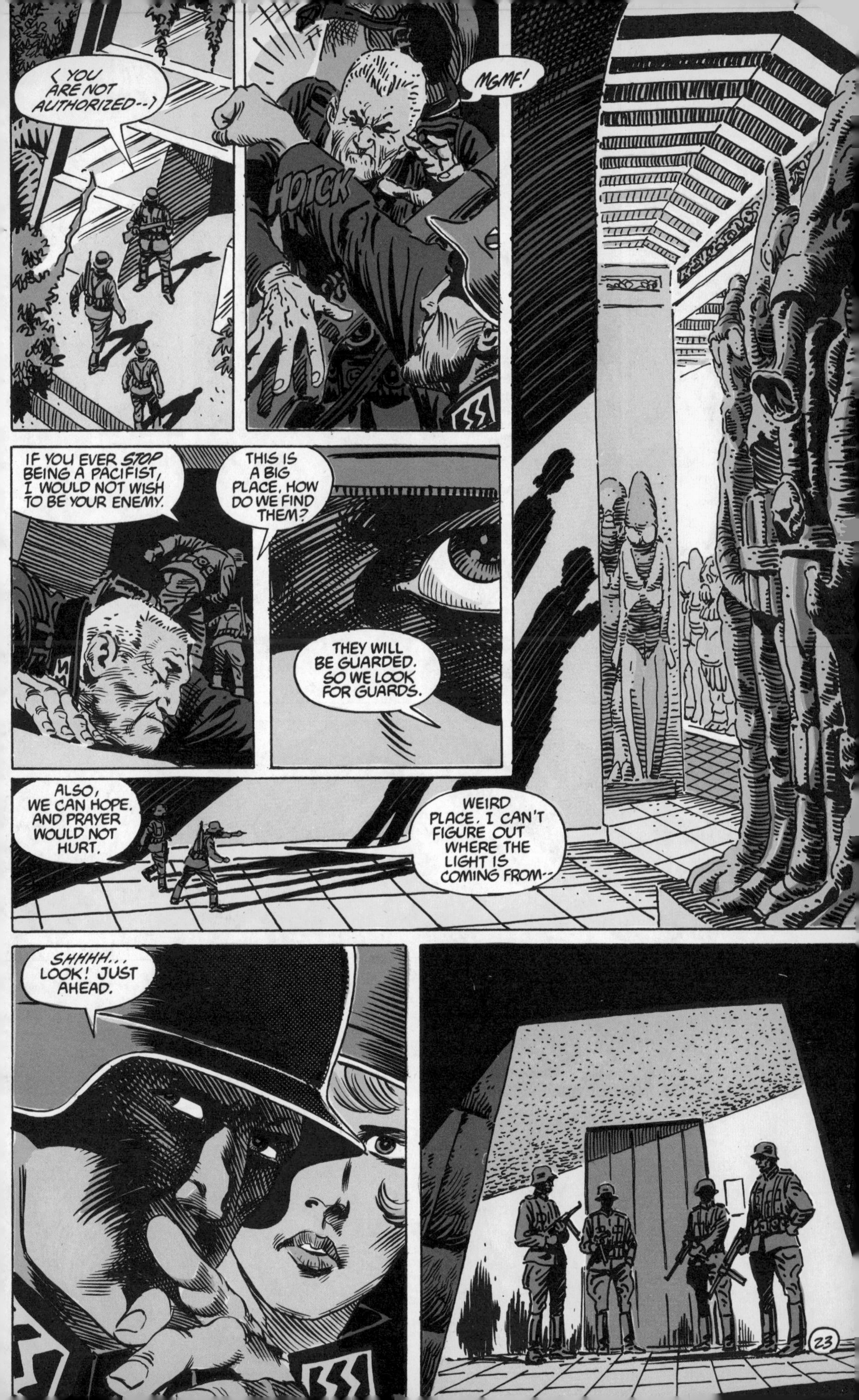

< YOU ARE NOT AUTHORIZED-->
MGMF!
HOTCK
IF YOU EVER STOP BEING A PACIFIST, I WOULD NOT WISH TO BE YOUR ENEMY.
THIS IS A BIG PLACE. HOW DO WE FIND THEM?
THEY WILL BE GUARDED. SO WE LOOK FOR GUARDS.
ALSO, WE CAN HOPE. AND PRAYER WOULD NOT HURT.
WEIRD PLACE. I CAN'T FIGURE OUT WHERE THE LIGHT IS COMING FROM--
SHHHH... LOOK! JUST AHEAD.
23

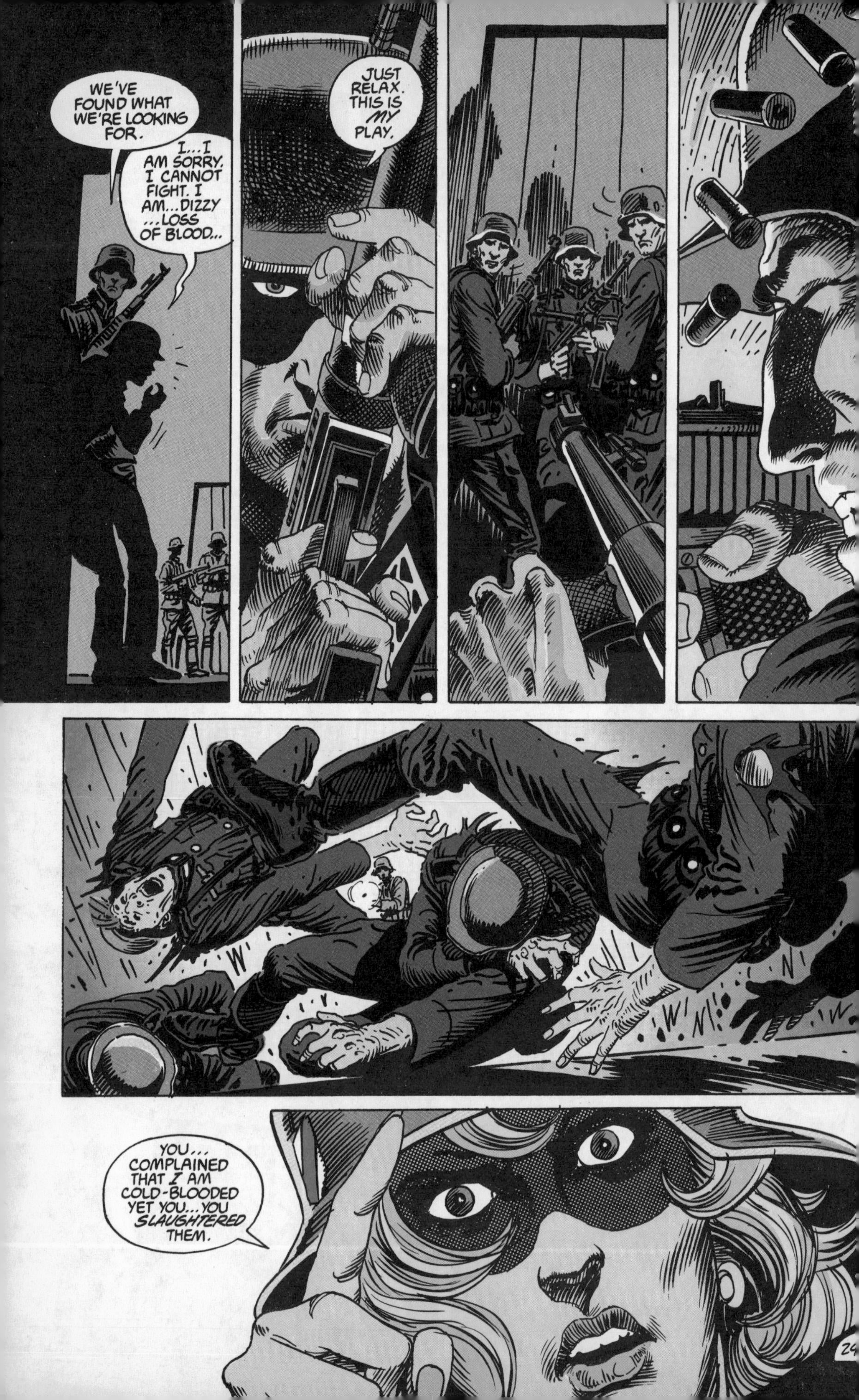
WE'VE FOUND WHAT WE'RE LOOKING FOR.
I...I AM SORRY. I CANNOT FIGHT. I AM...DIZZY ...LOSS OF BLOOD...
JUST RELAX. THIS IS MY PLAY.
YOU... COMPLAINED THAT I AM COLD-BLOODED YET YOU...YOU SLAUGHTERED THEM.

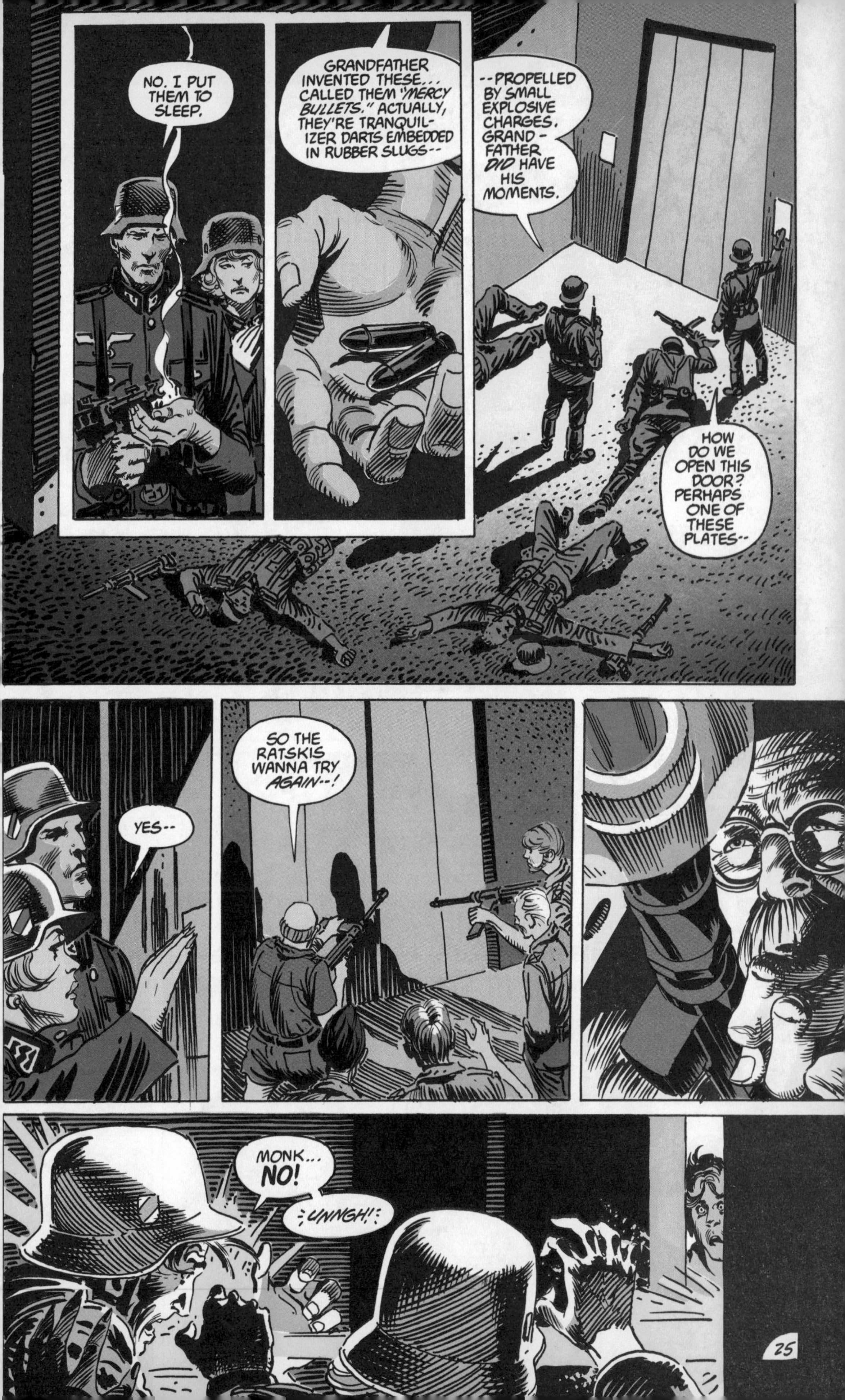
NO. I PUT THEM TO SLEEP.
GRANDFATHER INVENTED THESE... CALLED THEM "MERCY BULLETS." ACTUALLY, THEY'RE TRANQUILIZER DARTS EMBEDDED IN RUBBER SLUGS--
--PROPELLED BY SMALL EXPLOSIVE CHARGES. GRANDFATHER DID HAVE HIS MOMENTS.
HOW DO WE OPEN THIS DOOR? PERHAPS ONE OF THESE PLATES--
YES--
SO THE RATSKIS WANNA TRY AGAIN--!
MONK... NO!
UNNGH!

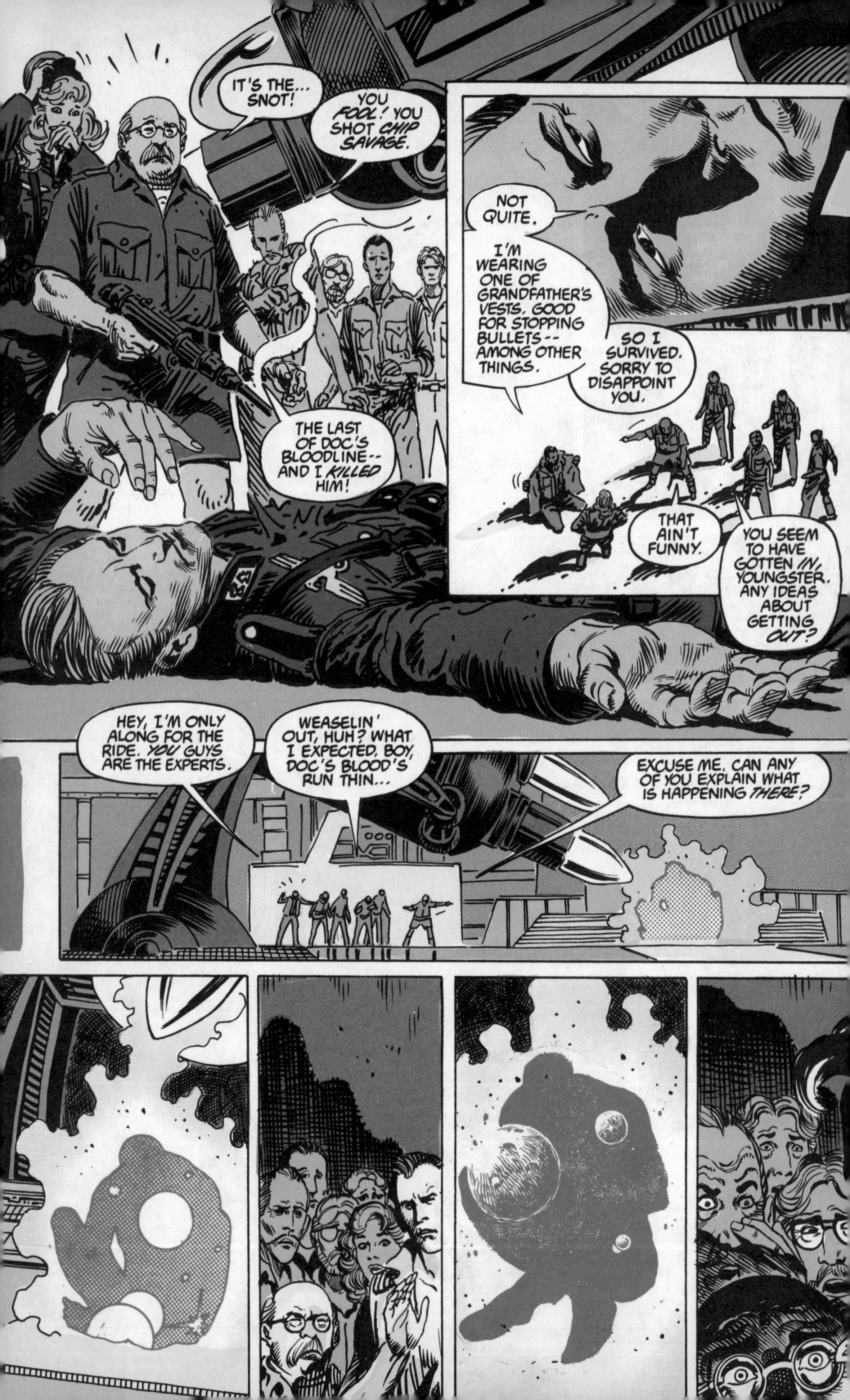
IT'S THE... SNOT!
YOU FOOL! YOU SHOT CHIP SAVAGE.
THE LAST OF DOC'S BLOODLINE-- AND I KILLED HIM!
NOT QUITE.
I'M WEARING ONE OF GRANDFATHER'S VESTS. GOOD FOR STOPPING BULLETS-- AMONG OTHER THINGS.
SO I SURVIVED. SORRY TO DISAPPOINT YOU.
THAT AIN'T FUNNY.
YOU SEEM TO HAVE GOTTEN IN, YOUNGSTER. ANY IDEAS ABOUT GETTING OUT?
HEY, I'M ONLY ALONG FOR THE RIDE. YOU GUYS ARE THE EXPERTS.
WEASELIN' OUT, HUH? WHAT I EXPECTED. BOY, DOC'S BLOOD'S RUN THIN...
EXCUSE ME. CAN ANY OF YOU EXPLAIN WHAT IS HAPPENING THERE?

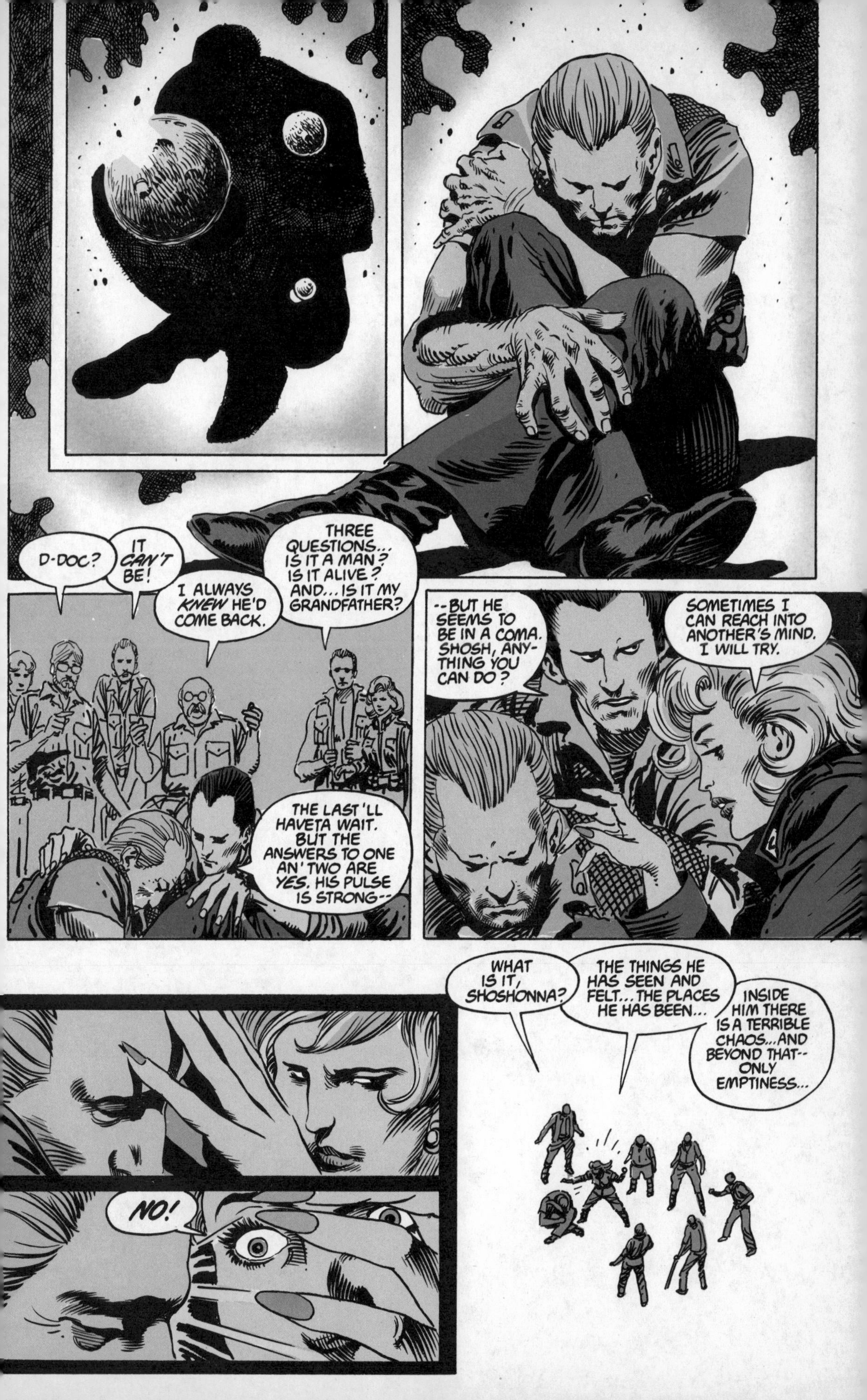
D-DOC?
IT CAN'T BE!
I ALWAYS KNEW HE'D COME BACK.
THREE QUESTIONS... IS IT A MAN? IS IT ALIVE? AND... IS IT MY GRANDFATHER?
THE LAST'LL HAVETA WAIT. BUT THE ANSWERS TO ONE AN' TWO ARE YES. HIS PULSE IS STRONG--
--BUT HE SEEMS TO BE IN A COMA. SHOSH, ANYTHING YOU CAN DO?
SOMETIMES I CAN REACH INTO ANOTHER'S MIND. I WILL TRY.
NO!
WHAT IS IT, SHOSHONNA?
THE THINGS HE HAS SEEN AND FELT... THE PLACES HE HAS BEEN...
INSIDE HIM THERE IS A TERRIBLE CHAOS...AND BEYOND THAT--ONLY EMPTINESS...

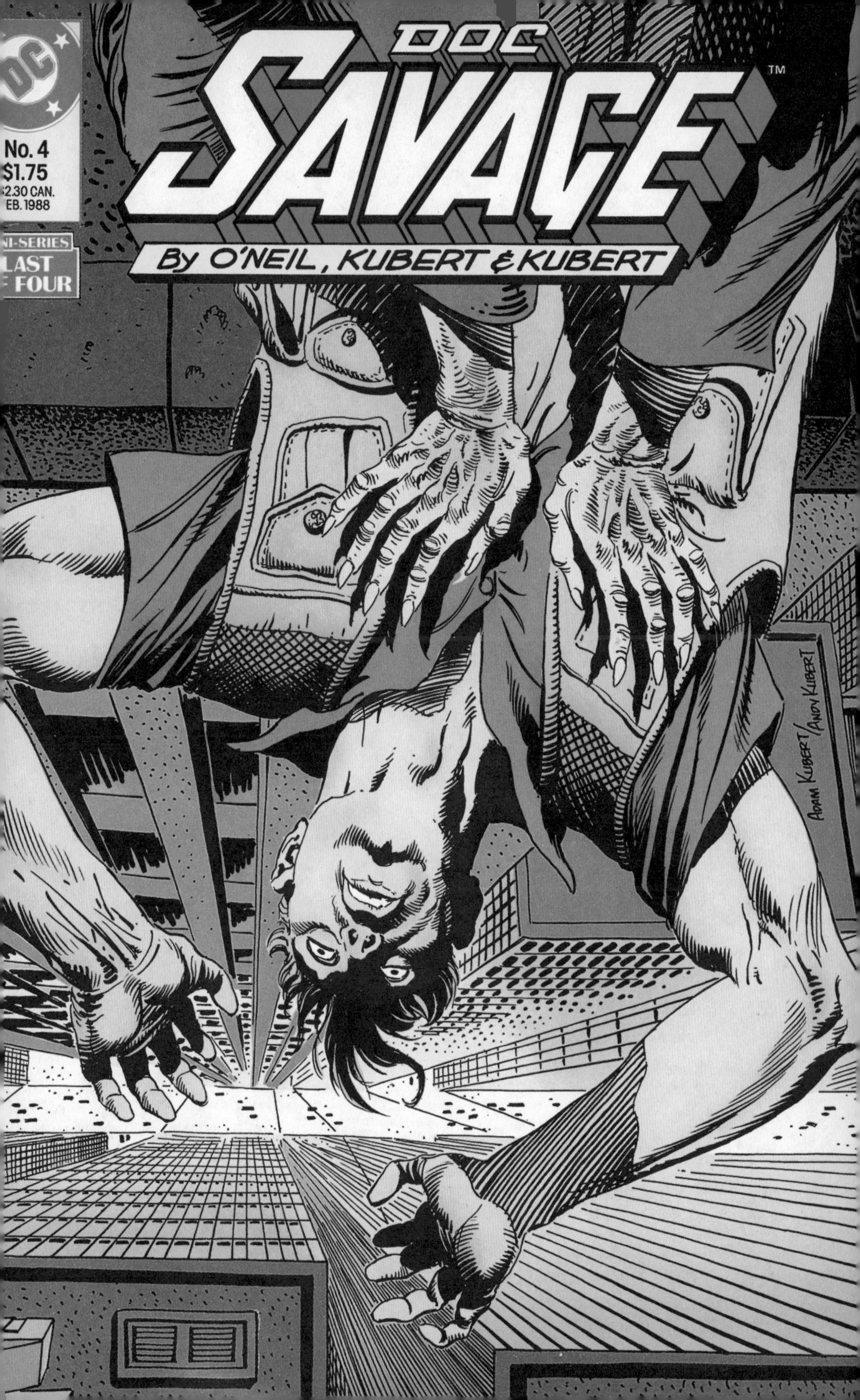

DC
No. 4
$1.75
$2.30 CAN.
FEB. 1988
DOC
SAVAGE
TM
MINI-SERIES
LAST OF FOUR
By O'NEIL, KUBERT & KUBERT
ADAM KUBERT/ANDY KUBERT

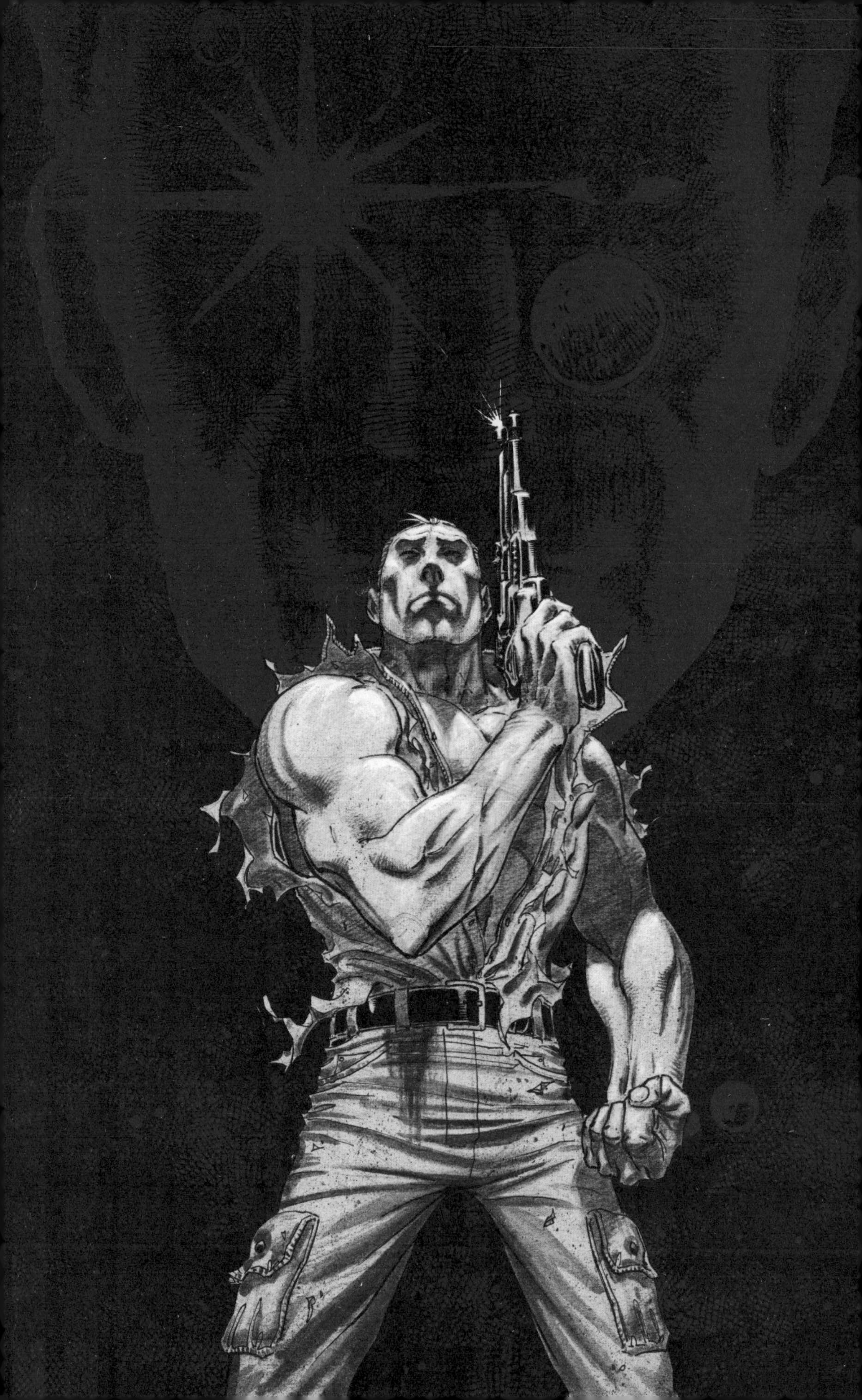

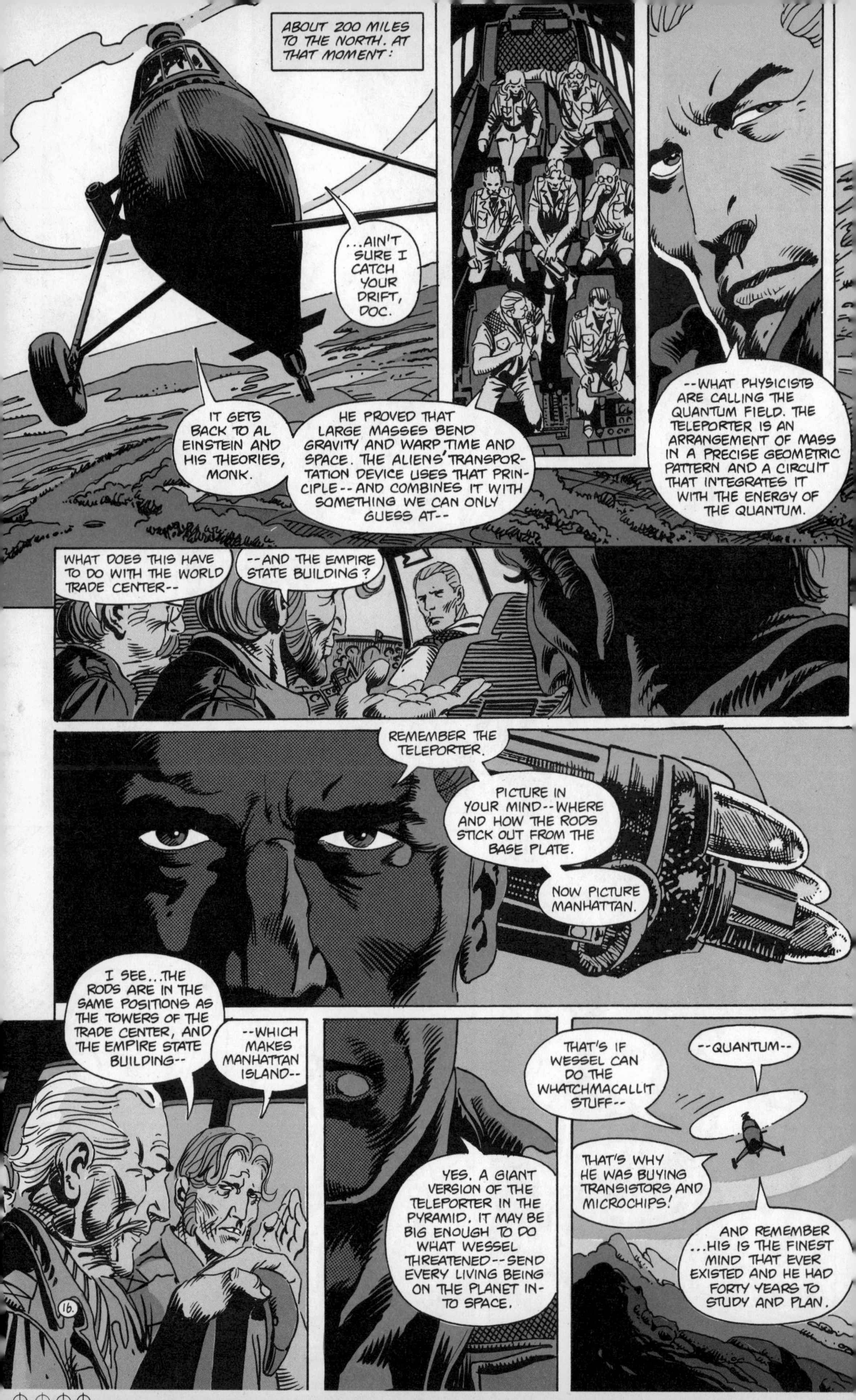
ABOUT 200 MILES TO THE NORTH. AT THAT MOMENT:
...AIN'T SURE I CATCH YOUR DRIFT, DOC.
IT GETS BACK TO AL EINSTEIN AND HIS THEORIES, MONK.
HE PROVED THAT LARGE MASSES BEND GRAVITY AND WARP TIME AND SPACE. THE ALIENS' TRANSPORTATION DEVICE USES THAT PRINCIPLE--AND COMBINES IT WITH SOMETHING WE CAN ONLY GUESS AT--
--WHAT PHYSICISTS ARE CALLING THE QUANTUM FIELD. THE TELEPORTER IS AN ARRANGEMENT OF MASS IN A PRECISE GEOMETRIC PATTERN AND A CIRCUIT THAT INTEGRATES IT WITH THE ENERGY OF THE QUANTUM.
WHAT DOES THIS HAVE TO DO WITH THE WORLD TRADE CENTER--
--AND THE EMPIRE STATE BUILDING?
REMEMBER THE TELEPORTER.
PICTURE IN YOUR MIND--WHERE AND HOW THE RODS STICK OUT FROM THE BASE PLATE.
NOW PICTURE MANHATTAN.
I SEE...THE RODS ARE IN THE SAME POSITIONS AS THE TOWERS OF THE TRADE CENTER, AND THE EMPIRE STATE BUILDING--
--WHICH MAKES MANHATTAN ISLAND--
YES. A GIANT VERSION OF THE TELEPORTER IN THE PYRAMID. IT MAY BE BIG ENOUGH TO DO WHAT WESSEL THREATENED--SEND EVERY LIVING BEING ON THE PLANET INTO SPACE.
THAT'S IF WESSEL CAN DO THE WHATCHMACALLIT STUFF--
--QUANTUM--
THAT'S WHY HE WAS BUYING TRANSISTORS AND MICROCHIPS!
AND REMEMBER ...HIS IS THE FINEST MIND THAT EVER EXISTED AND HE HAD FORTY YEARS TO STUDY AND PLAN.
16.

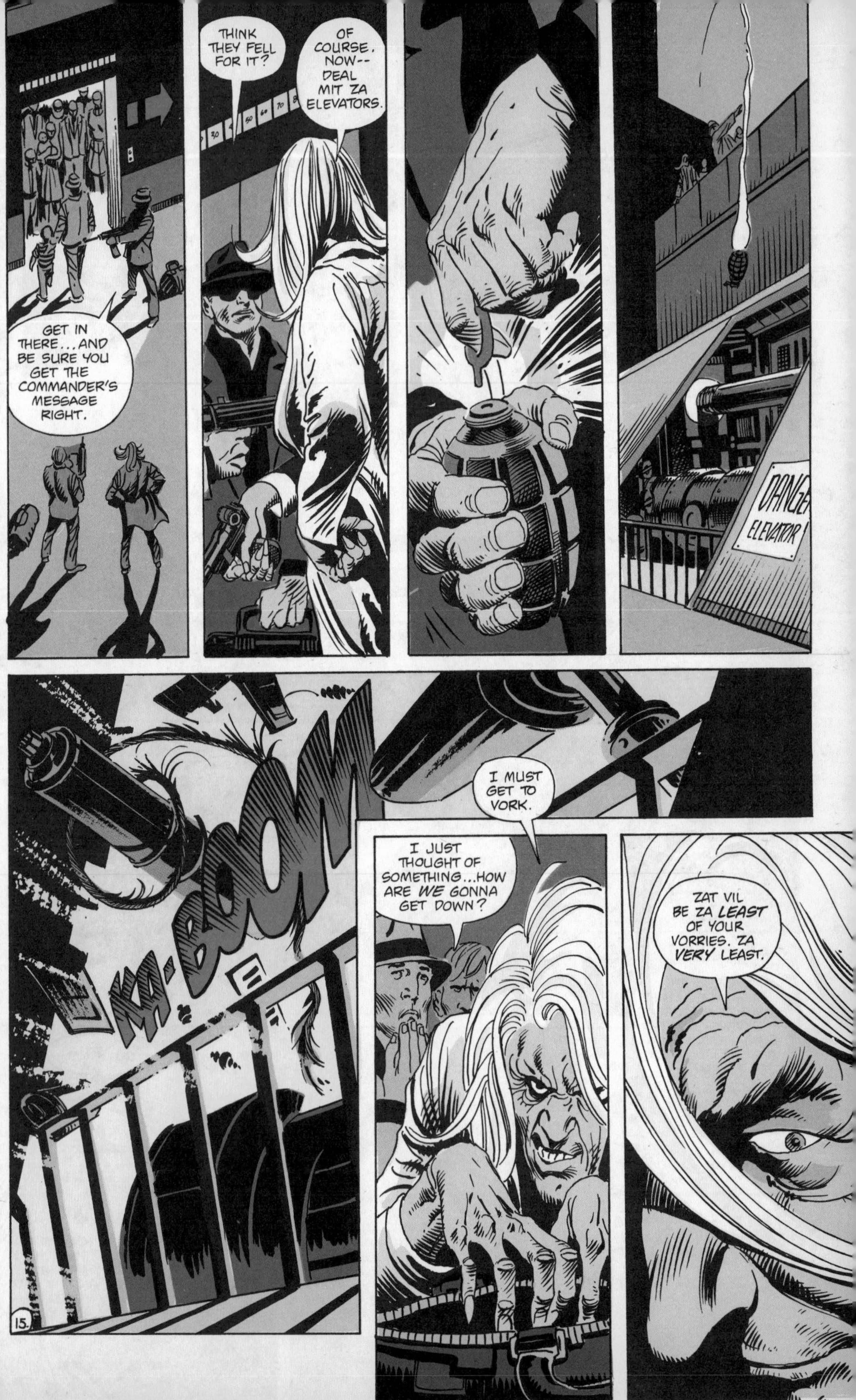
GET IN THERE... AND BE SURE YOU GET THE COMMANDER'S MESSAGE RIGHT.
THINK THEY FELL FOR IT?
OF COURSE. NOW-- DEAL MIT ZA ELEVATORS.
DANGE
ELEVATOR
KA-BOOM
I MUST GET TO VORK.
I JUST THOUGHT OF SOMETHING...HOW ARE WE GONNA GET DOWN?
ZAT VIL BE ZA LEAST OF YOUR VORRIES. ZA VERY LEAST.
15.

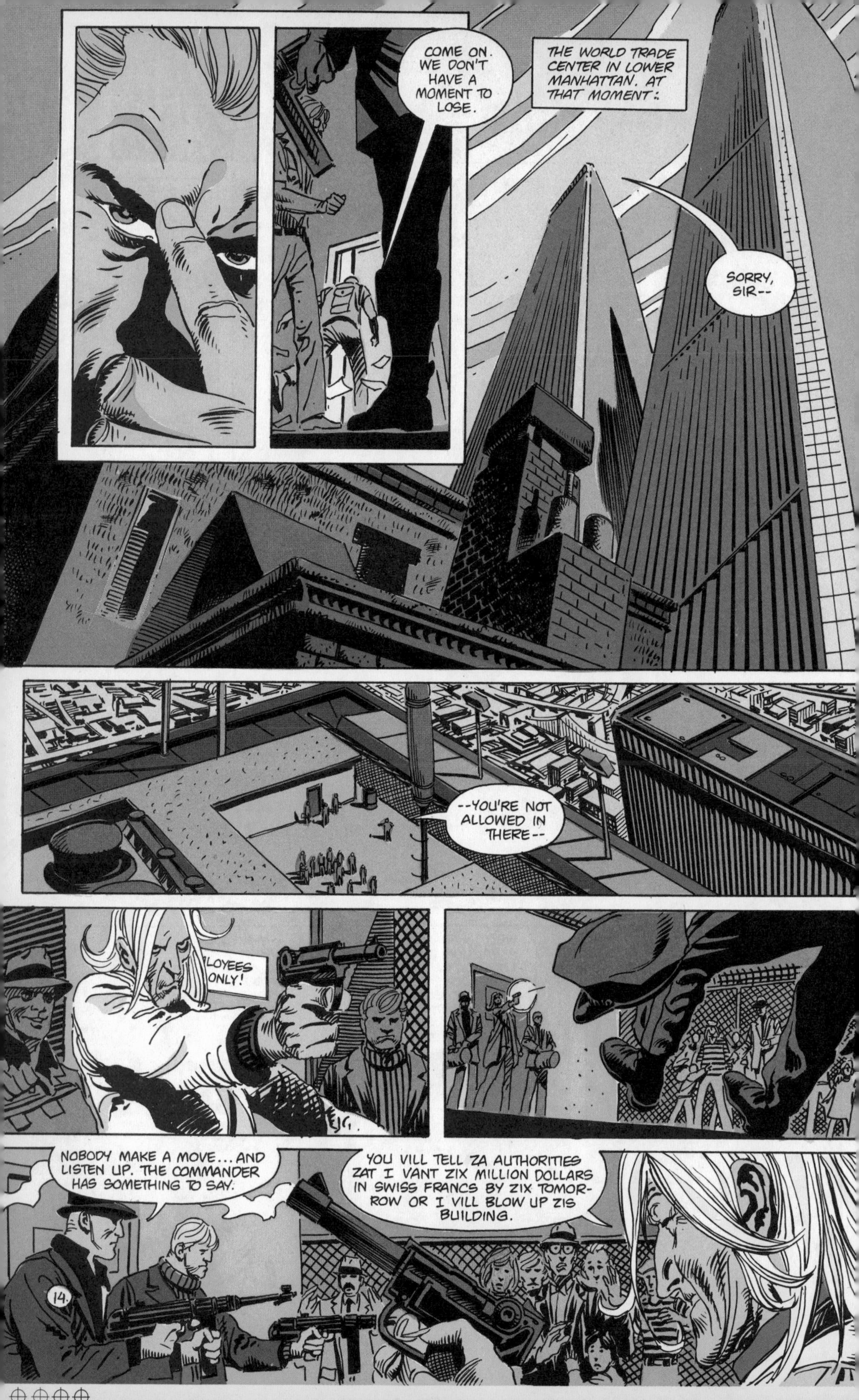
COME ON. WE DON'T HAVE A MOMENT TO LOSE.
THE WORLD TRADE CENTER IN LOWER MANHATTAN. AT THAT MOMENT:
SORRY, SIR--
--YOU'RE NOT ALLOWED IN THERE--
LOYEES ONLY!
NOBODY MAKE A MOVE... AND LISTEN UP. THE COMMANDER HAS SOMETHING TO SAY.
YOU VILL TELL ZA AUTHORITIES ZAT I VANT ZIX MILLION DOLLARS IN SWISS FRANCS BY ZIX TOMORROW OR I VILL BLOW UP ZIS BUILDING.
14.

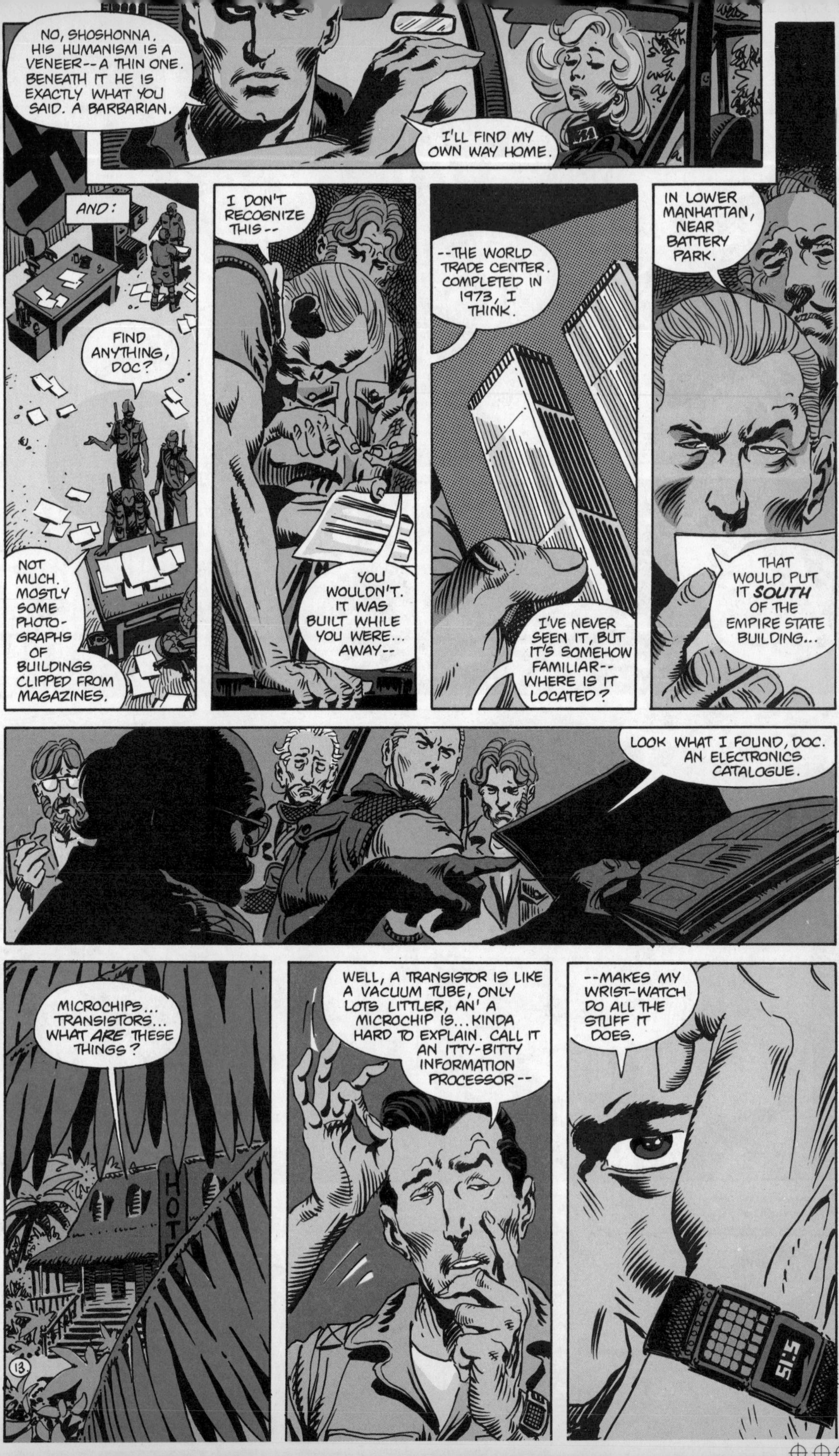
NO, SHOSHONNA. HIS HUMANISM IS A VENEER--A THIN ONE. BENEATH IT HE IS EXACTLY WHAT YOU SAID. A BARBARIAN.
I'LL FIND MY OWN WAY HOME.
AND:
FIND ANYTHING, DOC?
NOT MUCH. MOSTLY SOME PHOTOGRAPHS OF BUILDINGS CLIPPED FROM MAGAZINES.
I DON'T RECOGNIZE THIS--
YOU WOULDN'T. IT WAS BUILT WHILE YOU WERE... AWAY--
--THE WORLD TRADE CENTER. COMPLETED IN 1973, I THINK.
I'VE NEVER SEEN IT, BUT IT'S SOMEHOW FAMILIAR--WHERE IS IT LOCATED?
IN LOWER MANHATTAN, NEAR BATTERY PARK.
THAT WOULD PUT IT **SOUTH** OF THE EMPIRE STATE BUILDING...
LOOK WHAT I FOUND, DOC. AN ELECTRONICS CATALOGUE.
MICROCHIPS... TRANSISTORS... WHAT *ARE* THESE THINGS?
HOT
WELL, A TRANSISTOR IS LIKE A VACUUM TUBE, ONLY LOTS LITTLER, AN' A MICROCHIP IS...KINDA HARD TO EXPLAIN. CALL IT AN ITTY-BITTY INFORMATION PROCESSOR--
--MAKES MY WRIST-WATCH DO ALL THE STUFF IT DOES.
5:15
13

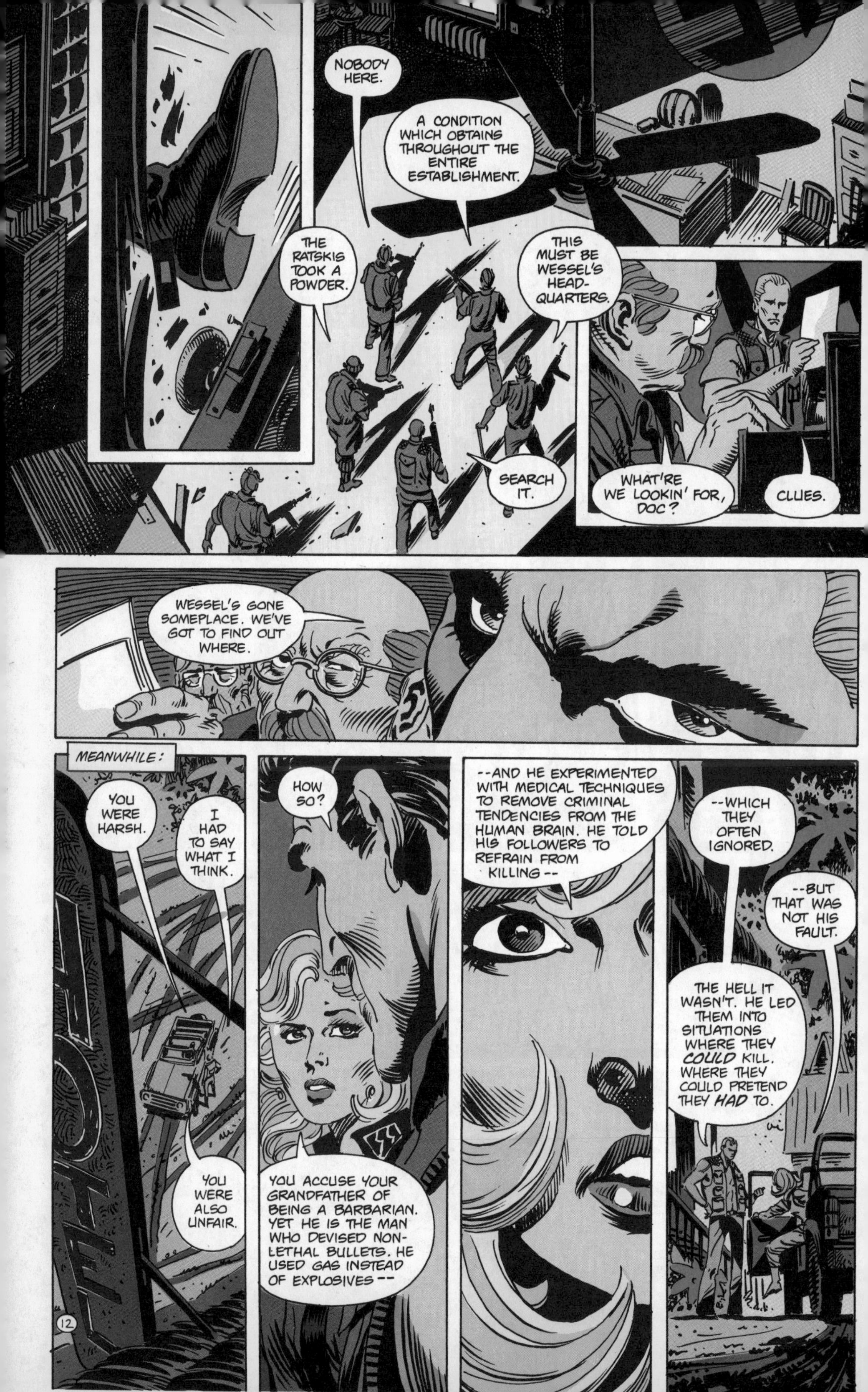
NOBODY HERE.
A CONDITION WHICH OBTAINS THROUGHOUT THE ENTIRE ESTABLISHMENT.
THE RATSKIS TOOK A POWDER.
THIS MUST BE WESSEL'S HEAD-QUARTERS.
SEARCH IT.
WHAT'RE WE LOOKIN' FOR, DOC?
CLUES.
WESSEL'S GONE SOMEPLACE. WE'VE GOT TO FIND OUT WHERE.
MEANWHILE:
YOU WERE HARSH.
I HAD TO SAY WHAT I THINK.
YOU WERE ALSO UNFAIR.
HOW SO?
YOU ACCUSE YOUR GRANDFATHER OF BEING A BARBARIAN. YET HE IS THE MAN WHO DEVISED NON-LETHAL BULLETS. HE USED GAS INSTEAD OF EXPLOSIVES--
--AND HE EXPERIMENTED WITH MEDICAL TECHNIQUES TO REMOVE CRIMINAL TENDENCIES FROM THE HUMAN BRAIN. HE TOLD HIS FOLLOWERS TO REFRAIN FROM KILLING--
--WHICH THEY OFTEN IGNORED.
--BUT THAT WAS NOT HIS FAULT.
THE HELL IT WASN'T. HE LED THEM INTO SITUATIONS WHERE THEY COULD KILL. WHERE THEY COULD PRETEND THEY HAD TO.
12

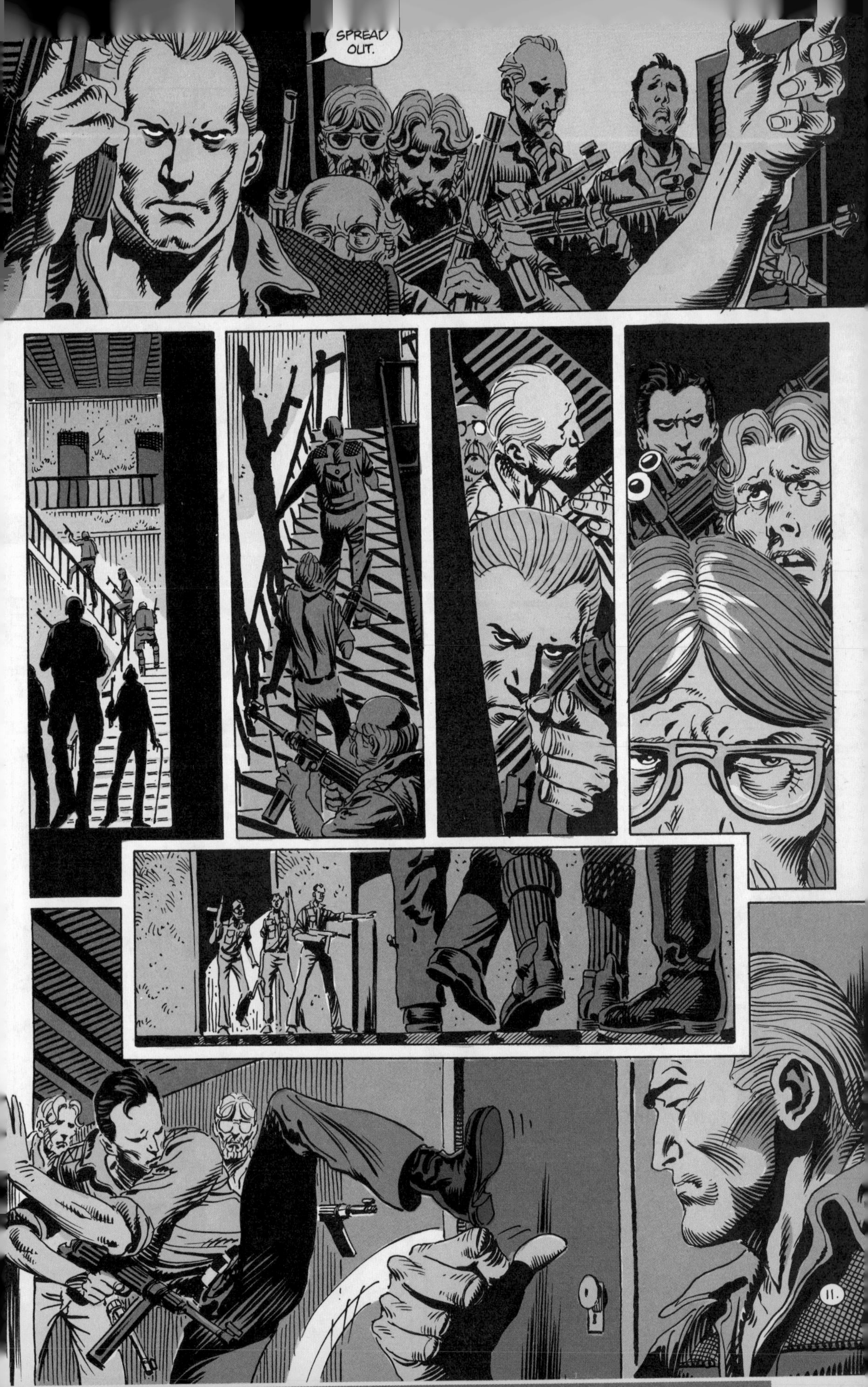
SPREAD OUT.
11.

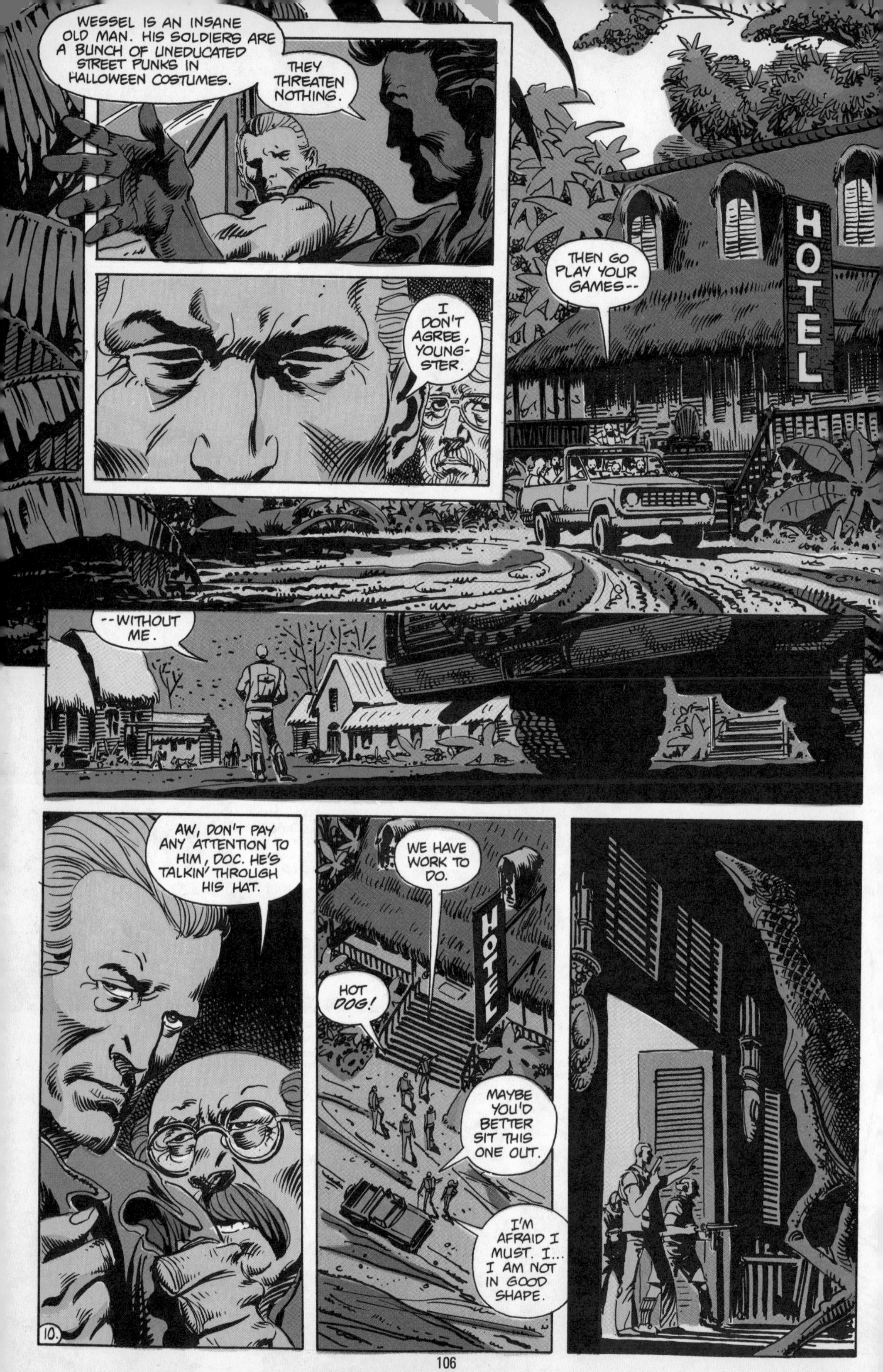
WESSEL IS AN INSANE OLD MAN. HIS SOLDIERS ARE A BUNCH OF UNEDUCATED STREET PUNKS IN HALLOWEEN COSTUMES.
THEY THREATEN NOTHING.
I DON'T AGREE, YOUNGSTER.
HOTEL
THEN GO PLAY YOUR GAMES--
--WITHOUT ME.
AW, DON'T PAY ANY ATTENTION TO HIM, DOC. HE'S TALKIN' THROUGH HIS HAT.
10.
WE HAVE WORK TO DO.
HOTEL
HOT DOG!
MAYBE YOU'D BETTER SIT THIS ONE OUT.
I'M AFRAID I MUST. I... I AM NOT IN GOOD SHAPE.

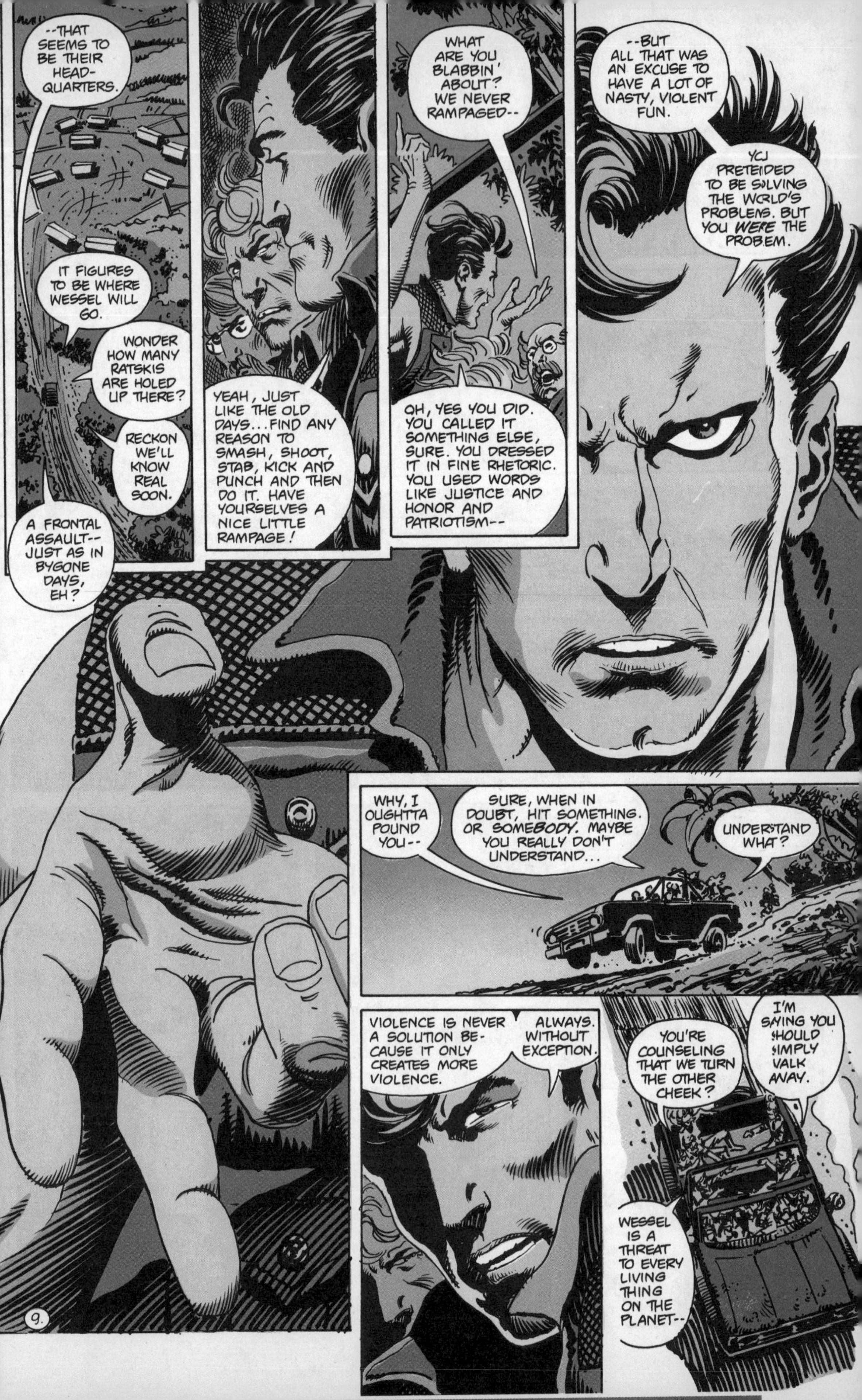
--THAT SEEMS TO BE THEIR HEAD-QUARTERS.
IT FIGURES TO BE WHERE WESSEL WILL GO.
WONDER HOW MANY RATSKIS ARE HOLED UP THERE?
RECKON WE'LL KNOW REAL SOON.
A FRONTAL ASSAULT--JUST AS IN BYGONE DAYS, EH?
YEAH, JUST LIKE THE OLD DAYS... FIND ANY REASON TO SMASH, SHOOT, STAB, KICK AND PUNCH AND THEN DO IT. HAVE YOURSELVES A NICE LITTLE RAMPAGE!
WHAT ARE YOU BLABBIN' ABOUT? WE NEVER RAMPAGED--
OH, YES YOU DID. YOU CALLED IT SOMETHING ELSE, SURE. YOU DRESSED IT IN FINE RHETORIC. YOU USED WORDS LIKE JUSTICE AND HONOR AND PATRIOTISM--
--BUT ALL THAT WAS AN EXCUSE TO HAVE A LOT OF NASTY, VIOLENT FUN.
YOU PRETENDED TO BE SOLVING THE WORLD'S PROBLEMS. BUT YOU WERE THE PROBLEM.
WHY, I OUGHTTA POUND YOU--
SURE, WHEN IN DOUBT, HIT SOMETHING. OR SOMEBODY. MAYBE YOU REALLY DON'T UNDERSTAND...
UNDERSTAND WHAT?
VIOLENCE IS NEVER A SOLUTION BE-CAUSE IT ONLY CREATES MORE VIOLENCE.
ALWAYS. WITHOUT EXCEPTION.
YOU'RE COUNSELING THAT WE TURN THE OTHER CHEEK?
I'M SAYING YOU SHOULD SIMPLY WALK AWAY.
WESSEL IS A THREAT TO EVERY LIVING THING ON THE PLANET--
9.

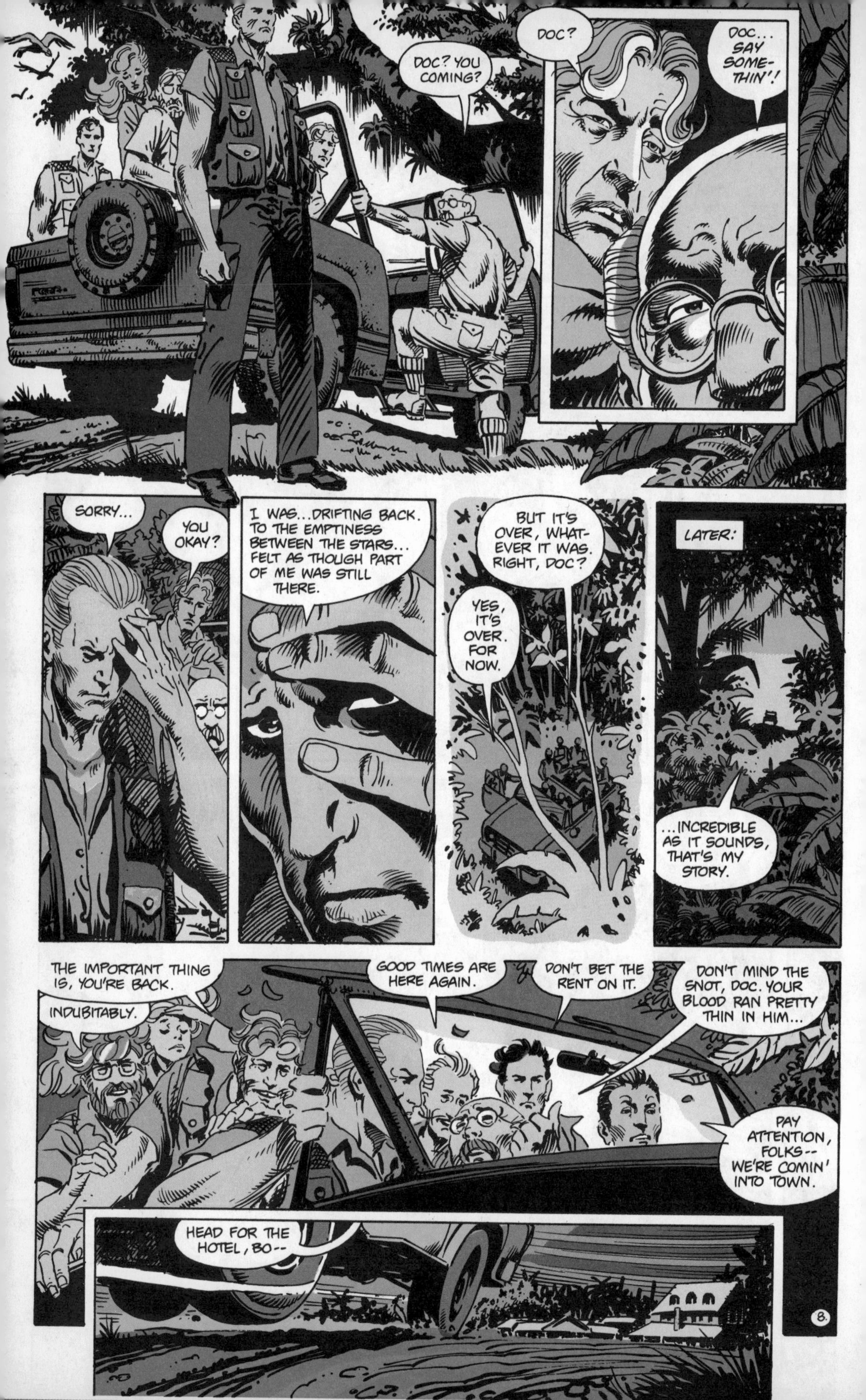
DOC? YOU COMING?
DOC?
DOC... SAY SOME-THIN'!
SORRY...
YOU OKAY?
I WAS...DRIFTING BACK. TO THE EMPTINESS BETWEEN THE STARS... FELT AS THOUGH PART OF ME WAS STILL THERE.
BUT IT'S OVER, WHAT-EVER IT WAS. RIGHT, DOC?
YES, IT'S OVER. FOR NOW.
LATER:
...INCREDIBLE AS IT SOUNDS, THAT'S MY STORY.
THE IMPORTANT THING IS, YOU'RE BACK.
INDUBITABLY.
GOOD TIMES ARE HERE AGAIN.
DON'T BET THE RENT ON IT.
DON'T MIND THE SNOT, DOC. YOUR BLOOD RAN PRETTY THIN IN HIM...
PAY ATTENTION, FOLKS-- WE'RE COMIN' INTO TOWN.
HEAD FOR THE HOTEL, BO--
8.

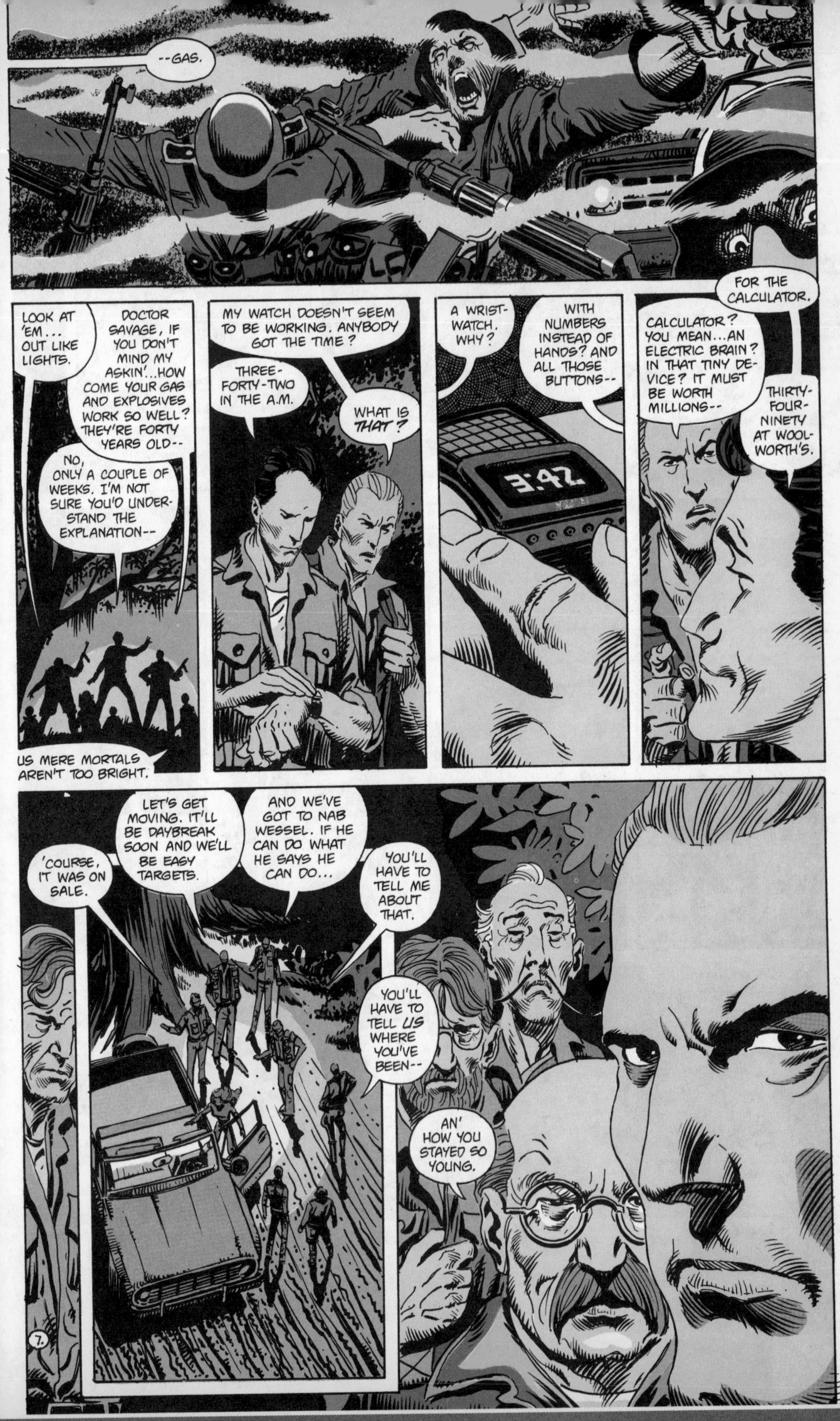
--GAS.
LOOK AT 'EM... OUT LIKE LIGHTS.
DOCTOR SAVAGE, IF YOU DON'T MIND MY ASKIN'...HOW COME YOUR GAS AND EXPLOSIVES WORK SO WELL? THEY'RE FORTY YEARS OLD--
NO, ONLY A COUPLE OF WEEKS. I'M NOT SURE YOU'D UNDERSTAND THE EXPLANATION--
US MERE MORTALS AREN'T TOO BRIGHT.
MY WATCH DOESN'T SEEM TO BE WORKING. ANYBODY GOT THE TIME?
THREE-FORTY-TWO IN THE A.M.
WHAT IS THAT?
A WRIST-WATCH. WHY?
WITH NUMBERS INSTEAD OF HANDS? AND ALL THOSE BUTTONS--
3:42
FOR THE CALCULATOR.
CALCULATOR? YOU MEAN...AN ELECTRIC BRAIN? IN THAT TINY DEVICE? IT MUST BE WORTH MILLIONS--
THIRTY-FOUR-NINETY AT WOOLWORTH'S.
'COURSE, IT WAS ON SALE.
LET'S GET MOVING. IT'LL BE DAYBREAK SOON AND WE'LL BE EASY TARGETS.
AND WE'VE GOT TO NAB WESSEL. IF HE CAN DO WHAT HE SAYS HE CAN DO...
YOU'LL HAVE TO TELL ME ABOUT THAT.
YOU'LL HAVE TO TELL US WHERE YOU'VE BEEN--
AN' HOW YOU STAYED SO YOUNG.
7.

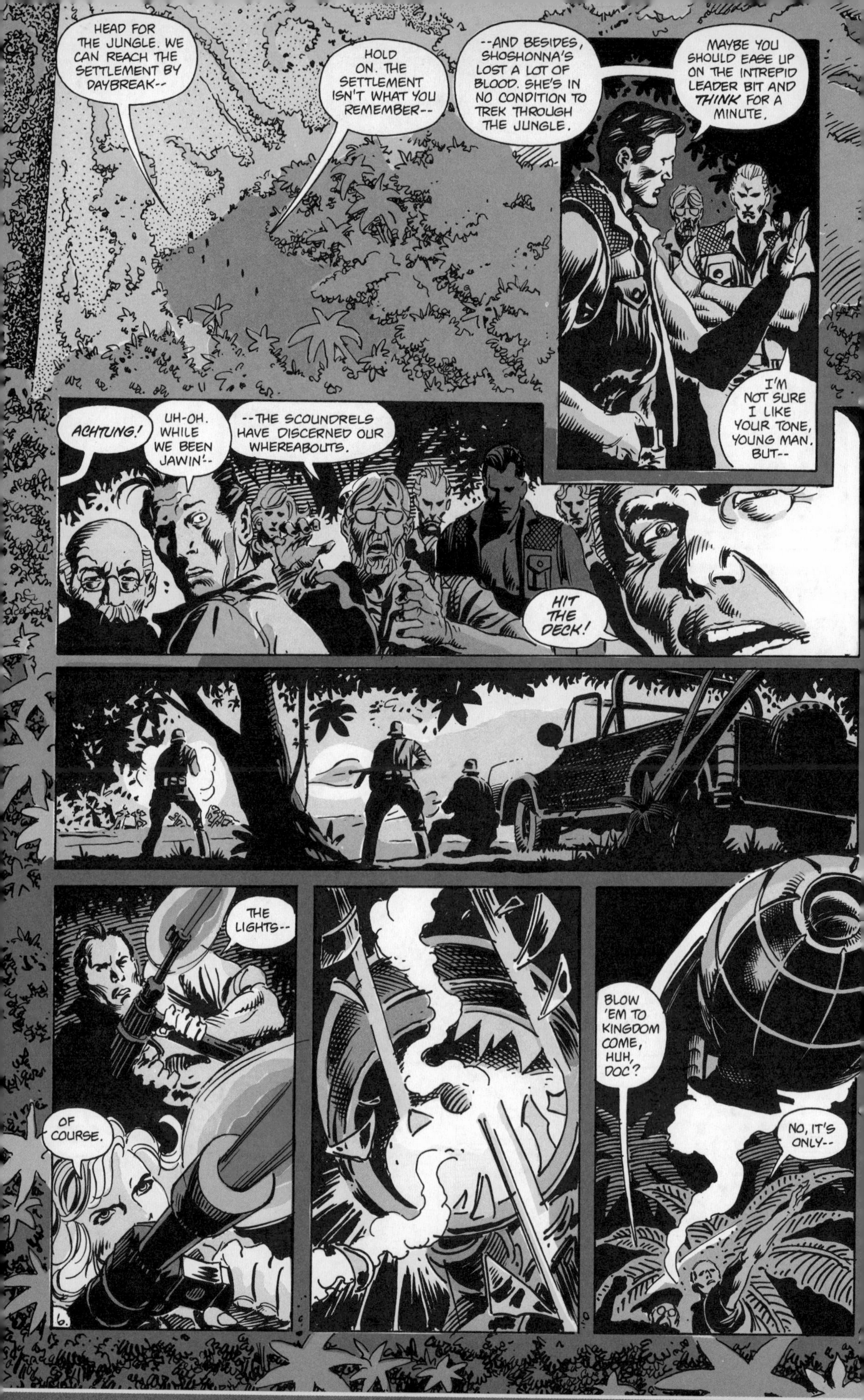
HEAD FOR THE JUNGLE. WE CAN REACH THE SETTLEMENT BY DAYBREAK--
HOLD ON. THE SETTLEMENT ISN'T WHAT YOU REMEMBER--
--AND BESIDES, SHOSHONNA'S LOST A LOT OF BLOOD. SHE'S IN NO CONDITION TO TREK THROUGH THE JUNGLE.
MAYBE YOU SHOULD EASE UP ON THE INTREPID LEADER BIT AND THINK FOR A MINUTE.
I'M NOT SURE I LIKE YOUR TONE, YOUNG MAN. BUT--
ACHTUNG!
UH-OH. WHILE WE BEEN JAWIN'--
--THE SCOUNDRELS HAVE DISCERNED OUR WHEREABOUTS.
HIT THE DECK!
THE LIGHTS--
OF COURSE.
BLOW 'EM TO KINGDOM COME, HUH, DOC?
NO, IT'S ONLY--

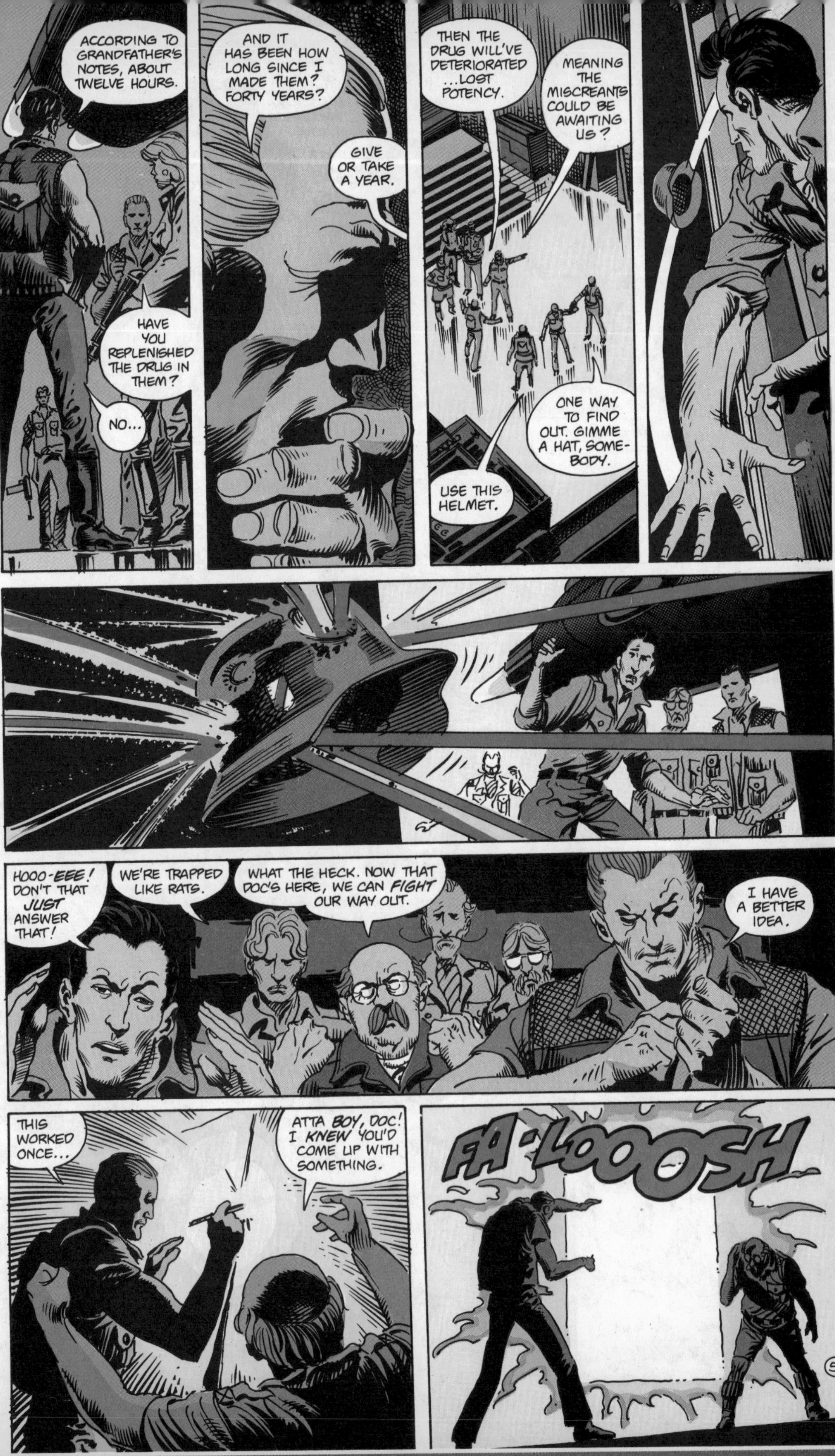
ACCORDING TO GRANDFATHER'S NOTES, ABOUT TWELVE HOURS.
HAVE YOU REPLENISHED THE DRUG IN THEM?
NO...
AND IT HAS BEEN HOW LONG SINCE I MADE THEM? FORTY YEARS?
GIVE OR TAKE A YEAR.
THEN THE DRUG WILL'VE DETERIORATED ...LOST POTENCY.
MEANING THE MISCREANTS COULD BE AWAITING US?
ONE WAY TO FIND OUT. GIMME A HAT, SOME-BODY.
USE THIS HELMET.
HOOO-EEE! DON'T THAT JUST ANSWER THAT!
WE'RE TRAPPED LIKE RATS.
WHAT THE HECK. NOW THAT DOC'S HERE, WE CAN FIGHT OUR WAY OUT.
I HAVE A BETTER IDEA.
THIS WORKED ONCE...
ATTA BOY, DOC! I KNEW YOU'D COME UP WITH SOMETHING.
FA-LOOOSH
5.

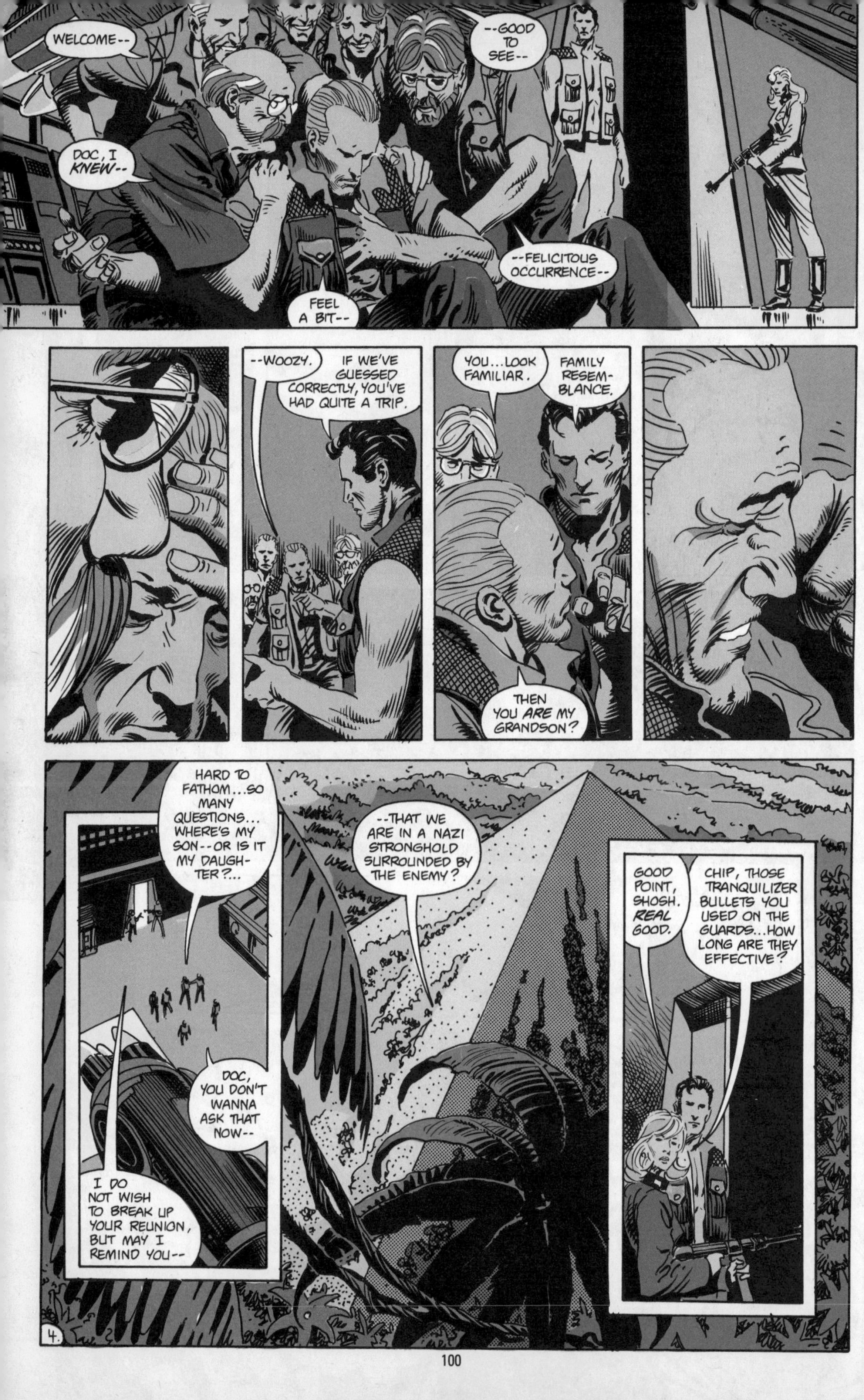
WELCOME--
--GOOD TO SEE--
DOC, I *KNEW*--
--FELICITOUS OCCURRENCE--
FEEL A BIT--
--WOOZY.
IF WE'VE GUESSED CORRECTLY, YOU'VE HAD QUITE A TRIP.
YOU...LOOK FAMILIAR.
FAMILY RESEMBLANCE.
THEN YOU *ARE* MY GRANDSON?
HARD TO FATHOM...SO MANY QUESTIONS... WHERE'S MY SON--OR IS IT MY DAUGHTER?...
--THAT WE ARE IN A NAZI STRONGHOLD SURROUNDED BY THE ENEMY?
DOC, YOU DON'T WANNA ASK THAT NOW--
I DO NOT WISH TO BREAK UP YOUR REUNION, BUT MAY I REMIND YOU--
GOOD POINT, SHOSH. *REAL* GOOD.
CHIP, THOSE TRANQUILIZER BULLETS YOU USED ON THE GUARDS...HOW LONG ARE THEY EFFECTIVE?
4.

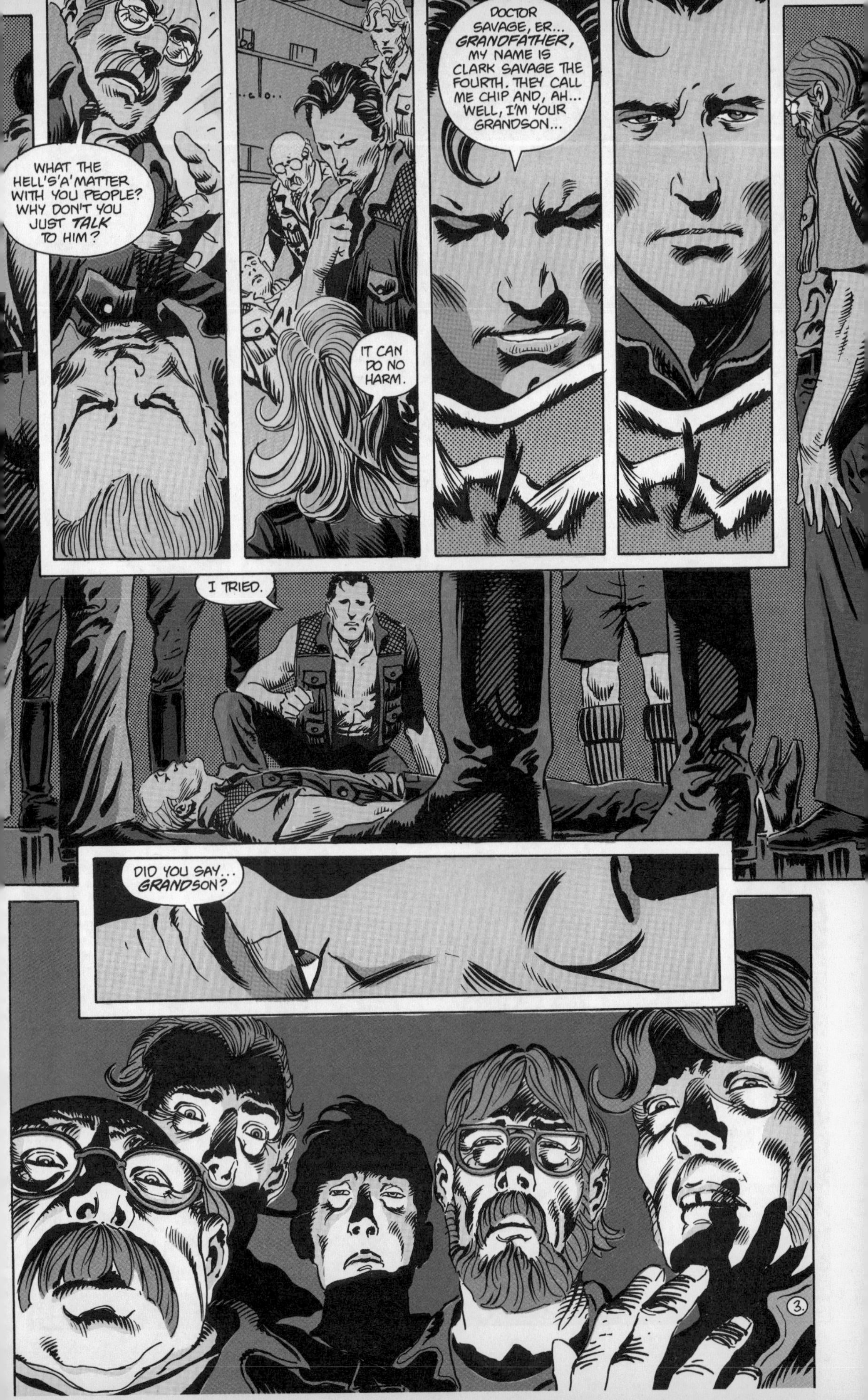
WHAT THE HELL'S'A'MATTER WITH YOU PEOPLE? WHY DON'T YOU JUST **TALK** TO HIM?
IT CAN DO NO HARM.
DOCTOR SAVAGE, ER... **GRANDFATHER**, MY NAME IS CLARK SAVAGE THE FOURTH. THEY CALL ME CHIP AND, AH... WELL, I'M YOUR GRANDSON...
I TRIED.
DID YOU SAY... **GRANDSON**?
3.

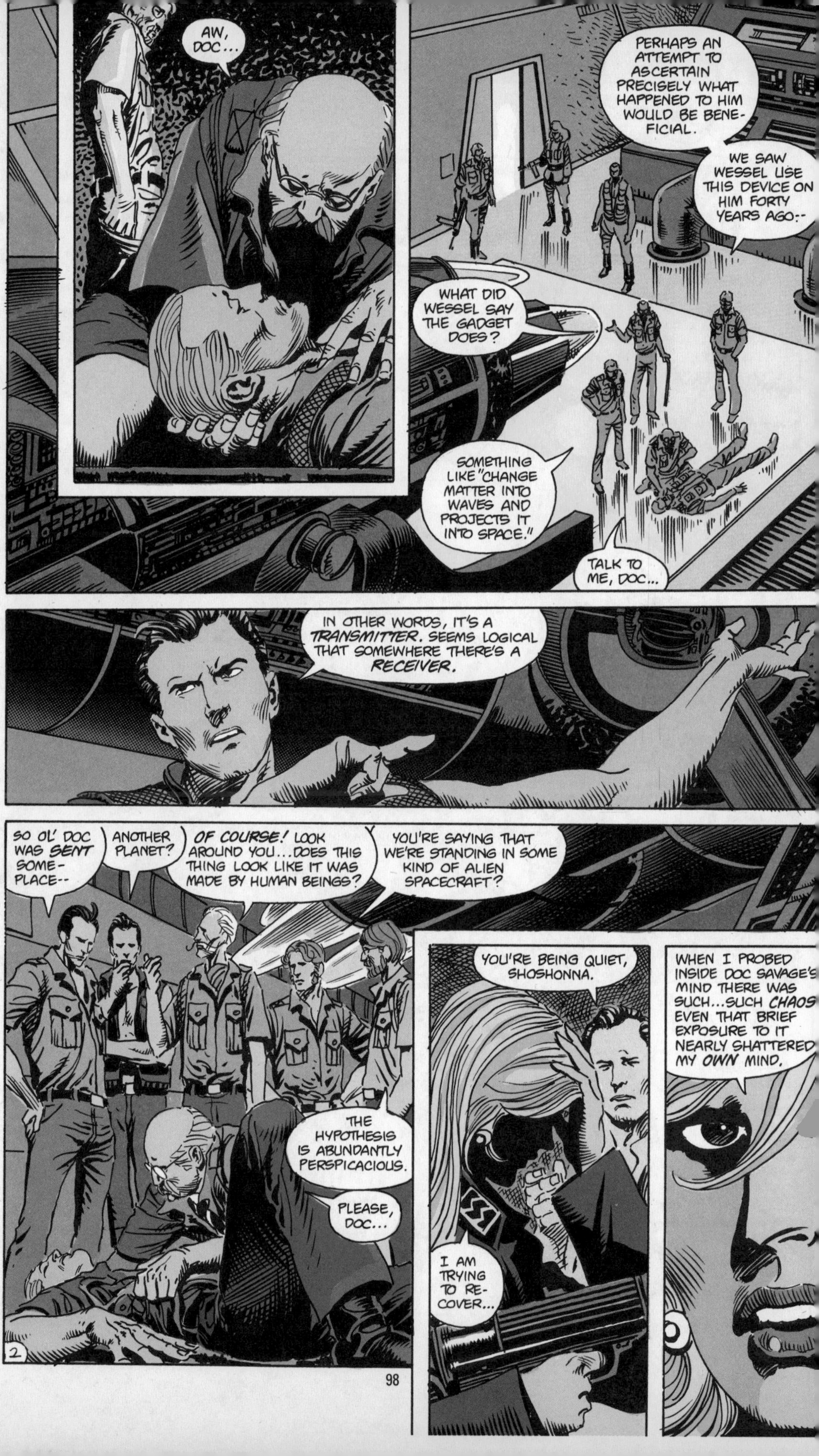
PERHAPS AN ATTEMPT TO ASCERTAIN PRECISELY WHAT HAPPENED TO HIM WOULD BE BENE-FICIAL.
WE SAW WESSEL USE THIS DEVICE ON HIM FORTY YEARS AGO:-
AW, DOC...
WHAT DID WESSEL SAY THE GADGET DOES?
SOMETHING LIKE "CHANGE MATTER INTO WAVES AND PROJECTS IT INTO SPACE."
TALK TO ME, DOC...
IN OTHER WORDS, IT'S A TRANSMITTER. SEEMS LOGICAL THAT SOMEWHERE THERE'S A RECEIVER.
SO OL' DOC WAS SENT SOME-PLACE--
ANOTHER PLANET?
OF COURSE! LOOK AROUND YOU...DOES THIS THING LOOK LIKE IT WAS MADE BY HUMAN BEINGS?
YOU'RE SAYING THAT WE'RE STANDING IN SOME KIND OF ALIEN SPACECRAFT?
THE HYPOTHESIS IS ABUNDANTLY PERSPICACIOUS.
PLEASE, DOC...
YOU'RE BEING QUIET, SHOSHONNA.
I AM TRYING TO RE-COVER...
WHEN I PROBED INSIDE DOC SAVAGE'S MIND THERE WAS SUCH...SUCH CHAOS EVEN THAT BRIEF EXPOSURE TO IT NEARLY SHATTERED MY OWN MIND.
2

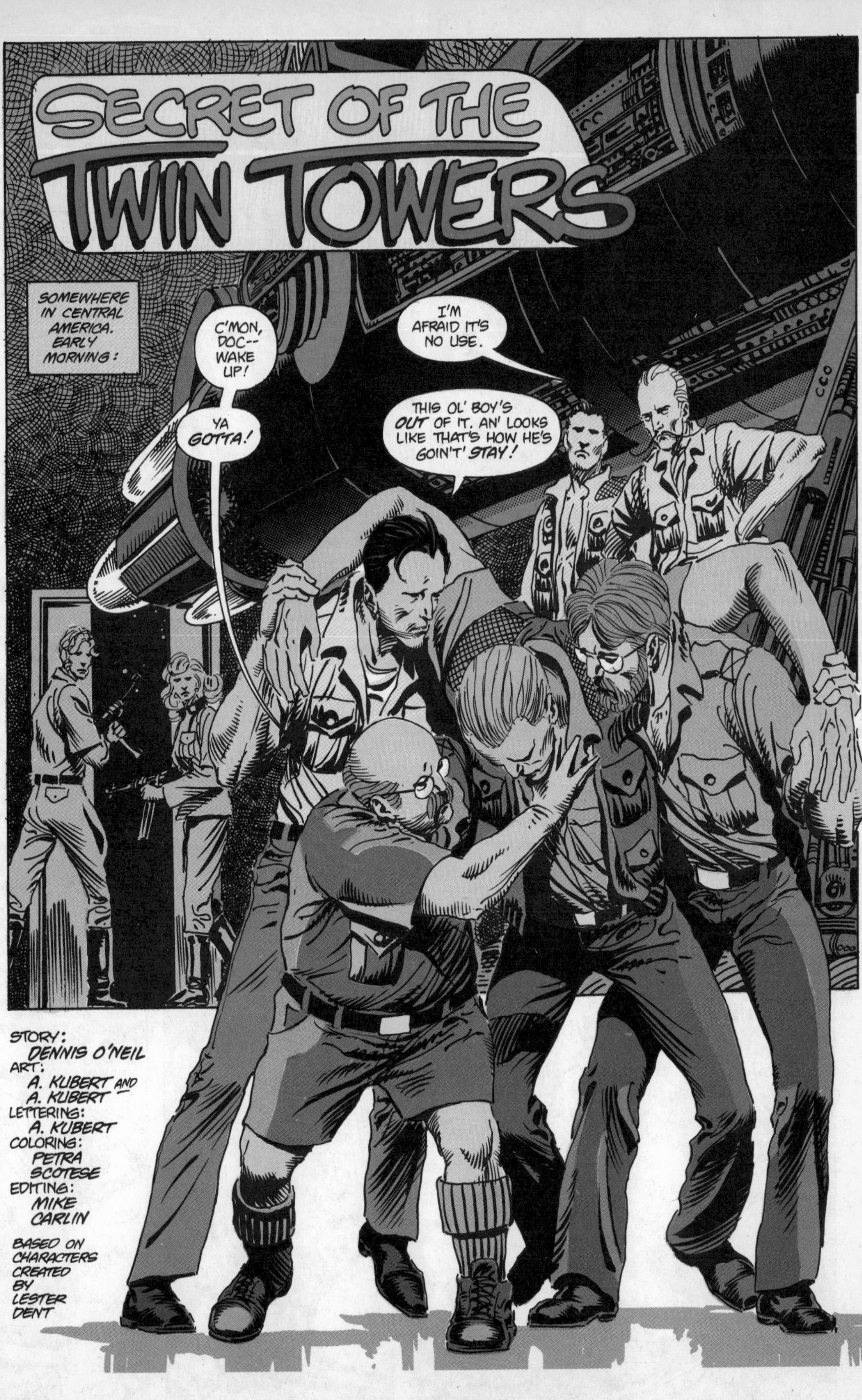
SECRET OF THE TWIN TOWERS
SOMEWHERE IN CENTRAL AMERICA. EARLY MORNING:
C'MON, DOC-- WAKE UP!
YA GOTTA!
I'M AFRAID IT'S NO USE.
THIS OL' BOY'S OUT OF IT. AN' LOOKS LIKE THAT'S HOW HE'S GOIN'T' STAY!
STORY: DENNIS O'NEIL
ART: A. KUBERT AND A. KUBERT
LETTERING: A. KUBERT
COLORING: PETRA SCOTESE
EDITING: MIKE CARLIN
BASED ON CHARACTERS CREATED BY LESTER DENT

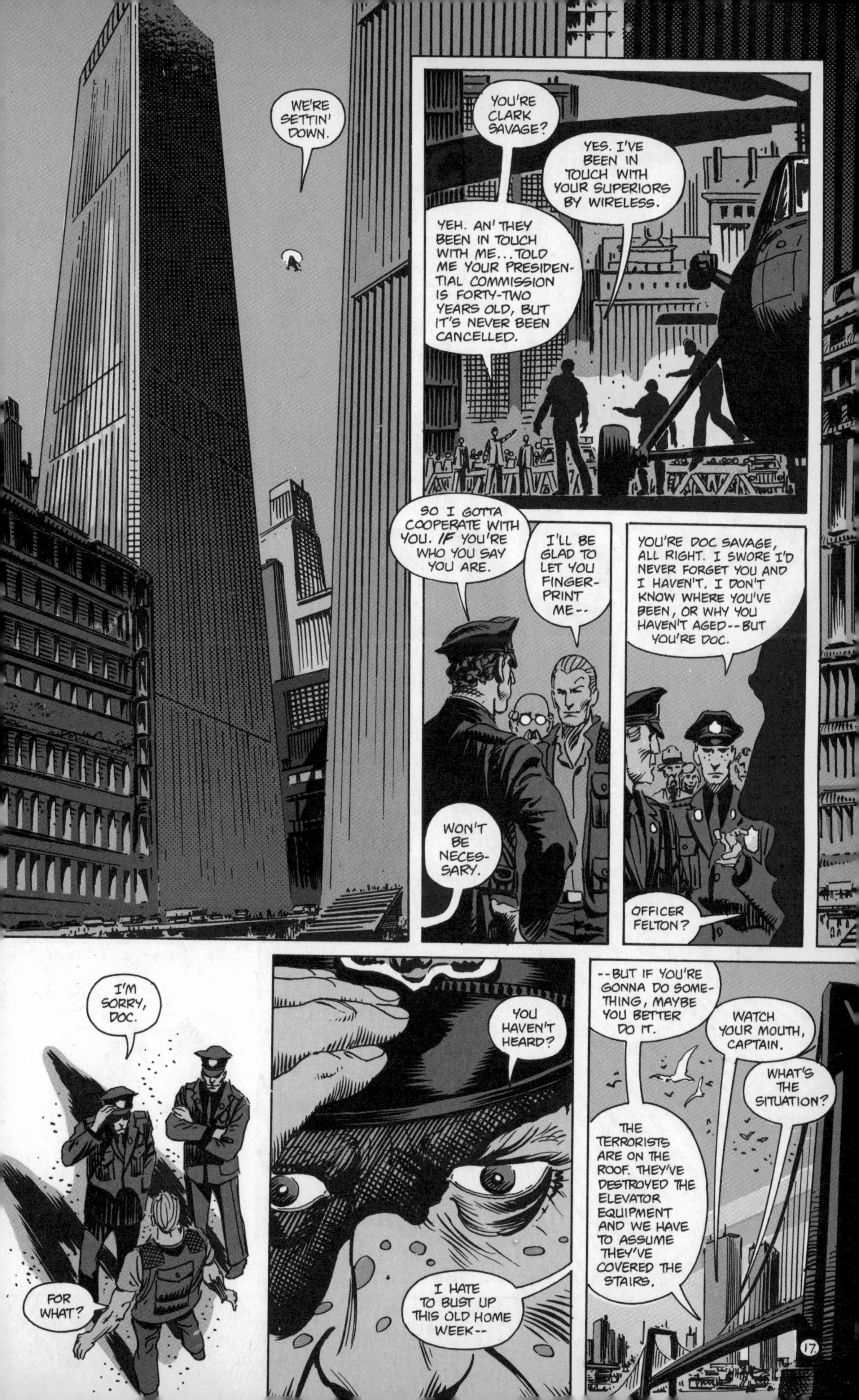
WE'RE SETTIN' DOWN.
YOU'RE CLARK SAVAGE?
YES. I'VE BEEN IN TOUCH WITH YOUR SUPERIORS BY WIRELESS.
YEH. AN' THEY BEEN IN TOUCH WITH ME... TOLD ME YOUR PRESIDENTIAL COMMISSION IS FORTY-TWO YEARS OLD, BUT IT'S NEVER BEEN CANCELLED.
SO I GOTTA COOPERATE WITH YOU. IF YOU'RE WHO YOU SAY YOU ARE.
I'LL BE GLAD TO LET YOU FINGERPRINT ME--
WON'T BE NECESSARY.
YOU'RE DOC SAVAGE, ALL RIGHT. I SWORE I'D NEVER FORGET YOU AND I HAVEN'T. I DON'T KNOW WHERE YOU'VE BEEN, OR WHY YOU HAVEN'T AGED--BUT YOU'RE DOC.
OFFICER FELTON?
I'M SORRY, DOC.
FOR WHAT?
YOU HAVEN'T HEARD?
I HATE TO BUST UP THIS OLD HOME WEEK--
--BUT IF YOU'RE GONNA DO SOMETHING, MAYBE YOU BETTER DO IT.
WATCH YOUR MOUTH, CAPTAIN.
WHAT'S THE SITUATION?
THE TERRORISTS ARE ON THE ROOF. THEY'VE DESTROYED THE ELEVATOR EQUIPMENT AND WE HAVE TO ASSUME THEY'VE COVERED THE STAIRS.
17

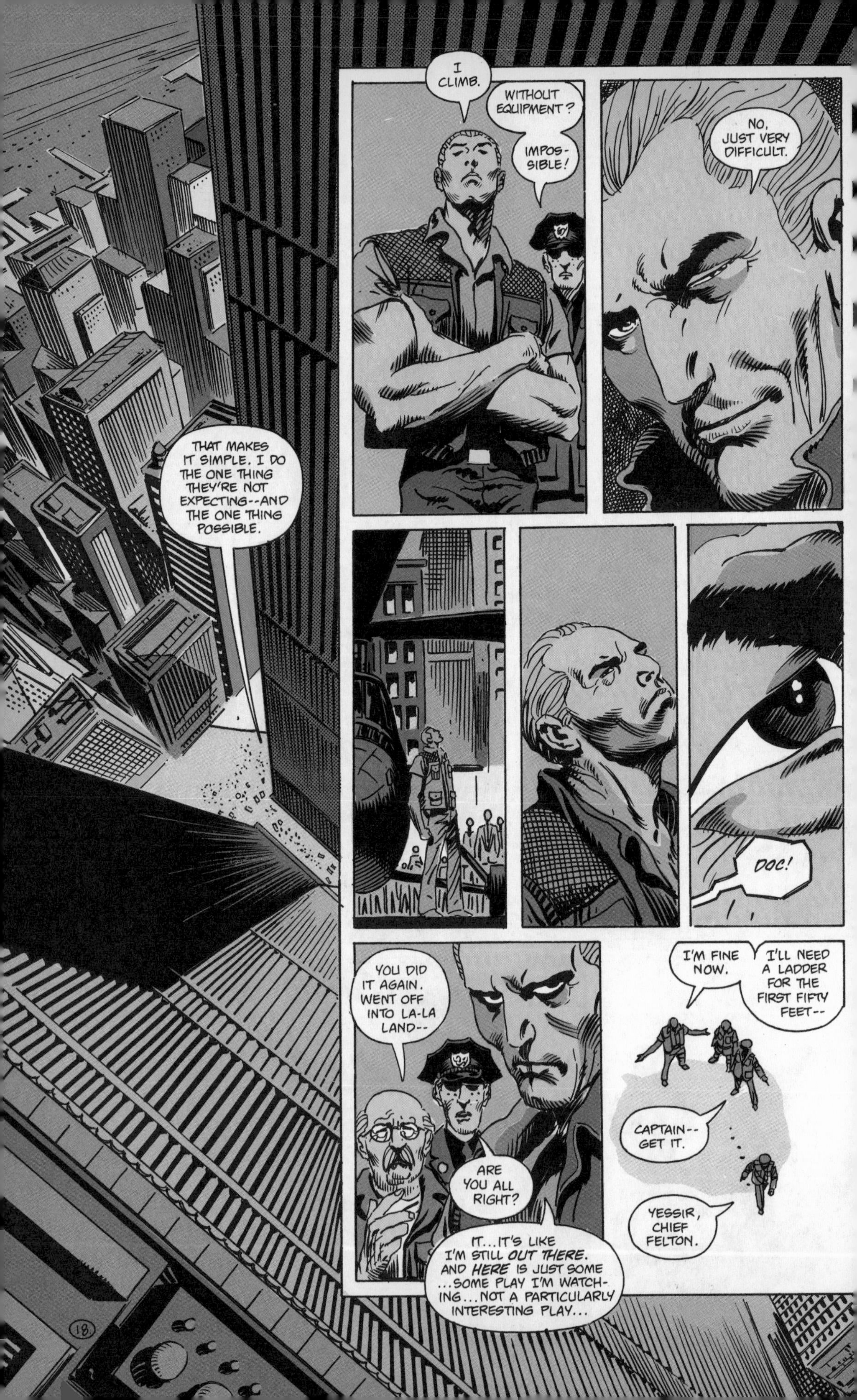
THAT MAKES IT SIMPLE. I DO THE ONE THING THEY'RE NOT EXPECTING--AND THE ONE THING POSSIBLE.
I CLIMB.
WITHOUT EQUIPMENT?
IMPOSSIBLE!
NO, JUST VERY DIFFICULT.
DOC!
YOU DID IT AGAIN. WENT OFF INTO LA-LA LAND--
ARE YOU ALL RIGHT?
IT...IT'S LIKE I'M STILL OUT THERE. AND HERE IS JUST SOME ...SOME PLAY I'M WATCHING...NOT A PARTICULARLY INTERESTING PLAY...
I'M FINE NOW.
I'LL NEED A LADDER FOR THE FIRST FIFTY FEET--
CAPTAIN--GET IT.
YESSIR, CHIEF FELTON.
18

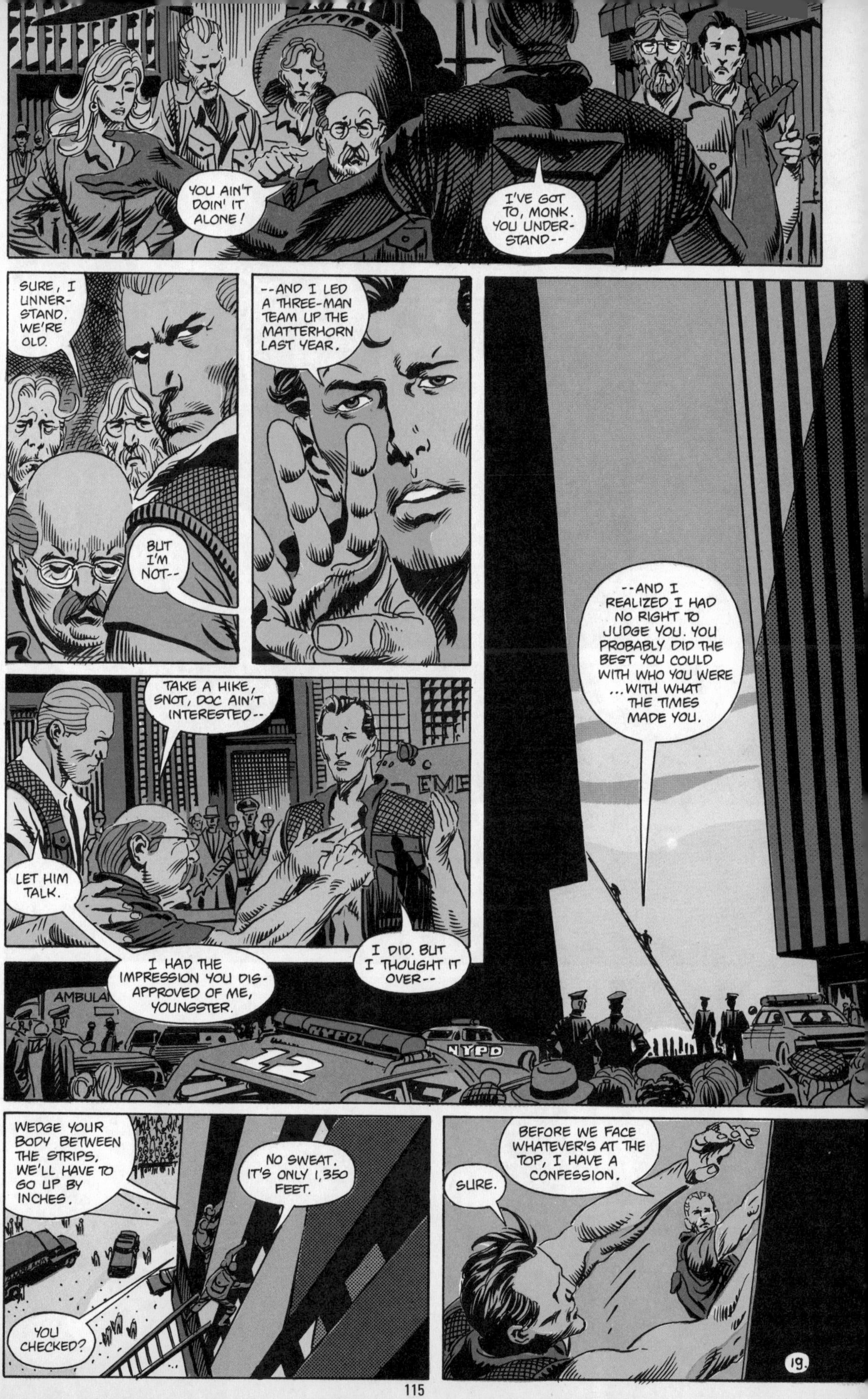
YOU AIN'T DOIN' IT ALONE!
I'VE GOT TO, MONK. YOU UNDERSTAND--
SURE, I UNNERSTAND. WE'RE OLD.
BUT I'M NOT--
--AND I LED A THREE-MAN TEAM UP THE MATTERHORN LAST YEAR.
TAKE A HIKE, SNOT, DOC AIN'T INTERESTED--
LET HIM TALK.
I HAD THE IMPRESSION YOU DISAPPROVED OF ME, YOUNGSTER.
I DID. BUT I THOUGHT IT OVER--
--AND I REALIZED I HAD NO RIGHT TO JUDGE YOU. YOU PROBABLY DID THE BEST YOU COULD WITH WHO YOU WERE ...WITH WHAT THE TIMES MADE YOU.
AMBULA
NYPD
NYPD
12
WEDGE YOUR BODY BETWEEN THE STRIPS. WE'LL HAVE TO GO UP BY INCHES.
NO SWEAT. IT'S ONLY 1,350 FEET.
YOU CHECKED?
BEFORE WE FACE WHATEVER'S AT THE TOP, I HAVE A CONFESSION.
SURE.
19.

I'VE ALWAYS CONSIDERED MYSELF AT LEAST PARTIALLY A FAILURE. I ALWAYS HATED USING VIOLENCE, BUT ALL TOO OFTEN I COULD THINK OF NO OTHER WAY TO DEAL WITH A SITUATION.

I HEAR YOU. I BELIEVE YOU.

YOU HOLDING UP?

DOING FINE.

HAVE YOU CHANGED YOUR MIND ABOUT WHETHER OR NOT WESSEL IS A THREAT?

LOOK, GRAND-FATHER, I SAW YOU MATERIALIZE FROM NOTHING IN THE PYRAMID.

IF *THAT* CAN HAPPEN... MAYBE THE REST CAN TOO.

AND IF WESSEL CAN DO AS HE SAYS, WELL...HE'S GOT TO BE STOPPED.

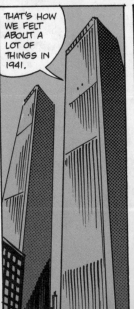

THAT'S HOW WE FELT ABOUT A LOT OF THINGS IN 1941.

ALMOST THERE.

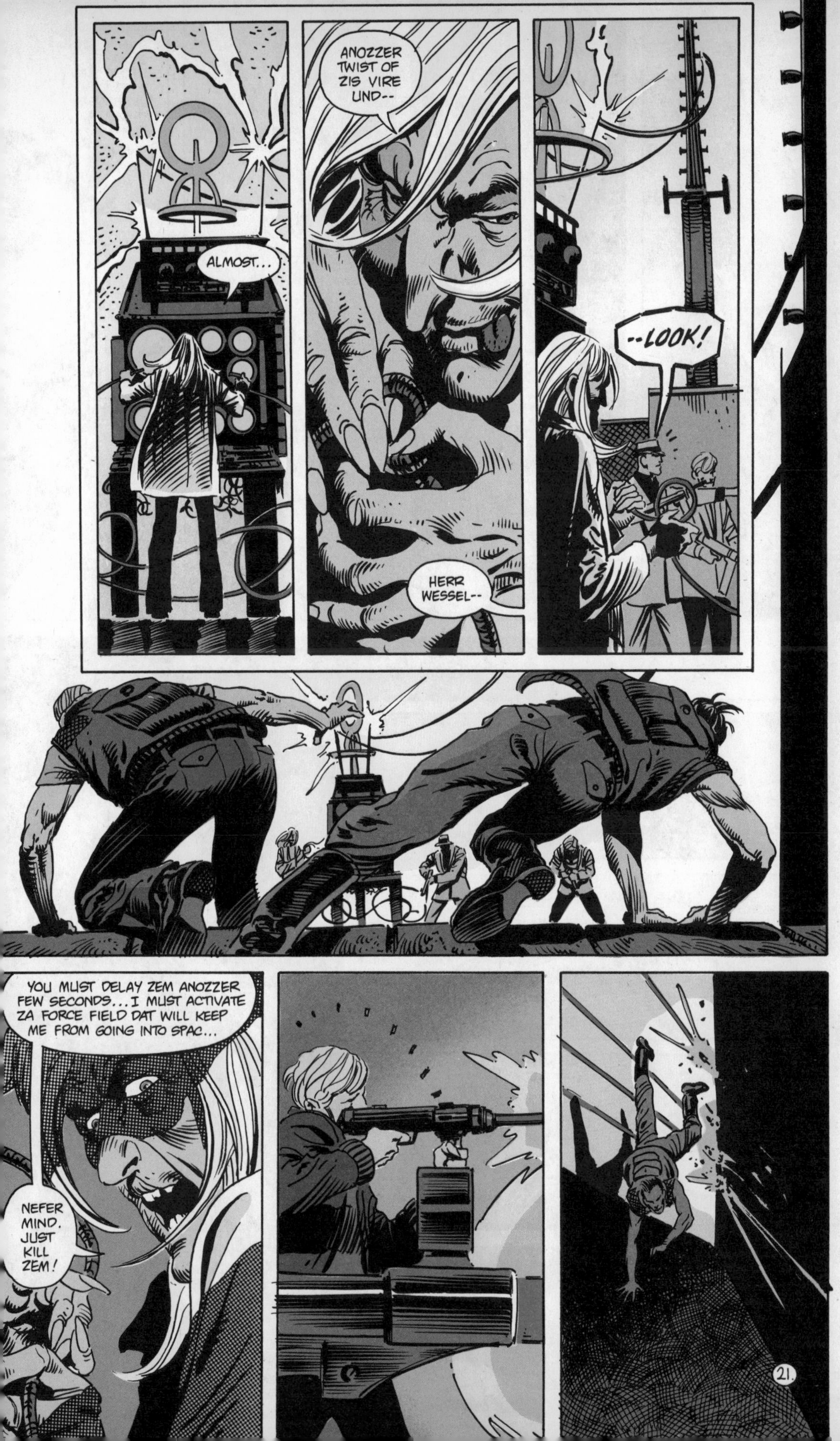
ALMOST...
ANOZZER TWIST OF ZIS VIRE UND--
HERR WESSEL--
--LOOK!
YOU MUST DELAY ZEM ANOZZER FEW SECONDS... I MUST ACTIVATE ZA FORCE FIELD DAT WILL KEEP ME FROM GOING INTO SPAC...
NEFER MIND. JUST KILL ZEM!
21.

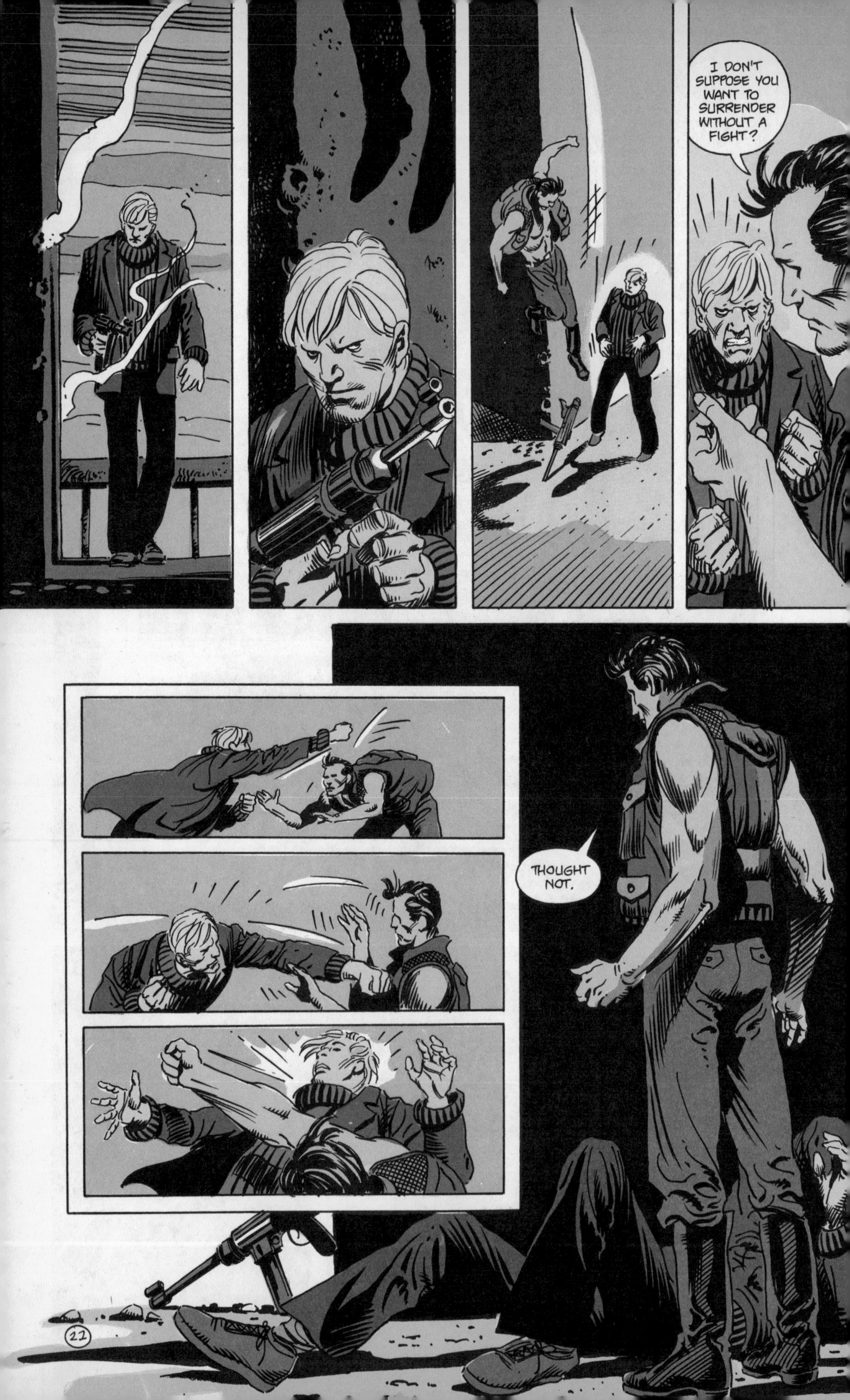

I DON'T SUPPOSE YOU WANT TO SURRENDER WITHOUT A FIGHT?
THOUGHT NOT.

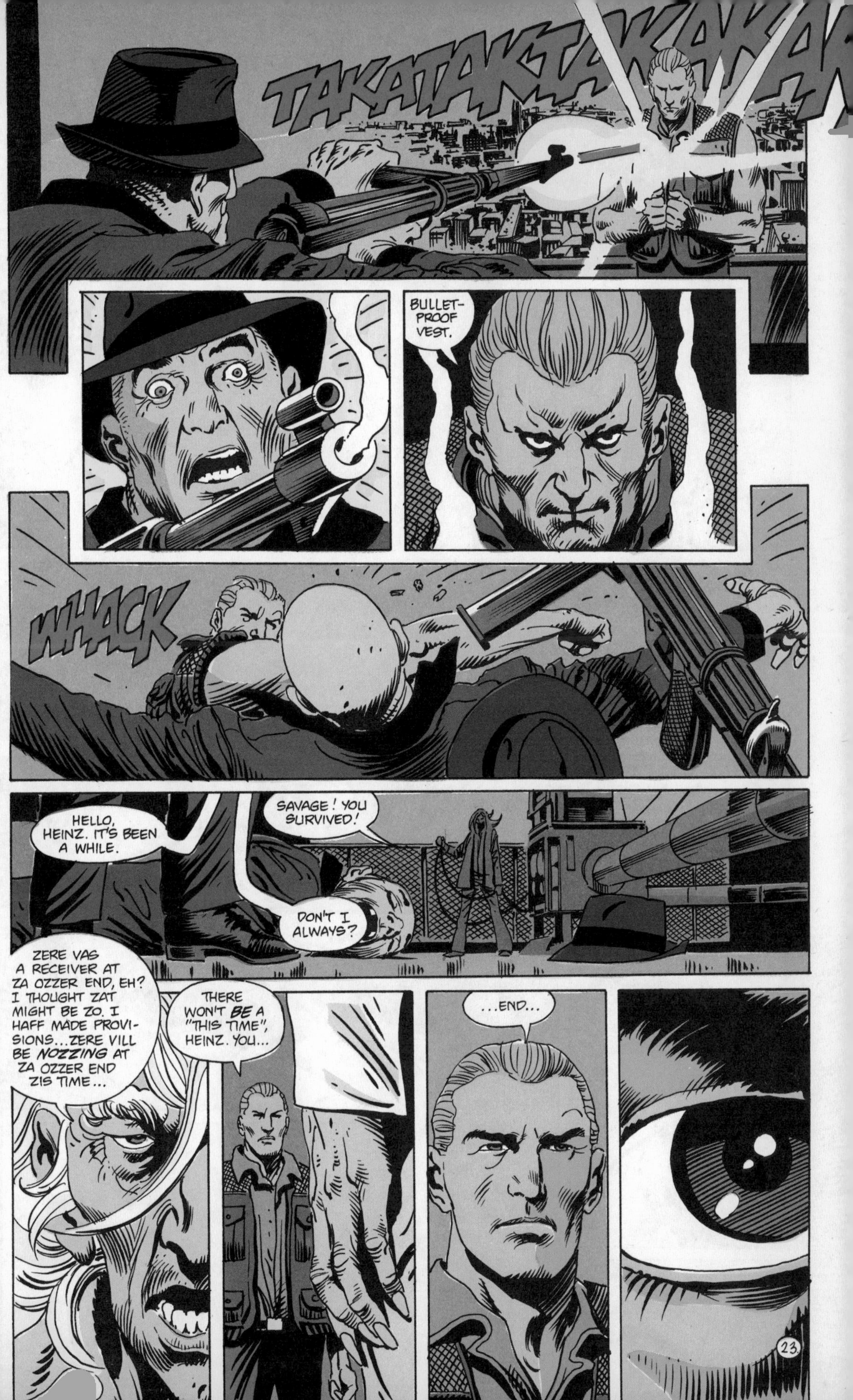
TAKATAKTAKTAKAK
BULLET-PROOF VEST.
WHACK
HELLO, HEINZ. IT'S BEEN A WHILE.
SAVAGE! YOU SURVIVED!
DON'T I ALWAYS?
ZERE VAS A RECEIVER AT ZA OZZER END, EH? I THOUGHT ZAT MIGHT BE ZO. I HAFF MADE PROVISIONS...ZERE VILL BE NOZZING AT ZA OZZER END ZIS TIME...
THERE WON'T BE A "THIS TIME", HEINZ. YOU...
...END...
23

SAVAGE?

NO!

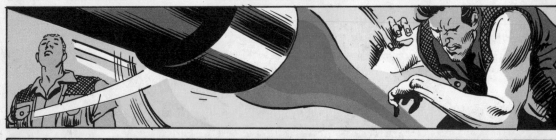

MY...
GRAND-
SON...

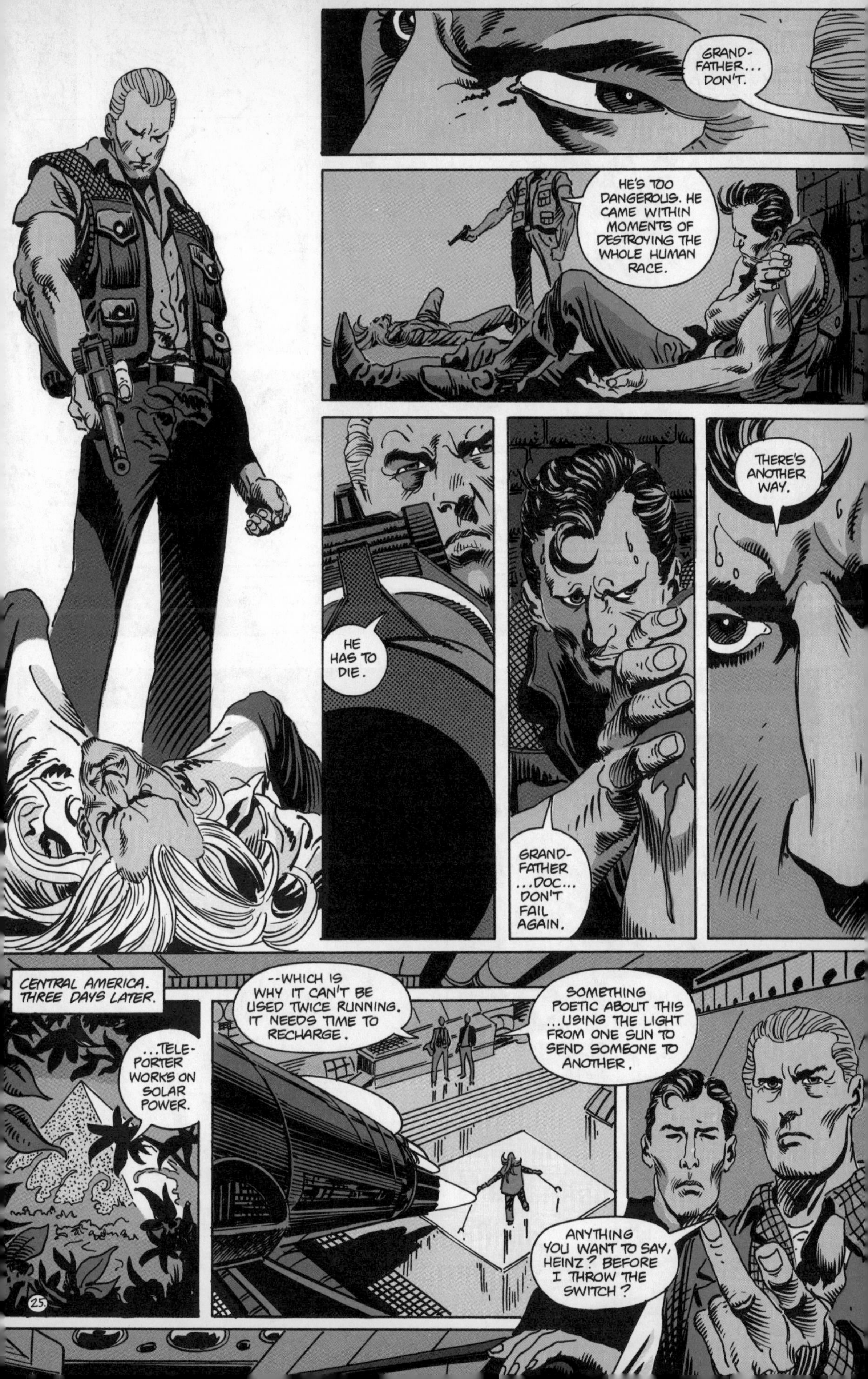

GRAND-FATHER... DON'T.
HE'S TOO DANGEROUS. HE CAME WITHIN MOMENTS OF DESTROYING THE WHOLE HUMAN RACE.
HE HAS TO DIE.
GRAND-FATHER ...DOC... DON'T FAIL AGAIN.
THERE'S ANOTHER WAY.
CENTRAL AMERICA. THREE DAYS LATER.
...TELE-PORTER WORKS ON SOLAR POWER.
--WHICH IS WHY IT CAN'T BE USED TWICE RUNNING. IT NEEDS TIME TO RECHARGE.
SOMETHING POETIC ABOUT THIS ...USING THE LIGHT FROM ONE SUN TO SEND SOMEONE TO ANOTHER.
ANYTHING YOU WANT TO SAY, HEINZ? BEFORE I THROW THE SWITCH?

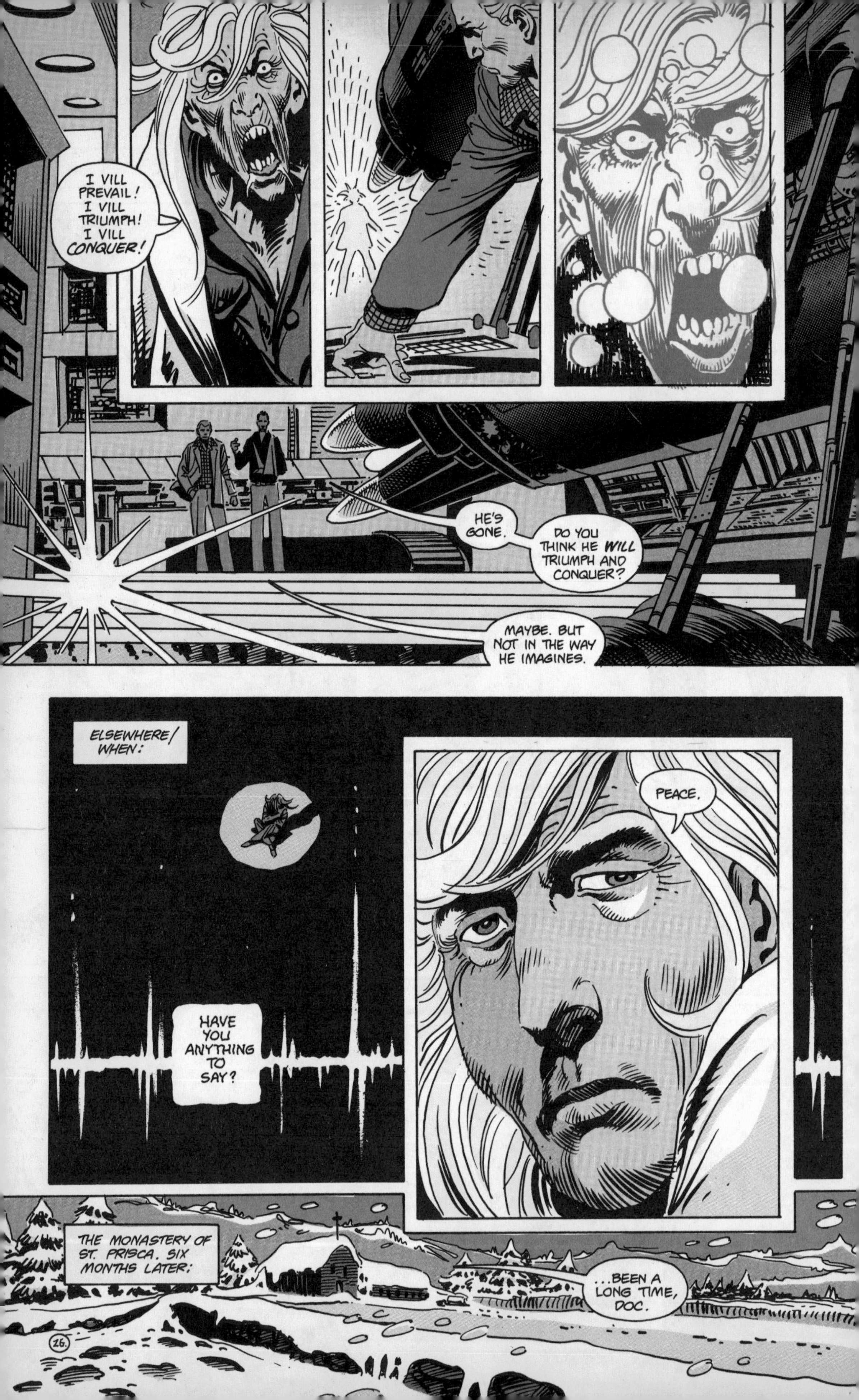
I VILL PREVAIL! I VILL TRIUMPH! I VILL CONQUER!
HE'S GONE.
DO YOU THINK HE WILL TRIUMPH AND CONQUER?
MAYBE. BUT NOT IN THE WAY HE IMAGINES.
ELSEWHERE/ WHEN:
HAVE YOU ANYTHING TO SAY?
PEACE.
THE MONASTERY OF ST. PRISCA. SIX MONTHS LATER:
...BEEN A LONG TIME, DOC.
26.

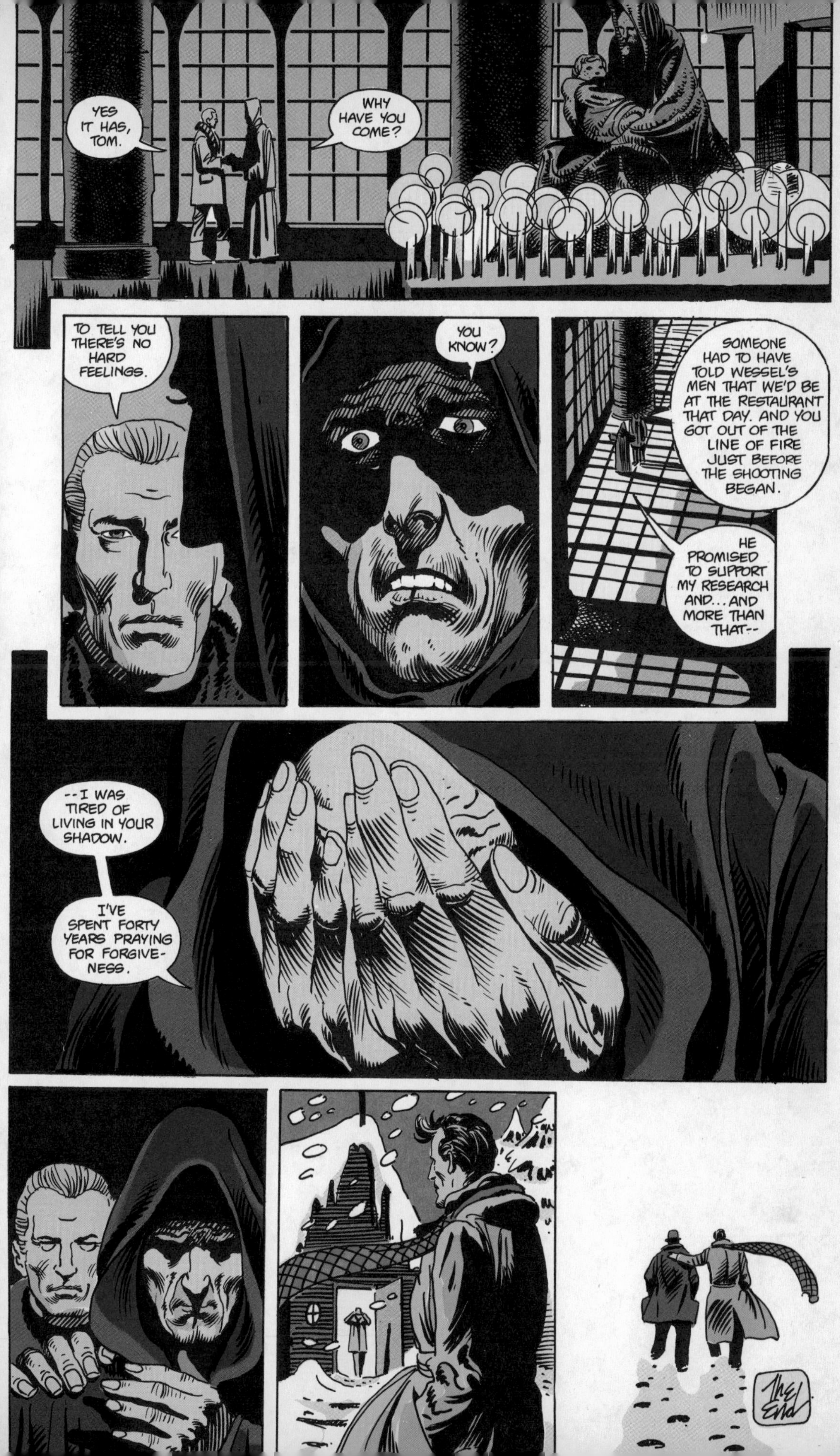
YES IT HAS, TOM.
WHY HAVE YOU COME?
TO TELL YOU THERE'S NO HARD FEELINGS.
YOU KNOW?
SOMEONE HAD TO HAVE TOLD WESSEL'S MEN THAT WE'D BE AT THE RESTAURANT THAT DAY. AND YOU GOT OUT OF THE LINE OF FIRE JUST BEFORE THE SHOOTING BEGAN.
HE PROMISED TO SUPPORT MY RESEARCH AND... AND MORE THAN THAT--
--I WAS TIRED OF LIVING IN YOUR SHADOW.
I'VE SPENT FORTY YEARS PRAYING FOR FORGIVE-NESS.
The End

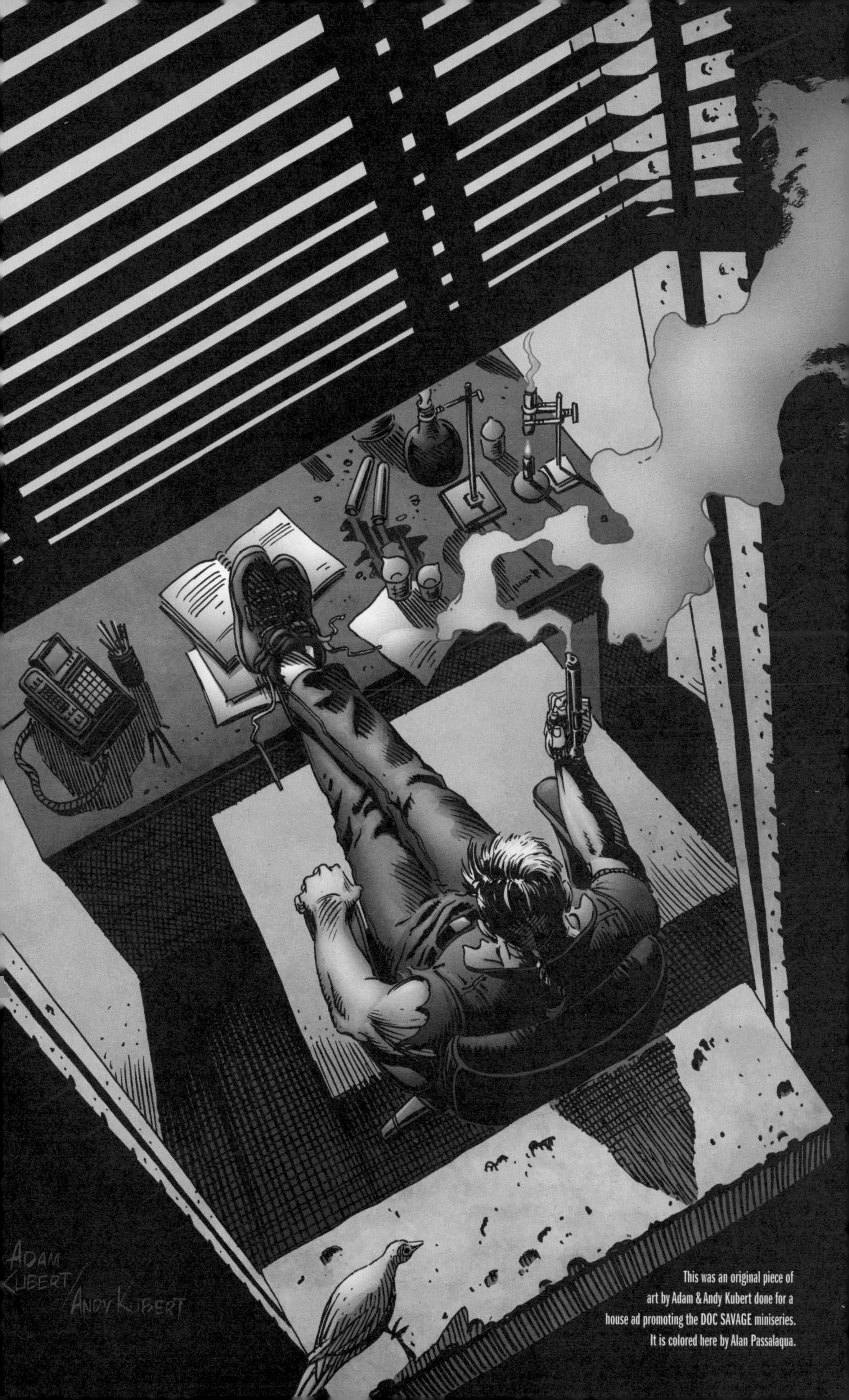
ADAM KUBERT/ANDY KUBERT

This was an original piece of art by Adam & Andy Kubert done for a house ad promoting the DOC SAVAGE miniseries. It is colored here by Alan Passalaqua.